The poetry of D. H. Lawrence has suffered from n▮▮▮ from controversy about its technical merit. In this, the first b▮ ▮▮▮▮rence's poetry in ten years, Ross C Murfin suggests that it ▮▮▮▮ ▮ither an entirely unconventional looseness nor a new formalism bu▮ ▮ther Lawrence's desire to use and yet to be disburdened of the past. Murfin studies Lawrence's poetry in the context of three major phases, or "lustres," in which the events and concerns of Lawrence's personal life converged with literary interests to determine his subjects and the poets who would influence him. Thus, because the powerful experiences of his youth were those of human love, the young Lawrence grappled with the great influence of Shelley. Similarly, after the poet's marriage to Frieda he turned from Subjectivity to the world of animate objects and to poets of the second lustre: Wordsworth, Coleridge, Keats, and Milton. Finally, as he prepared for death, Lawrence came under the liberating influence of Blake and Whitman. Throughout Lawrence's work, formal patterns set by Hardy, Swinburne, Keats, Wordsworth, and even Milton are intricately superimposed to create a language that seems free of all forms save those of common speech.

"This brilliant book is the best series of close readings of Lawrence's poems we have, as well as being the most intelligent placing of Lawrence's poetry in relation to the poetic traditions it echoes."—J. Hillis Miller, Yale University.

"This is a major contribution to our understanding of Lawrence's poetry, and of Lawrence's art in general. It is also a major contribution to the current critical debate about the nature of literary influences."—A. Walton Litz, Princeton University.

Ross C Murfin is an associate professor of English at the University of Miami and the author of *Swinburne, Hardy, Lawrence, and the Burden of Belief* (1978).

University of Nebraska Press: Lincoln and London

Ross C Murfin

The Poetry
of
D. H. Lawrence

Texts
&
Contexts

A portion of Chapter 1 was first published, in somewhat
different form, as "Hymn to Priapus: Lawrence's Poetry
of Difference," *Criticism* 22, No. 3 (1980).

Excerpts from *The Complete Poems of D H Lawrence*,
edited by F. Warren Roberts and Vivian de Sola Pinto,
copyright 1964, 1971 by Angelo Ravagli and C. M.
Weekley, as Executors of the Estate of Frieda Lawrence
Ravagli, reprinted by permission of Viking Penguin Inc.

The paper in this book meets the guidelines for
permanence and durability of the Committee
on Production Guidelines for Book Longevity of the
Council on Library Resources

Library of Congress Cataloging in Publication Data

Murfin, Ross C
The poetry of D. H. Lawrence

Includes bibliographical references and index.
1. Lawrence, D. H. (David Herbert), 1885-1930 –
Poetic works.   I. Title
PR6023.A93Z6897   1983   821'.912   82-10940
ISBN 0-8032-3080-X

Contents

Introduction

The Art of Interfluence

D. H. Lawrence describes his volume of poetry entitled *Look! We Have Come Through!* as a "story, or history, or confession, . . . the whole revealing the intrinsic experience of a man during the crisis of manhood, when he marries and comes into himself. The period covered is, roughly, the sixth lustre of a man's life."[1] Lawrence tended to think of his life in terms of crises, or lustres, and of himself as a kind of phoenix, dying and being reborn at regular intervals. In a preface written for his *Collected Poems* he speaks of his fifth lustre—when "I was twenty-five"—as a time when he nearly "dissolved away" but then "came back."[2]

The word *lustres* or *lustra* originally denoted quinquennial Roman purification rites, so Lawrence uses the term quite accurately to refer to the periods of upheaval, purification, and transition separating five-year stages of his own life. That the writer's personal life changed so radically so regularly is debatable; that Lawrence was a person who lived—and wrote—in definite stages is not. There were years in which he was above all a son and lover, years of being Frieda's husband, and years, finally, of being married but feeling alone. Lawrence went through poetic phases, novelistic phases, and phases in which he concentrated on prose nonfiction. There was even a time, during the First World War, when personal letters became the writer's primary means of literary self-expression.

Lawrence's powerful, unique, and still relatively neglected poetry is the subject of this study, and the poetic canon is as divisible into periods or phases as are the writer's life and *oeuvre*. Early volumes sought to express various kinds of passionate feelings. In *Birds, Beasts and Flowers,* Lawrence wrote almost exclusively about plants and animals; a few years later he embraced death as his primary subject. In the chapters to follow I will use the word *lustres* (somewhat less precisely than does Lawrence) to refer to three major phases of poetic development: one beginning in 1905 and ending in 1917, the next one drawing to a close in 1923, the final period ending with the poet's death in 1930.

Just as the contexts of an individual's personal life vary from stage to stage—Wordsworth speaks in his Great Ode of weddings and festivals giving way to mourning and funerals—so the literary contexts of poems written during one period of a writer's career differ from those of poems written in earlier or later periods or lustres. When Lawrence was a young man, the great crises of his life were romantic; he was torn between believing in the kind of bond that he had so long felt between himself and his mother (a "peculiar fusion of soul," he once called it)[3] and accepting a less idealistic definition of love, one that would recognize the essential loneliness—and integrity—of individual being. That the influence of Shelley was strong during the first lustre is no more surprising than the fact that Swinburne and Hardy also proved strong precursors during these early years. Through Shelley Lawrence could discover the extent of his own faith in epipsychic love, that love in which lover and beloved become, in Lawrence's words, "like one, so sensitive to each other that [they] never need . . . words."[4] With Swinburne as a contextual ally, Lawrence could articulate the difficulties he so often felt as he tried to live and write poems in a world that so constantly threatened the credibility of Shelley's more expansive claims about the powers and possibilities of romantic soul-union. Hardy, finally, became the poet Lawrence increasingly looked to and felt humbled by as he sought to break out of the confines of Romantic idealism, as he fought to come through to a new sensibility that would allow him to appreciate "flux, mutation in blossom, laughter and decay" through "the poetry of that which is at hand."[5]

Lawrence to a great extent succeeded in making the transition; with Swinburne's and Hardy's help, he left Shelley behind. After his marriage to Frieda the poet turned, first in letters, then through lyrics, to the world of objects as his subject. When he did so he found new mentors; with Wordsworth, Coleridge, Keats, and finally Arnold he sought both to know the natural world as in itself it really is and to articulate the various reasons why unmediated knowledge of the physical universe is so difficult to come by. Milton, for Lawrence as well as his Romantic and Victorian predecessors, proved to be one of those reasons; Lawrence finds himself doomed to heed "The voice of [his] education" in his most famous poem, "Snake," because whether he likes the serpent or is horrified by it, he likes or hates what Milton has made of it: "a god," a "king in exile," "one of the lords of life," "uncrowned in the underworld." When the poet attempts, at the end of the poem, to think of the snake he has just driven away, not as evil in an attractive or unattractive form, but rather as what Wordsworth might call a fellow inmate of the active universe, he finds his thoughts turning, once again, away from the very object that he would represent:

> I despised myself and the voices of my
> accursed human education.
>
> And I thought of the albatross. . . .

Romantic predecessors prove unfaithful comrades in the struggle to see and reveal the natural world: they prove to be of Milton's party without suspecting it.

Lawrence emerges from his fear that uninfluenced vision (and thus the "poetry of the incarnate Now")[6] is impossible, not by succeeding in his goal of apprehending the world of birds, beasts, and flowers with Adamic clarity but rather by coming to the conclusion that the original world that the poets are exiled from and should struggle to see is not a world of objects in the first place but is, rather, a realm of divinities for which objects are themselves only arbitrary signs. The result of his change in poetic perspectives is a new poetic lustre with new literary contexts; Blake and Whitman, especially Whitman, provide Lawrence with languages and basic structures to modify and combine to make the greater *Pansies* and *Last Poems*.

Because this is a study of the contexts out of which Lawrence wrote poems, and because it is at the same time about the threat to originality that inheres in those voices of education which must be allowed to speak again if the new poet is to express his own difference, Harold Bloom's theoretical writings in and since *The Anxiety of Influence* have proven very useful to me. I would suggest, however (and I hope without sounding anxious myself), that for several important reasons this book on Lawrence's poetry is only quasi- or perhaps neo-Bloomian in its approach. Because I see Lawrence as his own precursor, I am often interested both in the way in which a poet rewrites his own poems of an earlier lustre and in the way in which that act of rewriting is made possible by the turn to new precursors. Because Lawrence was a novelist and essayist as well as a poet, I sometimes believe novels by influential predecessors lie behind Lawrence's poems (Hardy's *Tess of the d'Urbervilles* casts shadows over Lawrence's "Hymn to Priapus"), and I occasionally consider the complex interrelationship between the sensibility of a poem (such as "Snake") and novels written by Lawrence, earlier and later (*Women in Love, The Plumed Serpent*).

I also swerve from Bloom's methodology by considering biographical as well as literary contexts. Indeed, not only do I treat certain biographical facts as if they were as important to the shape and structure of certain poems as were the texts of strong precursors, but I also believe and suggest that personal and literary-historical contexts are often inseparable; it was Shelley that the young Lawrence both wrote against and was greatly influenced by *because* the powerful experiences of Lawrence's youth were experiences of the manifold varieties of human love. And Lawrence loved—and feared annihilation by—his lovers in the way that he did *because* he was under Shelley's sway. Similarly, the poet's marriage to Frieda was no small part of the reason for the turn from subjectivity as the object of poetry to the world of animate objects as his primary poetic subject. Frieda's great marriage-struggle was to get Lawrence to love her as something other than a self-manifestation, and the trials of marriage—which coincided with changes in literary interests, allegiances, and priorities—were as responsible for turning the poet's view outward, away from his own feelings and toward that uncomprehended otherness of the world, as were the new precursors of the second lustre. So interinvolved are the events of Lawrence's personal and artistic life, in fact, that the word *interfluence* sometimes proves less inadequate than *influence* in such a study as this, for the views of influential artistic predecessors helped shape the events of Lawrence's life, events which, in turn, altered the poet's perceptions of the world and caused him to turn to new literary mentors while rewriting his own old poems and novels in new forms.

Finally, this investigation into Lawrence's poetry and its contexts fails the test of Bloomian orthodoxy because it believes that the poet can liberate himself from the anxiety of influence, and is interested, therefore, in the ways in which self-liberation, and subsequent originality, may be achieved. In the final third of the book, I argue that some very strong precursors are far less inhibiting to the ephebe than others. Blake, because of his morality of the casual and his casual style, is one such predecessor. Whitman proved to be another poet whose very influence could be liberating. Lawrence, as he prepared for death by writing last poems, turned to those poems by Whitman which are themselves acts of preparation for letting go—and not attempts at self-immortalization.

Another way in which the poet may step out of the penumbrae of past poems is by synthesizing a new style and sensibility from the antithetical meanings and methods of dead predecessors. Lawrence emerges from his anxiety over having neither Shelley's spiritual idealism nor Hardy's great "sensuous understanding"[7] by effectively combining their poetries into one which sees the spirituality of sex and the degree to which divinity inheres in desire. He similarly forges a new and casual poetic style by breaking up the seven-beat anapestic and dactylic couplets of Swinburne and fitting them to quatrains like Hardy's, quatrains that alternate four-beat and trimeter lines.

As any student of Lawrence's poetry knows, there has been a long-standing, three-sided debate between critics who denigrate Lawrence's lyrics for being frenzied, hysterical, and without craftsmanship (R. P. Blackmur founded this school); those who believe the poems to be carefully and even rather traditionally crafted (Harold Bloom takes this position in an early essay written in response to Blackmur); and still others, led by W. H. Auden, who hold the view that technique is not the *sine qua non* of all great poetry. This study seeks, with some help from Bloom's more recent, theoretical writings, sometimes to moderate, sometimes to complicate, the existing debate by suggesting that what a few critics have taken for entirely unconventional looseness and what others have seen as a new formalism may in fact be the product of Lawrence's simultaneous desires to use and to be free of the past. Formal patterns set by Hardy, Swinburne, Keats, Wordsworth, and even Milton are intricately superimposed to create a language that seems free of all forms save those of common speech.

I have sought, in writing this book, to strike several kinds of balances. Although my focus is on poetic precedents and my theoretical model adapted from Harold Bloom's, I seek not to challenge but rather to reaffirm in new ways the view that Lawrence's themes and prosodies are unique to poetic tradition. If originality may be defined as the radical reorganization of tradition, then this study of Lawrence's complex modes of resynthesizing the past will surely enhance the poet's reputation as a great original. Another balance this study seems to strike is between general theory and specific literary history. At times my argument takes Lawrence as a model in order to advance the thesis that even the most original of modern poets produces works that are shaped by the contexts of the past; at times I am advancing a literary-historical argument about the way in which the poetics of a single modernist poet relates to the poetics of previous epochs.

The third kind of balance I am seeking to strike is between intensive analysis and wide coverage. Those who do not share my great enthusiasm for Thomas Hardy and D. H. Lawrence often tell me that Lawrence, like Hardy, published far too many poems. Although there is not a single one of them that I would wish out of print, I do grant that some of Lawrence's poems may be more worthy of extended critical discussion than others. Of those that lend themselves to analysis and explication, some are particularly interesting to the critic exposing intricacies of contextual plot. For these reasons, I have taken the liberty of making two lyrics the focus of separate chapters while covering, in other chapters, dozens of poems that are important to an understanding of Lawrence but less rich contextually.

Whatever imbalances there may be in this book are, I hope, justified not only by its interests and purpose but also by the fact that Sandra Gilbert, in *Acts of Attention*, has already done the work of providing us with an interesting and even-handed treatment of Lawrence's poetic corpus. I am greatly indebted to her and to Tom Marshall, whose study entitled *The Psychic Mariner* first proved Lawrence's poems worthy of a serious, book-length appreciation.

While on the subject of debts, I should say that to Professors Carlos Baker, Martin Battestin, Harold Bloom, Leslie Brisman, Robert Caserio, A. Dwight Culler, Paul Fry, Cecil Lang, Walton Litz, Hillis Miller, Robert Shaw, and James Winn I owe many thanks for the time, advice, and assistance that they have offered me over the years. My wife, parents, and children have—in different ways—provided support and encouragement. A grant from the American Council of Learned Societies made possible a marvelous year in Lawrence's Italy, where this book was gratefully written.

University of Miami
Coral Gables, Florida

Chronology

1905   Lawrence composes his earliest poems, "Guelder Roses" and "Campions."

1909   Jessie Chambers submits his first poems to *The English Review*. Lawrence enters into a relationship with Helen Corke that is to last until 1912.

1910   Lawrence's mother dies.

1912   Lawrence meets and travels on the Continent with Frieda Weekley, née von Richthofen

1913   *Love Poems and Others* and *Sons and Lovers* are published.

1914   Lawrence and Frieda marry. World War I breaks out. Lawrence writes his *Study of Thomas Hardy*.

1915   *The Rainbow* is published. The Lawrences move from London to Cornwall.

1916   *Amores* is published.

1917   *Look! We Have Come Through!* is published. The Lawrences are expelled from Cornwall on suspicion of spying.

1918   Lawrence publishes *New Poems*.

1919   Lawrence visits Turin and Lerici, Italy, en route to Florence. Joined by Frieda, he travels to Rome and Capri. *Bay* is published.

1920   *Women in Love* is published, also the American Edition of *New Poems*, which contains an "Introduction" later to be called "Poetry of the Present."

1920–21   The Lawrences live in Taormina, Sicily, where many of the finest poems on *Birds, Beasts and Flowers* are written, including "Snake." After travelling to Sardinia with Frieda in January of 1921, Lawrence spends July alone in Zell-am-See, Austria, where he writes "Fish." *Sea and Sardinia* is published in December.

1922   The Lawrences move to Taos, New Mexico, via Ceylon and Australia, where Lawrence works on *Kangaroo.*

1923   Lawrence lives in New Mexico, then Mexico, working on *The Plumed Serpent.* Frieda returns alone to Europe. *Birds, Beasts and Flowers* and *Studies in Classic American Literature* are published.

1925   Seriously ill with "malaria" (and tuberculosis), Lawrence returns to Europe and begins to write *Pansies.*

1926–27   The Lawrences live at the Villa Mirenda, outside Florence, where Lawrence writes *Lady Chatterley's Lover. Etruscan Places* is written after a 1927 walking tour of tombs and museums.

1928   *Lady Chatterley's Lover* is published. The Lawrences leave Tuscany for the south of France.

1929   Lawrence publishes *Pansies,* writes *Nettles,* and begins both an essay and a volume of poems to be published posthumously as *Apocalypse* and *Last Poems.*

1930   *Nettles* is published. Lawrence dies in Vence, France.

1931   *Apocalypse* is published.

1932   Richard Aldington and Giuseppe Orioli publish posthumously Lawrence's *Last Poems.*

First Lustre: 1905–17   Poetic Loves

Chapter One

A Text and Some Contexts

Everyone who knows about D. H. Lawrence knows about his early relationships with at least four women: his mother; the slight, sensitive girl named Jessie Chambers; Helen Corke, companion of the Croydon years; and Frieda, the aristocratic German woman who became his wife. Of course, the young man who felt drawn to and sometimes antagonized by these women was also an artist beginning a career. He had tempestuous literary as well as personal affections, and so strong were some of them that they were far more than developing tastes. They were self-identifying passions.[1]

Shelley, Swinburne, and Hardy were the predecessors that Lawrence wrote about in the strongest terms during what I will be referring to as his first poetic lustre, the period beginning in 1905, when he wrote his first poems, and ending in 1917 with the publication of *Look! We Have Come Through!* In the 1914 *Study of Thomas Hardy,* Lawrence mixes strong objections to his Dorsetshire senior with assessments like the one in which he declares Hardy to have a "feeling," an "instinct," and a "sensuous understanding deeper than that, perhaps, of any other English novelist."[2] Two years later he says in a letter that Swinburne "is very like Shelley, full of philosophic spiritual realisation and revelation. . . . I put him with Shelley as our greatest poet. He is the last fiery spirit among us."[3]

But it was Shelley, the no-longer-living member of the young Lawrence's first trinity of mentors, with whom the poet was most deeply and troublingly involved during the first of his three major poetic periods. "I feel you laughing—and you know what a Sensitive Plant is a young, sentimental man of some slight ability and much vanity," he declares in a 1908 letter to Blanche Jennings (*Collected Letters*, p. 4) just after asking her to read the typescript of *The White Peacock*. In a later letter he speaks of one of his characters, a girl with "soul," as being the kind of girl he "could read Shelley to . . . and she would look at me with grand understanding eyes" (ibid., p. 11). Since Lawrence as a young writer and Lawrence as a young lover were roles that shared many scenes and even lines—his first writings were to no small extent about his relations with women he knew, even as those relationships were to no small extent grounded in literary discussion—it is hardly surprising to learn that Shelley's poetry had some bearing on Lawrence in love.

The love he shared with Helen Corke, a woman we know he read Swinburne to and may suspect he read Shelley to during the years in which he wrote *The White Peacock*,[4] was certainly a love conceived in terms of if not to a great extent modeled upon an ideal of love expressed by Shelley. In "Epipsychidion" the Romantic poet addresses Emily, the woman from whom he is to be forever separated by convent walls:

> We shall become the same, we shall be . . .
> One passion in twin-hearts, which grows and grew,
> Till like two meteors of expanding flame,
> Those spheres instinct with it become the same,
> Touch, mingle, are transfigured; ever still
> Burning, yet ever inconsumable:
> In one another's substance finding food,
> Like flames too pure and light and unimbued
> To nourish their bright lives with baser prey,
> Which point to Heaven and cannot pass away:
> One hope between two wills, one will beneath
> Two overshadowing minds, one life, one death,
> One Heaven, one Hell, one immortality,
> And one annihilation.
> (lines 573–87)

In a letter he wrote in 1910, Lawrence describes his feelings for Helen in terms of fire, apartness and union, timelessness, a private world, stars, meteors, and eventual endings. Although the prose is more mundane, it bears more than a slight resemblance to Shelley's inspired lines:

An old fire burned up afresh, like an alcohol flame, faint and invisible. . . . It is the old girl, who has been attached to me so long. . . . She knows me through and through, and I know her—and—the devil of it is, she's a hundred and fifty miles away. . . . She lifts up her face to me and clings to me, and the time goes like a falling star, swallowed up immediately; it is wonderful, that time . . . should be swept up with one sweep of the hand. . . . She is coming to me for a weekend soon; we shall not stay here in Croydon, but in London. The world is for us, and we are for each other—even if only for one spring—so what does it matter! (*Collected Letters*, p. 60)

To say that Lawrence thought of Helen in terms of Shelley's idealized Emily is not to say that she was in any way the figment of a poetic imagination in search of a subject. Kenneth Rexroth is surely wrong to suggest that Lawrence essentially invented her, that she was no less but little more than his image of the gnostic demi-goddess, his envisioned priestess of ideal love.[5] So interinvolved were Lawrence's life and art that such assessments are wide of the mark; one need only say that Lawrence was reading Shelley, drawn to Helen, and unwilling or unable to keep the two fascinations apart.

It was the love he expressed for his mother, though, that Lawrence couched in the most Shelleyan terms. And since the love between the young writer and Jessie Chambers was a pale and belated version of that sublimated, mutual adoration of mother and son, it was Jessie whom the poet described as a kind of failed epipsyche. He tells Rachel Annand Taylor, in another letter dated 1910, that he has "just broken" his "betrothal of six-years standing" on a day when his sick "mother has only a fortnight longer. . . . We have been great lovers" (ibid., p. 68). And he goes on to speak of souls in love that recall Shelley's "spheres instinct" with the same elements:

I was born hating my father: as early as ever I can remember, I shivered with horror when he touched me. . . .

This has been a kind of bond between me and my mother. We have loved each other, almost with a husband and wife love, as well as filial and maternal. We knew each other by instinct. She said to my aunt—about me:

'But it has been different with him. He has seemed to be part of me.'—And that is the real case. We have been like one, so sensitive to each other that we never needed words. It has been rather terrible and has made me, in some respects, abnormal.

I think this peculiar fusion of soul (don't think me high-falutin) never comes twice in a life-time—it doesn't seem natural. When it comes it seems to distribute one's consciousness far abroad from oneself, and one understands! I think no one has got 'Understanding' except through love. . . .

[Jessie] is the girl I have broken with. She loves me to madness, and demands the soul of me. . . .

Nobody can have the soul of me. My mother has had it, and nobody can have it again. Nobody can come into my very self again, and breathe me like an atmosphere. (Ibid., pp. 69–70)

Frieda, whom Lawrence was to meet two years later and eventually marry, was by all accounts not a woman who got—or wanted—Lawrence's soul. Nor did Lawrence seem to want hers. "It is a great thing for me to marry you," he wrote her in May of 1912, "not a . . . passionate coming together."

I know in my heart 'here's my marriage.' It feels rather terrible —because it is a great thing in my life. . . . It's the very strength and inevitability of the oncoming thing that makes me wait, to get in harmony with it.

. . . It's a funny thing, to feel one's passion . . . steady, and calm . . . , instead of a storm. . . . I am realizing things that I never thought to realize. Look at that poem I sent you—I would never write that to you. (Ibid., p. 121)

We do not know whether the poem Lawrence had sent Frieda — the poem that must have been about a "passionate coming together"—was a poem by Shelley or one of Lawrence's own, Shelleyan "Helen" poems. (It was presumably, in Lawrence's words to Rachel Taylor, "high-falutin.") What we can infer, however, is that in the mind of this young man whose love was poetry and whose early poetry was much about love, a change in love's definition demanded a change both in poetic mode ("I would never write that to you") and, presumably, a change of poetic models.

A complete understanding of Lawrence's poetry will eventually require us to examine fully the poet's long and troubled commitment to Shelley. However, because Lawrence's work is most fascinating contextually at those points in his life where a change in the way he lived seems to have begun to demand changes both in his style and in his allegiances towards the poetic past, it is best to begin by examining a poem written at or beyond the midpoint of a poetic lustre. In such a poem, influences other than the predominant one are brought into play. Consequently, that contextual complexity underlying Lawrence's finest and most original poems is most evident.

The poem I have chosen, the intricately crafted and yet deceptively casual-seeming "Hymn to Priapus," may be called a poem written late in Lawrence's first lustre for several reasons. Although first composed as early as 1912—the year the poet wrote to speak of his "oncoming" marriage—the "Hymn to Priapus" was not readied for publication until 1917. (Only nine poems were written between 1914 and 1917;[6] any poem written after the midpoint of what I am calling the first poetic lustre was therefore one of the last pieces to be written before Lawrence's change in poetic direction.) Although it is possible that Lawrence had not yet met Frieda when he set down his first draft of the "Hymn," the poem makes clear the fact that its author's Shelleyan ideal of love is waning, even moribund. Finally, the "Hymn to Priapus" may be called a late first-lustre poem because the first draft was written over a year after the death of Lawrence's mother in December of 1910, and that date marked the end of a five-year lustre in Lawrence's personal life. "I was twenty-five," the poet writes, when "from the death of my mother, the world began to dissolve around me, beautiful, iridescent, but passing away substanceless. Till I almost dissolved away myself. . . . Then slowly the world came back."[7] "Hymn to Priapus," in other words, was written after that "purification" that divides roughly in half the first major poetic lustre, the period during which Lawrence devoted his rapidly developing talents as a singer to the subject of love in its manifold varieties.

*   *   *

The speaker of the "Hymn to Priapus," like the speakers in all the other lyrics in D. H. Lawrence's volume of poems entitled *Look! We Have Come Through!,* may be taken to be Lawrence himself. He tells us he danced "at a Christmas party / Under the mistletoe"

> Along with a ripe, slack country lass
> Jostling to and fro.

At the dance or, more likely, after the dance, the country lass "slipped through" the speaker's "arms on the threshing floor," where he found her "Sweet as an armful of wheat." As if words like "armful" and images of "threshing" a "ripe . . . country" woman on the "floor" were not explicit enough to convince us of what has transpired, Lawrence plays blasphemously with Christ's words at the Last Supper. She "was broken / For me, and ah, it was sweet," he says wittily, making absolutely clear the fact that "this is [her] body" that the "big, soft country lass" has broken for the remission of his appetites.

Lawrence leaves the barn (as well as the woman) behind, and as he goes home through a silent country landscape, he feels "Fulfilled" but also "alone." Part of that feeling of loneliness stems from guilt and even a feeling that some sin has transpired, a fact suggested clearly through the strategically placed word, "commission," and even more subtly and potently through the speaker's representation of the constellation Orion as a father figure. He sees "the great Orion standing / Looking down," the "witness" of his "first beloved / Love-making" (which in Lawrence, after Freud, could refer to a child's Oedipal affair). Orion

> Now . . . sees this as well,
> This last commission.
> Nor do I get any look
> Of admonition.
>
> He can add the reckoning up
> I suppose, between now and then,
> Having walked himself in the thorny, difficult
> Ways of men.

Having partaken of the sensual fulfillments offered by a rustic woman and wondered if his father would have words of "admonition," the speaker lapses in the later stanzas of the poem into thoughts of his mother, that sweeter, better love who now

> lies undergro|und
> With her face upturned to mine,
> And her mouth unclosed in the last long kiss
> That ended her life and mine.

"She fares in the stark immortal / Fields of death," the speaker bitterly complains, and "I in these goodly, frozen / Fields. . . .[8] She is a Proserpine or Persephone, Lawrence implies, only she is a Proserpine lost forever to Plutonian darkness. He, the "frozen" inhabitant of sterile "fields," is powerless to bring her to light or love again.

It is not necessary to have read either the letters or biographies of Lawrence to know that the dead beloved is the writer's recently deceased mother, whom he "loved with husband and wife love." *Look! We Have Come Through!*—the volume in which the "Hymn to Priapus" appears—contains at least four poems that seek to be, in the words of one title, "Everlasting Flowers for a Dead Mother." Neither is it so dangerous a procedure to read Lawrence with the poet's personal history in mind as it might be to see some other poet's lyrics as having biographical contexts as definitive and important as the literary ones. Lawrence himself says, in the "Preface" to *Collected Poems*, that "if we knew a little more of Shakespeare's self and circumstance, how much more complete the Sonnets would be to us, how their strange, torn edges would be softened and merged into a whole body."[9] He could hardly have argued with Graham Hough, who implies that Lawrence's career, poems, and novels may be read as commentaries on one another. "If . . . we simply read the three volumes of his collected verse straight through," Hough writes in *The Dark Sun*, "they assume the status of a running commentary to the course of development outlined in the novels."[10]

Sons and Lovers, the novel Lawrence was writing in the very year that he wrote the first draft of the "Hymn to Priapus," might seem to offer little that would identify the old love in the poem as Lawrence's mother. Indeed, F. B. Pinion, the only critic until now who has sought to identify the first beloved at all, uses the novel to suggest that it is to Jessie Chambers that the poet's thoughts are turning during his lonely walk home from the dance.[11] In *Sons and Lovers,* the constellation "Orion was for [Paul and Miriam] chief in significance among constellations."[12] But the first beloved of the "Hymn" is quite literally dead—underground—and therefore it seems impossible that the constellation could be reminding Lawrence of Miriam's original. It seems far more likely that Orion can suggest both Paul's love for Miriam in *Sons and Lovers* and Lawrence's love for his mother in the "Hymn to Priapus" because, in life as in his novel, it was for his mother that Lawrence (Paul Morel) first felt the kind of love that he was to feel for Jessie Chambers (Miriam Leivers). Paul likes to sit in church "next to Miriam, and near to his mother, uniting his two loves under the spell of the place of worship";[13] in the novel, in other words, the affection for Miriam is part of a single, spiritual experience, one that had its origins before he met her. And although the constellation Orion looks down on Paul as he leaves Miriam to embark on the lonely, nighttime walk of the eighth chapter of *Sons and Lovers,* it is to his mother that Paul is returning, both in thought and in deed.

The literary contexts provided by other Lawrence poems strengthen the hypothesis that the old love in the "Hymn to Priapus" is the poet's mother. Proserpine, or Persephone, is several times a mother figure in Lawrence's poetic canon. The Persephone of the very late lyric "Bavarian Gentians" is said by Tom Marshall to be "not merely an image of Lawrence's soul; she is the mother within, the mother whose frustration and despair he felt so deeply." Marshall goes on to speculate, in *The Psychic Mariner,* that the poet came to associate his "aspiring, spiritual" mother with Persephone because she alternately accepted and "failed to accept her husband as the natural man he was."[14]

But it is Lawrence's prose, more than his poetry or his fiction, that best identifies the dead beloved of the "Hymn" as Mrs. Arthur Lawrence. "What is the use of a mother's sacrificing herself for her children," Lawrence asks in a work entitled *The Symbolic Meaning,* "if after her death her unappeased soul shall perforce return upon the child and exact from it all the fulfillment that should have been attained in the living flesh and blood and was not?"[15] The memory that returns to the speaker of the "Hymn to Priapus" exacts the price of just such an unappeased mother's soul.

The recollection of the spiritual love that Lawrence is powerless to bring back breeds a powerful form of what might be called secondary impotence. Any man who spends his time after lovemaking thinking morbid thoughts about his unforgettable mother cannot have been "fulfilled" by his sexual experience as an adult, no matter what he may claim to the contrary. The impossible love for the mother, as symbolized by the deathbed kiss, seems to have rendered the poet incapable, for a while at least, of enjoying his own loves in his own time. It has, indeed, turned the course of life against life itself:

> Something in me remembers
> And will not forget.
> The stream of my life in the darkness
> Deathward set!

I take this stanza to refer, in part, to the returning memory of that "long last kiss / That ended her life and mine." If we suspect, however, that the reference is also to the moment of the poet's own conception, the sexual act between father and mother that brought him into being, the impact of the stanza is greatly heightened though its import is little changed. For to be so burdened by the past that coitus triggers "memories" of one's own conception is to be a man always driven by reality back into the womb and into the world of the deep, parental past, now quiet like Orion in the blackness of the heavens, now peaceful and still in the "stark immortal / Fields of death" that stretch beyond the reach of our "frozen / Fields."

One thing is certain. The poem, however richly suggestive and even moving it may be, does not seem much of a "Hymn to Priapus." It cannot be said to celebrate the sexual relationship abandoned after only three stanzas, and however much Lawrence might hold to a neo-Freudian view of the family, we can hardly suppose that "Priapus" is a figure for the relationship which the poem seems more interested in and certainly talks in more "hymnal" language about, the love between mother and son. Where, then, is Lawrence taking us? What has he written a poem about?

One possible answer to this question—and the kind of answer that any study of Lawrence's literary contexts must be interested in—emerges when we remember that the mother exerts an immortal, controlling influence over the life of her son; that the imagery of the poem ("underground," "Fields of death") associates the mother with the goddess Proserpine; that Swinburne, whom Lawrence once ranked with "Shelley as our greatest poet" wrote not a "Hymn to Priapus" but a "Hymn to Proserpine"; and that the elder poet's hymn treated the subject of two kinds of love, one current but unsatisfactory, the other wonderful but dead. The "Hymn to Priapus," although fascinating in its own right in a number of ways that I will mention later, is a particularly compel-

ling example of the kind of poem that generates meanings through
its interplay with other poems. Through his title, Lawrence might
lead us to expect a poem that is a paean to a simple and primal
urge. After we have been surprised by the lines that follow, how-
ever, we may take the title as an illustrative admission. The
"Hymn to Priapus" is a revisionary "Hymn to Proserpine" that half
develops and half covers over the traces of a Victorian original.
That is work, Lawrence makes us realize, that has first to be done
before any convincing hymns to sexual being can be sung.

In Swinburne's powerful poem, the speaker, upon the proclama-
tion in Rome of the Christian faith, weeps for the passing of the old,
Olympian order (whose gods, once "fair," are now "broken"). He
also decries the elevation of a new, pale, son of man who is now
"crowned in the city" but whose "days are bare" and "device is
barren" to a man raised a passionate devotee of those older, more
majestic deities who were "more than the day or the morrow, the
seasons that laugh or that weep." The speaker especially laments
the passing of Proserpine,

> our mother, a blossom of flowering seas,
> Clothed round with the world's desire as with
> raiment, and fair as the foam,
> And fleeter than kindled fire, and a goddess, and
> Mother of Rome.

Who or what has replaced this "mother" of "desire" in the new
scheme of things? A mere girl, Mary, a mere "maiden men sing as a
goddess" and have "crowned . . . where another was queen."

In despair, with no object worth desire or devotion in the present
and no viable goddess of love left over from the previous epoch, the
speaker admits that his life, nurtured in a time and in a view of
things now forever past, is now meaningless. "I am sick of singing"
and "fain" only "to rest," the Swinburnian speaker sighs (for
Swinburne, too, was raised on faiths which were, in his lifetime,
"dethroned and deceased, cast forth, wiped out in a day"). He
longs only for "sleep"; he would "look to the end," the time in
which he will forever join the "hidden head" of Proserpine in
"death." "I will go," he says, "as I came," to "abide" in the "earth"
with "my mother." In a companion poem, entitled "The Garden of
Proserpine," Swinburne associates this death and this mother

with "Pale beds of blowing rushes / Where no leaf blooms or blushes," and he ends his prayer in the garden on a note of thanks

> That no life lives for ever;
> That dead men rise up never;
> That even the weariest river
>> Winds somewhere safe to sea.

Swinburne's Proserpine poems would seem to be important sources of Lawrence's images, themes, and larger poetic structures in the "Hymn to Priapus." The elder poet's characterization of life as a weary flow from origins to the finality of death informs both Lawrence's memory of that "stream of [his] life in the darkness . . . set" and his lament, which may ultimately be an anxious hope, that his parents will "rise up never," will never return to repossess him, to offer "admonition," to "add the reckoning up." The dead mother who is also a lover and a deity, who "fares in the stark immortal / Fields of death" with her "underground . . . face upturned" to her son's, clearly descends from Swinburne's Proserpine, at once a mother and goddess of desire whose "head" is now "hidden" in death, in a "Pale" garden where "no leaf blooms or blushes." Lawrence's poem, like Swinburne's, is founded upon a structure of diametrical opposition: there are two women representing two kinds of love, one available but unmeaningful, the other, maternal one "Clothed round with . . . desire" but out of present reach. The speakers of both poems, caught between an unrecallable past and an unfulfilling present, live in memory. Each of them, consequently, tends to see life as a flow from origins towards death.

There are still more parallels to be drawn. In Swinburne's hymn, "love is sweet for a day" but soon "grows bitter"; Lawrence says of his bliss on the "threshing floor," "ah, it was sweet"; but soon he thinks of his "first beloved / Love-making" and remembers that it soon became a "bitter-sweet / Heart-aching." Lawrence completes the symbolism Swinburne began by associating his minimally loved country lass with wheat (she's an "armful of wheat") and even with the "bread" of Christ's body ("was broken / For me"). Swinburne had associated his most dearly loved mother with "green grapes" in order to contrast her with Christ, from whose blood the "Sweet . . . wine" of mercy and sacrifice is made. The important thing for the reader to be aware of, however, is not the number of echoes, parallels, and debts but, rather, the reason for their existence. Lawrence intends to discuss, poetically, the situation of being torn between two sensibilities, two visions of things. *Look! We Have Come Through!*, as its title indicates, is a volume about the arduous struggle for emergence, spiritual and aesthetic. Swinburne, in his Proserpine poems, gave Lawrence a poetic system with which to do so. Through appropriation of Swinburne's poetic structure Lawrence can make the following claim through an unstated but powerful analogy: mere sexual experience with a "ripe" country lass at a Christmas dance is, for him, for the moment, as pale, grey, empty—even barren—as the living cult of the Galilean, Christ, was to the speaker of Swinburne's hymn, raised in adoration of a beautiful old goddess whose time has passed, nurtured in a world that now lies dead and buried.

To anyone who has been at all intrigued by the Oedipal relation that Harold Bloom believes to obtain between the literary precursor and ephebe, it would be tempting, at this point, to see Swinburne as the father, or as one of the fathers, figured by Orion. Lawrence says of the downward-looking constellation:

> He has done as I have done
> No doubt:
> Remembered and forgotten
> Turn and about.

It was Swinburne, after all, who like Lawrence "knew" both a "Proserpine" and an unmeaningful alternative. Swinburne's speakers, in poems like "The Leper," preferred to kiss the dying, finally the dead, rather than to embrace the living present. Through "Laus Veneris"—whose speaker first "turned" to follow a brand-new God, Christ, but then "returned" to the Olympian Venus whose reign had ended—Swinburne proved that, as a poetic and spiritual father, "He has done as [Lawrence has] done." Therefore, Swinburne surely would not censure Lawrence for his "Turn and about," his turn from "the stark immortal / Fields of death" and to the "ripe wheat" of the present (the turn that Lawrence chronicles as he moves from his first to his second stanza), his about-face and consequent *return* to the worship of that which was living but is now dead.

Any such identification of Orion with Swinburne, however, is bound to be less than fully convincing. For one thing, Orion seems to represent some kind of judgement that Lawrence would dread; words like "no doubt" and "suppose" make the eighth and ninth stanzas into little more than uncertain statements of hope that the ascendant Orion would approve of the speaker's "commission[s]." Swinburne, having himself chosen the decadent way, would prove a most unlikely judge of Lawrence. For another thing, Swinburne is not the only Victorian to inform Lawrence's "Hymn." Indeed, Thomas Hardy's very different kind of poetry, which in many ways proves the more challenging source of inspiration for Lawrence, must be faced off against or even married to the Swinburnian strain of Victorian lyric if Lawrence is to come through, if he is to generate the new ethos needed to replace the passing Shelleyan one.

The earthy, erotic scene that Lawrence suddenly drops in stanza 5 of the "Hymn to Priapus" and thus leaves provocatively unfulfilled and incomplete is one that can be found energetically set forth in *Tess of the d'Urbervilles* (1891). In that novel, Hardy describes a barn dance attended by villagers and farmhands of the Tantridge region:

> Through this floating fusty *debris* of peat and hay, mixed with the perspirations and warmth of the dancers, and forming together a sort of vegeto-human pollen, the muted fiddles feebly pushed their notes, in marked contrast to the spirit with which the measure was trodden out. They coughed as they danced, and laughed as they coughed. Of the rushing couples there could barely be discerned more than the high lights—the indistinctness shaping them to satyrs chasing nymphs—a multiplicity of Pans whirling a multiplicity of Syrinxes; Lotis attempting to elude Priapus, and always failing.[16]

The passage from *Tess*, certainly, is enough to suggest that Hardy was the first-comer to the world of the barn and to its sensual, country Lotises, that Lawrence is thus a son with a juvenile passion for something that isn't his. If Hardy is the Priapus that never fails in his rustic relations, a procreative force in a primeval world, then Lawrence, as a second-generation barnyard guest, proves to be something of an Oedipal dancer. The country lass and the dead mother are thus, in a horrible sense, psychologically inseparable, a fact which may suggest that Lawrence suspects here what he will come to fear later, namely, that all his attempts at new creation begin in incest, that the words and things out of which he would attempt to bring or make something original are always his own parents.

The passage from *Tess*, however, is not the most convincing, let alone the exclusive, evidence of Hardy's powerful precedence. In the process of examining all the Swinburnian images, myths, and diametrical patterns present in Lawrence's poem, we may have felt that the "Hymn to Priapus" doesn't look or sound or feel very much like Swinburne. Take a stanza like

> Something in me remembers
> And will not forget.
> The stream of my life in the darkness
> Deathward set!

This sounds somewhat less like Swinburne's

> Though art more than the day or the morrow, the seasons
>   that laugh or that weep;
> For these give joy and sorrow; but thou, Proserpine,
>   sleep

and more like one "Ditty" by Thomas Hardy:

> Upon that fabric fair
>   "Here is she!"
> Seems written everywhere
>   Unto me!

or another:

> And we were left alone
> As Love's own pair;
> Yet never the love-light shown
> Between us there!
> ("At an Inn")

> Face unto face, then, say,
> Eyes my own meeting,
> Is your heart far away,
> Or with mine beating?
> ("Between Us Now")

> Yet, Dear, though one may sigh,
> Raking up leaves,
> New leaves will dance on high—
> Earth never grieves!
> ("Autumn in King Hintock's Park")

On closer inspection, we find that what Lawrence has in fact done is to compromise the very regular anapestic hexameter couplets of Swinburne's "Hymn to Proserpine" with Hardy's looser stanza form. If we rewrite the following quatrain from Lawrence's "Hymn to Priapus,"

> He can add the reckoning up
> I suppose, between now and then,
> Having walked himself in the thorny, difficult
> Ways of men.

in the form of a rhyming couplet, the secondary presence of Swinburne begins to be noticeable;

> ˘ ˘ ´ ˘ ´ ˘ ˘ ´ ˘ ´ ˘ ˘ ´
> He can add the reckoning up I suppose, between now
> ˘ ´
> and then,
> ˘ ˘ ´ ˘ ´ ˘ ˘ ´ ˘ ´ ˘ ˘ ´ ˘
> Having walked himself in the thorny, difficult ways of
> ´
> men.

Swinburne's presence, nonetheless, remains secondary, not just because it is felt only when Lawrence's lines are so altered but also because it is the meaning and implications of Hardy's art—not his rhythms—that preoccupy the later poet in the "Hymn to Priapus." One of Hardy's *Wessex Poems* that Lawrence no doubt knew well, "The Dance at the Phoenix," tells of a woman whose girlhood "had hardly been / A life of modesty"; by sixteen she had known half the "troopers of / The King's-Own Cavalry." At age sixty, lying in bed next to the sleeping husband to whom she has always been faithful, she hears some soldiers making merry at the Phoenix Inn. "'Alas for chastened thoughts!'" she says, and soon she has left the house, her "springtide blood" aflow. Hardy describes her ensuing night of "unchastening," her reentry into the life of her youth (like a Lawrentian phoenix rising from its ashes even as it dies), through the metaphor of "dancing." She "soared and swooped" until the

> chime went four,
> When Jenny, bosom-beating, rose
> To seek her silent door.

Because such moments of ecstasy have no place in what we deem mature life, because the social repercussions that will inevitably follow such a night's revelry would end the old woman's life as she has come to know it, morning finds Jenny dead.

Hardy published a number of other poems about "dancing," most of them in the same volume, *Time's Laughingstocks*, in 1909, the year of Swinburne's death and three years before Lawrence composed his "Hymn." "The Night of the Dance" describes a man's anticipation of festivities to come in an old "thatch" barn where "sparrows flit" and "owls . . . whoo from the gable[s]." He seems to sense that "Sweet scenes are impending here" (Lawrence will later say "ah, it was sweet!") and "That She will return" his vows tonight in "Love's low tongue." As the speaker thinks these amorous thoughts and awaits the anticipated hour, it would seem, he thinks, that "The cold moon . . . centers its gaze on me." Like the star that "witness[es]" Lawrence's doings and thoughts,

> The stars, like eyes in reveries,
> Their westering as for a while forborne,
> Quiz downward curiously.

"After the Club Dance," another and perhaps the most important influence on the "Hymn to Priapus" that can be found in Hardy's 1909 volume, is the narrative of a woman walking home alone from a rural dance. There she, like the "soft country lass" of Lawrence's poem, has been "broken" for some fellow. And he, it now seems, blames her for allowing him the pleasure he himself sought:

> Black'on frowns east on Maidon
> And westward to the sea,
> But on neither is his frown laden
> With scorn, as his frown on me!
>
> At dawn my heart grew heavy,
> I could not sip the wine,
> I left the jocund bevy
> And that young man o'mine.

The roadside elms pass by me —
Why do I sink with shame
When the birds a-perch there eye me?
They too have done the same!

The poet delivers his ironic commentary indirectly through the confused mind of the girl. She is an "innocent" in the way that Tess Durbeyfield is, for Hardy, "A Pure Woman." She knows—or thinks she knows—her indulgences to be perfectly natural. What is more, she knows her young man has "done the same" as she. She cannot understand why pleasure should turn to "scorn" and why her spirits, recently high, should now have to "sink with shame." Whether or not the last, exclamatory line of the poem is a triumph for the speaker is not clear. But the poet's triumph is: Hardy's ironic structure celebrates natural energies and scorns those perverse laws of society which would always identify their manifestation as corrupt.

Thus, although several poems by Hardy together with Swinburne's Proserpine poems can be seen providing some of the poetic building blocks of Lawrence's "Hymn," Hardy is far more to the poem than a way of expressing, analyzing, and coming to terms with life, an artistic problem, or both. He is, rather, the reason why terms need to be come to. In generating a sensibility, a world view, he generated the crisis Lawrence's poem depicts, responds to, and in a sense *is*. That sensibility—an appreciation for the sensual, for the quick throb of the physical in everything—is one that greatly compels Lawrence. This much we know from his criticism of Shelley, who, according to the *Study of Thomas Hardy* that Lawrence was to write two years after completing the "Hymn to Priapus," was primarily a bloodless and bodiless abstraction.[17] What we see in the "Hymn to Priapus," however, is Lawrence's fear that he himself may be something of an old-fashioned, asensual abstraction. How, then, is Lawrence to continue the work that Hardy began? How is *he* to develop Hardy?

Although I will ultimately be arguing that Lawrence succeeds in radically reoriginating tradition, it is important first to consider some of the ways in which Hardy might seem to offer a kind of anachronistic advance on a poet forty-five years his junior. Hardy's poem about the old woman who thrills to "The Dance at the Phoenix," like Lawrence's "Hymn to Priapus," relates the dances of sex and death. But where Lawrence's poem is threatened by morbidity, Hardy's is witty and satiric. The "death" of Jenny, after all, cleverly signifies on one hand a renewed, orgasmic intensity of life and on the other the killing guilt which society instills. Hardy's Jenny, like the speaker of Lawrence's poem, might seem to want to revivify a dead past, but the important difference is this: whereas Jenny's search for a dead past becomes an intensely living present, Lawrence's plunges him into gloomy thoughts of a love lost to time. The treatment of incest in Lawrence's poem is reminiscent of Hardy's somewhat quieter exploration, and again the predecessor manages a brighter tone. At "The Dance at the Phoenix," young men dance in high spirits and reckless abandon with a woman their fathers once "knew," a woman old enough to be their mother. At Lawrence's Christmas dance, the poet's sub-liminal recognition that his dance follows the same steps that his father's did (whether or not one accepts the suggestion that Lawrence has been the guest of a barn and a girl to whom Hardy was the original "Priapus") causes him to drown his poem in guilt and self-consciousness unknown to Hardy's more ebullient ballad.

Or take "The Night of the Dance." Hardy's ballad is excited, optimistic, poetic foreplay to the "sweet scene" to come, the dance in which "She will return" the speaker's love in "Love's low tongue." Even the "gaz[ing]" moon and "quiz[zing]" stars reflect the protagonist's present curiosity, not doubts or questions about the past or the future. Lawrence, by positioning a poem seven or eight hours after the setting of the poem Hardy has published some three years earlier, opts for a postclimactic scenario that betrays his lack of optimism, his mixed feelings, about both the sensual dance and the sensual poetry he would enjoy.

In the "Hymn to Priapus," then, Lawrence at once represses and indulges a fear. The fear is that, rather than proving his own poetic viability by recalling, developing, and thus extending poetic his-tory (however much he is determined by it), he takes one step forward only to fall two steps back to the position of Swinburne, whose "new words" were responsible for pointing Hardy (by Hardy's own admission) on the way of his own poetic quest.[18] In talking about this level of the poem, it is not necessary to read the "mother" of the "Hymn to Priapus" as an autobiographical figure, although on the more literal level, discussed earlier, she is admit-tedly that. Speaking of the symbolic identity of the mother in

Lawrence's "Hymn," one might risk reductivity by saying she represents the nourishing sensibility which Lawrence's letters indicate he associated with his mother, namely, that Romantic past from whose grave he would turn but to which he, like Swinburne, continually returns in acts of homage.

Space does not permit a full discussion of Swinburne's symbolism, but that poet's debt to an engendering Romantic sensibility is immense, and when Swinburne's personae retreat to the body of a dead or dying woman or a goddess whose sway has waned— whether it be Venus or a leprous lover or, most often, Proserpine— they usually act out Swinburne's ever-present longing for poetic decadence, to return to the service of the moribund Romantic muse. "A Ballad of Life," for instance, is written in praise of a lady who holds an instrument "strung with the subtle-coloured hair / Of some dead lute-player / That in dead years had done delicious things." When the lady revives the dead lute-player's dead songs, Lust and Fear and Shame are suddenly transformed from "grey old miseries" of flesh and blood into holy images of freshness and hope. "Now assuredly I see / My lady is perfect, and transfigureth / All sin and death," Swinburne's speaker cries out, "Making them fair as her own eyelids be." The lady would seem to be a Romantic idea, akin to the "seraph of Heaven! too gentle to be human" addressed in the opening lines of Shelley's "Epipsychidion," a lady whose presence could at once metamorphose the grey dimness of experience and the poems that capture it in song. "All shapes look glorious which thou gazest on!" Shelley claims:

> Ay, even the dim words which obscure thee now
> Flash, lightning-like, with unaccustomed glow.

The lady of "A Ballad of Life" might also be likened to the mother figure in Blake's "The Land of Dreams." In his famous essay on Blake, Swinburne dwells on the poem and quotes the lines in which a child speaks:

> O what is the Land of Dreams?
> What are its Mountains & what are its Streams?
> O Father, I saw my Mother there,
> Among the Lillies by waters fair.[19]

Such a lady, such a mother fair, reappears in "A Ballad of Death," Swinburne's dark and funereal pronouncement of the death of the divine romantic mother whose powers he succeeded in pretending were still viable in "A Ballad of Life" and, indeed, whose depicted ability to reorder reality gave life to that earlier, visionary poem. Love's lute, which transformed reality in the more optimistic piece, has in "A Ballad of Death" been abandoned, left hung on a tree where it can only intone the raw reality of "Love and Time and Sin" (lines 11–13). "A Ballad of Death" closes with its poet declaring his intent to "seek out Death's face ere the light altereth / And say 'My master that was thrall to Love / Is become thrall to Death'" (lines 107–9). This is very nearly Lawrence's position in the "Hymn to Priapus" vis-à-vis his once-enthralling mother, whether we take her to be in part a representation of a Romantic sensibility or not. He knows that having been "thrall to Love" he must, now that "Love" is dead, either abandon his worship of her or become "thrall to Death."

My identification of Lawrence's dead mother as a kind of Romantic ideal or muse, I suppose, implies the Romantic and, more specifically, Shelleyan ideal of love. It is, after all, into "Love" that lust and fear and shame are transformed by the lady in "A Ballad of Life," a lady who bears more than a passing resemblance to Shelley's beloved Emily. And the young Lawrence's view of his relation with his mother—as one that fuses souls and distributes consciousness—is expressed in terms of a Romantic definition of love. But once we see how closely Lawrence associates his familial and literary pasts, it may not be necessary to limit our definition of what the Romantic mother stands for to a Romantic ideal of love or, perhaps more accurately, to the ideal of Romantic love. For one thing, it must have been something like the more generally Romantic failure of "the aspiring, spiritual woman" to accept the merely natural, to use Tom Marshall's words, that allowed the special relation between mother and son to develop in the first place. For another thing, the word *love* itself, with which Lawrence associates both Romanticism and his mother, has a broad definition in Lawrence's poetic canon. What Lawrence often means by *love* when he is thinking about a Romantic sensibility is a faith that objects reflect the soul's deepest thoughts and feelings and that souls reflect each other in harmonious, metaphysical unity. The fish in his poem "Fish" (1923) is startlingly unlike a Coleridgean water snake that comes by with his "head up, steering like a bird." It is different, Lawrence tells us, in that the fish is utterly "loveless"—and unlovable—in his liveliness. No doubt thanks to Coleridge, Lawrence's imagination can go out to a water serpent. It can go out full of heartfelt thoughts, thoughtful feelings in exalted moods, feelings of kinship, even feelings of brotherhood. As for the fish, however, it can be touched but not loved. "My heart," Lawrence admits after trying, "couldn't own" him:

> . . .*there are limits*
> *To you, my heart . . .*
> *Fish are beyond me.*

In the last analysis, Lawrence's relationship with his barnyard dancer in the "Hymn to Priapus" is memorable not so much because it offered some specific sexual achievement but because it was fishy, that is, because it was loveless in Lawrence's general sense of the word. Through the dance the poet achieves no spiritual or psychic or imaginative union at all, no connection whatsoever between self and other save the purely physical, the Priapan, one. The other remains "beyond" his heart, unknown and unowned. The contact leaves the poet "Fulfilled and alone"; physical connection has been satisfactorily established, but no psychic or metaphysical correspondence has been sensed, felt, achieved, or imposed. The alternative epistemology which the dead mother represents is the old one which allows for spiritual as well as physical and temporal interfluence, a vision of things like the one Wordsworth represents symbolically in the second book of *The Prelude* through a description of the relationship between mother and child:

> Blest the infant Babe,
> (For with my best conjecture I would trace
> Our Being's earthly progress), blest the Babe
> Nursed in his Mother's arms, who sinks to sleep
> Rocked on his Mother's breast; who with his soul
> Drinks in the feelings of his Mother's eye!
> For him, in one dear Presence, there exists
> A virtue which irradiates and exalts
> Objects through the widest intercourse of sense.
> No outcast he, bewildered and depressed.

Thomas Hardy, writing some ninety years after Wordsworth,

gives voice to a mother, a Nature, which regrets that man ever dreamed of a Nature so vastly meaningful and beneficent, a Nature, in other words, which regrets that she was ever conceived of as a mother who could speak to, irradiate, exalt man and his moral sense. She deplores the fact that for years man insisted on seeing her "sun as a Sanct-shape," her "moon as the Night-queen," her "stars as august and sublime." His "mountings of mindsight," the "range of his vision," now reach so high that, the saddened mother laments, man only "finds blemish / Throughout my domain." So, she declares,

> Let me grow, then, but mildews and mandrakes,
> And slimy distortions,
> Let nevermore things good and lovely
> To me appertain.

Hardy's poem, entitled "The Mother Mourns," describes a fictional mother dying, a man-projected mother who was thought to reflect man's highest hopes and most fanciful dreams, a "Nature" who was once far more than just some "country lass" to be "broken" for man but who is now as carelessly used as she once was revered and exalted. ("My species are dwindling," Hardy's mother protests before she lapses into silence; "my forests grow barren," "my leopardine beauties are rarer, / My tusky ones vanish.")

In coming to a Hardy piece like "The Mother Mourns" from a poem such as the "Hymn to Priapus," however, we suddenly become dissatisfied enough with the literary anxiety that permeates one level of Lawrence's work to look beyond it and discover a deeper lever of significance. Anyone, after Lawrence, who considers carefully the Hardyan "Mother"—whether specifically in this particular poem or generally in any one of the elder author's many lyrics treating once-worshipped deities or ideals—cannot help feeling it an oversimplification to state that Hardy views the mothering past as moribund and fictive, something we are well-rid of. The more we look at a lyric like "The Mother Mourns" the more we decide that its sensibility is more deeply ambivalent than Lawrence's own. After all, Lawrence speaks in his own voice and admits, though he laments, the passing of a maternal sensibility. But doesn't Hardy, by letting his "Mother" deliver her own lament and sing her own swan song, put himself in a terribly compromised position? Although he admits that his mother may speak no divine messages, he will not give up the idea that she may still speak to man. Although he lets his mother confess that man's mind far eclipses nature's dumb indifference, he also gives her the tone of a miffed deity critical of man, an insulted goddess who will write on the tablets of an inspired poet.

Lawrence, by remembering Thomas Hardy and protesting, implicitly, his own insufficiency in a work like the "Hymn to Priapus," sends us into the texts of the precursor with a particular point of view that allows or causes us to see them in a new light. Thinking of Lawrence's own predicament, we are led to realize that his forerunner's lyrics turn from and yet sneak back towards an old romantic sensibility considerably more quickly even if somewhat less obviously than do Lawrence's own. The genius of a poem such as the "Hymn to Priapus" is that it unmakes its own "anxiety" by positing the Hardyan source. As it does so it propels us into a whole new awareness of Thomas Hardy's world view, Lawrence's inter-reactions with it, and the nature of the emerging—and emergent—results.

I have spoken of Hardy's "Mother" poems as if they were the point at which Lawrence jolts us into a critical reassessment of Hardy's sensibility. My choice is, of course, arbitrary. Another reader might first experience a revisionary recollection during contemplation of some of the images and terms that are absent in Lawrence's poem but that are to be found in Hardy's description of the barnyard dance in *Tess*, namely, *"debris,"* "vegeto-human," "trodden," "cough[ing]," "indistinctness," and "failing." Still another might become aware of these images after first being made aware, by the authorial-philosophical perspective of the "Hymn to Priapus," of the total absence of such a viewpoint in "After the Club Dance," the poem in which a young girl asks why she should feel guilty for having indulged in an activity that all Nature takes delight in. Does Hardy's artistic decision to present no more than a young girl's half-guilty questions derive from his own strong convictions of her innocence? Or does his reluctance to speak a line in his own voice grow out of a simultaneous willingness and inability fully to leave behind the punitive values of the age that bore him?

The significant fact about Lawrence's poem, then, has little to do with whether the doubts it may raise about Hardy stem primarily from its differences with one old "dancing" passage or another. It has little to do with whether the view Lawrence affords us of Hardy's living Romantic "Mother" causes, is caused by, or is simultaneous with the questions we may find ourselves raising about the depths of Hardy's earthy sensuality. The important revelation made by the "Hymn to Priapus," rather, is the critical assessment of that sensibility by the more modern poet's central self, the poet's highly original act of understanding that although in Hardy there are elements of a modern sensibility, the Hardyan sensibility as it stands is not the way of the future. Lawrence has sensed that to make sexual encounter into a more simple, natural indulgence than it has been, or to imply that but for Christian society and its muddle-headed ideals the Tess Durbeyfields of the world should have no serious misgivings about what happens in barns or under the darkness of the primeval trees, may be to bring more Priapan enjoyment into a Victorian world but it is *not* to offer a new world view. To intimate that the coming together of a man and a woman is analogous to a madcap dance at the Phoenix or a tying up of the garter before "jog[ging] on again" down "Crim-mercrock Lane" (which is what Hardy makes it in a poem called "The Dark-Eyed Gentleman"), even to suggest that it is or should be the same as what "the birds a-perch" in the "roadside elms" have so often done, is not to revise drastically the prevailing education. It is, rather, to offer but another version of the old, old story which holds that the earthy, sensual life is not a thing to be valued or prized. Far from being the locus of divine mystery, it is just about as common as it can be. Lawrence walks away from his casual sexual encounter with a Hardyan subject to return, in thought, to an absent mother. He does so not because the encounter was sexual but, rather, because it was casual. Put another way, the poet ends up in a dark no-man's-land that is outside two realms—the realm of the barn and the realm of the dead— because something in him has managed to make a connection between the two. Speaking of the "anxious" level of the "Hymn to Priapus," I said that Lawrence connects the living lass with the dead mother because of his fear as a poet that, in the words of Hardy's "Dance at the Phoenix," the world in which he "dances" is a world his "father knew." At the deeper level of discourse the same connection is inevitably made, but its meaning is different. Lawrence mentally connects the two women because something in him senses that the image of a discardable reality is the look that old, Romantic ideals project from just beyond the grave.

In his *Study of Thomas Hardy,* Lawrence suggests that Hardy developed a wonderful, residual, primitive strain of sensuality that existed in Shelley but that Shelley repressed almost out of his poems. Speaking of Shelley's poem "To a Skylark," Lawrence says that although "Shelley wishes to say" that "the skylark is a pure, untrammelled spirit," the line "Bird thou never wert," together with the very regular metrics and rhyme scheme of the poem, suggest that the Romantic predecessor knows "that the skylark *is* in . . . fact a bird" and that birds *are,* in fact, "concrete, momentary thing[s]."[20] If we think of Hardy's poem entitled "Shelley's Skylark," a lyric in which the recycled organic remains of the bird that Shelley never even saw are pictured "throb[bing] in the myrtle green," we can hear that primitive strain in Hardy that Hardy had heard in Shelley and amplified. That strain, in turn, is recombined by Lawrence with the strain of spirituality that had stood opposed, in Shelley, to the world of earthy sensuality and that Hardy had sought to reject for reasons of its opposition. Beginning with the basic rhetorical model of Swinburne's "Hymn to Proserpine," which allows the poet to position himself between half-tenable philosophies (the Christianity available is far less attractive than the Hellenism that is not), Lawrence emerges from the Victorian's situation of self-division with what he hopes will be a new poetics of living. Starting with an almost indeterminate act of self-criticism, he ends up recalling from destructive eminence two dreams that amount to what Hardy might call "twin halves of one . . . august event" ("The Convergence of the Twain," line 30)—Shelley's spiritual love and Hardy's demystified (or casual) sex. What he will be left with, when the radical project has been completed, is a new creation presided over by a new, quasi-Greek Sex-God or Priapus. "Life is a process of rediscovering backwards," Lawrence will come to write in *Sea and Sardinia* in 1921. "It is a . . . rediscovery one must make before one can be whole at all, move forwards."[21] In his posthumously published work entitled *Apocalypse,* Lawrence will put this even more succinctly when he declares that "every profound new movement makes a great swing backwards to some older, half-forgotten way of consciousness."

When we arrive at this level of understanding of the "Hymn to Priapus," we can make sense both of the conclusion and of the title of Lawrence's poem. When it is seen solely as the work of a poet obsessed with influence anxiety, the "Hymn to Priapus" makes us wonder just how it is that "Desire comes up, and contentment." The poem, furthermore, leaves us wholly unsatisfied by the answer Lawrence provides to the last question he poses:

> How is it I grin then, and chuckle
> Over despair?
>
> Grief, grief, I suppose and sufficient
> Grief makes us free
> To be faithless and faithful together
> As we have to be.

But as the statement of a poet who by having been "faithless and faithful together" to the several influences of his past is making a profound new movement out of a double sense of dissatisfaction and into a unified sense of contentment-in-liberty, these lines make sense enough. Perhaps even more important, they return us as far as the most literal level of the poem with a new understanding that can perhaps best be expressed by the following analogy. Critical dissatisfaction, that necessary corraborative of free will that we might define as the essential operation of the self, allows the capable young poet to be faithless and faithful together to the various "instincts" with which recent tradition has provided him and by so doing to begin the generation both of a half-forgotten way of consciousness and what Lawrence, in an essay, will soon call the "Poetry of the Present."[23] In the same manner, the grief which the adolescent inevitably feels as the richly essential parent-child connection gradually or suddenly breaks down and necessarily more random and tenuous relations form is an essential stage in the development of the adult being. That adult will be one who has put by both Oedipal desire and casual indulgences and created, in the process, a Priapan life in which desire and the lost mystery of involvement can "come up" together. For the young person who can be at once faithful and faithless to two forms of love at the point of early adulthood, the deep and hymnable significance of old relations can be recalled in the double sense. They can be removed from destructive presence by being remembered in such a way that they can combine with—and re-form—new relations. Lawrence's last stanza quietly suggests that such a reformation has taken place. Whereas the penultimate stanza is still self-conscious and introspective in the way that all the previous ones have been ("How much do I care? / How is it grin . . . ?"), the final quatrain has a steady, relaxed, matured, conversational tone ("Grief, grief, I suppose . . . makes us free"). The change in sound may not imply that an interlocutor has come on the scene, but it does seem to suggest that the speaker might now be ready for one.

The analogy I have been using, relating as it does a poet's act of recalling other poets and his own development as an individual, inevitably suggests something even larger, more important. The critical reinterpretation of old texts is always deeply inter-involved with the formation, in grief, of a profound "new" ethos. The rereading and rewriting of literatures, the analogy may be understood to suggest by something *like* analogy, is necessary to mankind's significant development, that is to say, to the deepening of human identity and the understanding of that identity. Literature is the field in which, coming to understand something of the possible dynamics of the past as it informs the present, we have ideas that amount to the plotting of the future.

*   *   *

Lawrence's "Hymn to Priapus" is a very rich poem, and its richness is not limited to what might be called its thick contextual plot. Although the poem has been less discussed than many of the other lyrics published in *Look! We Have Come Through!* and far less than the poems in *Birds, Beasts and Flowers,* it has not gone unnoticed by several important critics of Lawrence's work. What has interested past students of the poem, moreover, is not the affinity of the work with its several literary-historical antecedents, but, rather, what might generally be called its style.[24]

Sandra Gilbert's *Acts of Attention* is generally acknowledged to be the most significant book-length study of Lawrence's poetry. In a chapter aptly titled "The Burden of Self-Accomplishment: Preparation for Change," she singles out the "Hymn" as one of several early "apparently conventional rhyming poems [that] are really a good deal more transitional than they appear." Comparing the rhymes of this poem with those of earlier poems such as "Tease," Professor Gilbert remarks that the "skillfully irregular rhythms and unobtrusive rhymes in

> My love lies underground
> With her face upturned to mine,
> And her mouth unclosed in the last long kiss
> That ended her life and mine,

or

> Now I am going home
> Fulfilled and alone,
> I see the great Orion standing
> Looking down

suggest that [Lawrence] is now consciously trying to write a poem that will, as he later advised Catherine Carswell, 'use rhyme accidentally, not as a sort of draper's rule for measuring lines off.'"[25]

What Lawrence meant by accident, Gilbert goes on to explain, was really something like poetic design—redefined. "Design in art," Lawrence writes in an essay that Gilbert quotes, "is a recognition of the relation between . . . various elements in the creative flux. You can't *invent* a design. You recognize it, in the fourth dimension, that is, with your blood and your bones, as well as your eyes."[26] "Certainly," Gilbert concludes, "the best of the rhymes that link the uneven lines of 'Hymn' seem not to have been imposed on the poem but rather 'recognized' by the poet as a part of his attentive meditation on 'faithless and faithful' grief."[27]

Gilbert's judicious response to Lawrence lies somewhere near the middle of a spectrum of critical points of view, most of which explicitly or implicitly carry on the work of denying R. P. Blackmur's by now famous claim that Lawrence utterly lacked craftsmanship or any concern for poetic form and that he was, consequently, a merely "hysterical" poet. On one end of the critical spectrum are the defenders who seek to deny the charge that Lawrence lacks craftsmanship by denying that all great poetry rests on craftsmanship. Some poets are "pilgrims," not "citizens," Auden writes; Karl Shapiro says that "Lawrence . . . broke through the facade of artistry and literary affectation and stood at the doorway of poetry itself"; and R.G.N. Salgado argues that Lawrence ignored the claims of formal patterns, especially metrical ones, and in his better poems thereby achieved "unmediated, naked vision."[28]

A different kind of critical defender insists that Lawrence's poems *are* adequately long on technique—or that they are, at least, quite traditional in ways that Blackmur either cannot or will not see. "When Lawrence's imagination is fully engaged, his technique does not fail him," Keith Sagar says in *The Art of D. H. Lawrence,* and Graham Hough thinks that Lawrence's work only "partly fails from a formal point of view."[29] Harold Bloom, in his famous early response to Blackmur's charges, says that although "Lawrence may have believed in 'expressive form,'" Lawrence's "poetry, largely, does not." According to Bloom, lines which Blackmur calls frenzied can be formally analyzed and found to be "slow with irony." As for the iconoclastic pose Lawrence often struck, Bloom borrows a sentence from Frye's *Anatomy of Criticism* and counters that "Lawrence, as a Romantic poet, was compelled by the conventions of his mode to present" his poetry as "self-generated."[30]

In his essay entitled "D. H. Lawrence: The Single State of Man," A. A. Alvarez preceded Sandra Gilbert in striking a middle course between those who would rescue Lawrence by asserting the needlessness of form and tradition and those who would do so by making him formal and/or traditional. Alvarez sees Lawrence's art as rhythmical in a controlled way, but he says the rhythms grow out of the poet's thoughts and feelings and thereby resist "set meter." The "inner pressure of disturbance gives to every one" of Lawrence's poems "its own form," Alvarez suggests,[31] and like Gilbert, he supports his view of what Lawrence was doing by quoting from Lawrence's own prose. "It has always seemed to me," the poet writes in the foreword to *Pansies,* "that a real thought . . . , not an argument, can only exist easily in verse, or in some poetic form. There is a didactic element about prose thoughts that makes them repellent, slightly bullying."

Neither Sandra Gilbert nor A. A. Alvarez uses the word *casual* to describe the controlled forms of this poetry whose "ease" is its "tact."[32] The adjective, however, would seem to apply well, for Lawrence uses rhymes that, in Gilbert's words, seem not to have been imposed and rhythms that, according to Alvarez, arise as if naturally from inner feelings, thoughts, pressures, disturbances.

What I hope I have shown, in my discussion of the transitional "Hymn to Priapus," is that the "easy" existence of thought in a verse form that seems barely half-conventional in its rhythms and rhymes is also the hard-won result of marrying separate conventions, traditions, and practices of poetic craftsmanship and creating in the process a "free," "debonair," casual poetry for the present that is also a new hybrid of past forms. The stanzas that Gilbert sets forth as examples of a poetry halfway between "conversational roughness" and "smooth artifice"—a poetry, therefore, on which little seems to have been imposed—are also stanzas that interweave Swinburne and Hardy and end up sounding, and being, new. The rhythm of "My love lies underground /With her face upturned to mine" may sound casual, but the casualness derives from a tension between anapests ("With her face") and iambs ("upturned to mine"), between unpunctuated hexameter and two ballad lines of unequal length (the second line is trimeter, but the first could conceivably be called a four-beat line), between Hardy's influence, therefore, and Swinburne's.

Thus, although I have resisted identifying the Orion of Lawrence's "Hymn" with a specific poetic precursor, I am perfectly ready to admit that the more recent writings of Harold Bloom have provided Lawrence critics with a way of resolving an old debate in which Bloom himself once took sides. What Blackmur deems to be frenzy and what his opponents call a new kind of craftsmanship may also be understood as the working out of Lawrence's desire, perhaps subconscious, simultaneously to acknowledge and be free of a literary past. Graham Hough's claim that Lawrence's poems "are so independent of literary tradition" that "ordinary categories will hardly serve us"[33] is therefore only half true. Lawrence may be a great original, but his poems are no less responsive to literary tradition than are Hardy's or Swinburne's or even Shelley's, and some of the newer categories by which we understand literary influence can show us that this is so. Even Blackmur himself seems in some way to sense the tensions in his claim that Lawrence is an untraditional hysteric without craftsmanship. After pointing out a half-Hardyan stanza and commenting that even "Hardy would have been ashamed" of its "lopsided metrical architecture," Blackmur continues to use, almost interchangeably, three terms to describe Lawrence's work: "commonplace language," "low formalism," and "ritual frenzy."[34] Now these are vastly different terms that ought not to have been used so generally in describing one poet's work. "Low" is a valuative word, but if we admit its partial accuracy, then we cannot also believe Lawrence's work to be frenzied or hysterical. In truth, Lawrence's is a formalism that creates, as it were, a commonplace language that Hardy might not have been happy with, and it does so by fusing Hardy's ballad to the long and, if anything, overly-polished lines of Swinburne.

But Lawrence's past is more than just literary. It must also be spoken of in the way that Lawrence speaks of Thomas Hardy; it is "madly personal."[35] Or rather, in Lawrence's case the two pasts, literary and personal, were so inseparable that mothers could be loved in a Shelleyan way and then later come to suggest a tradition in a poem. Because Lawrence's personal and literary backgrounds are often best understood in terms of their interfluences with one another—and because the contexts of Lawrence's poetry are at once the incidents of a life, the poems of certain precursors, and the previous works that Lawrence himself had written as his personal and literary interests interacted—this study will proceed chronologically. Because Shelley was the poet most often relied on and contested during the lustre that began to draw to a close after Lawrence met Frieda, the next chapter of this study will consider the shape of Shelley's influence.

Chapter Two

Recalling the Future

"It is a curious thing," Lawrence muses in an essay entitled "Making Love to Music," "but the ideas of one generation become the instincts of the next. . . . What is her dream, this slender, tender lady just out of her teens . . . ? Because what her dream is, that her children, and my children, or children's children, will become. It is the very ovum of the future soul, as my dream is the sperm."[1] "Making Love to Music" is about dancing, but it might as well be about poetry, for if there is one belief that Lawrence is to hold to throughout his career it is that the "instinct" of any young poet is a composite of the dreams and ideas of the poetic parents.

In the poetry Lawrence wrote during his first lustre, it is Shelley who most often compels Lawrence's thinking and writing. Even in those works in which Thomas Hardy figures prominently, Shelley's importance to Lawrence can be felt. In the "Hymn to Priapus" the attempt to be more Hardyan is equally an attempt to redirect Shelleyan reverence towards the mysteries of the body. To call Shelley the major contextual component of Lawrence's first-lustre poetry is, of course, not to say that Shelley's world view is happily accepted or fully confirmed. Rather, it is to say that Shelleyan dreams are the most powerful instincts the young love poet has; that they are, indeed, the dream instincts that Lawrence, because of Shelley, believes he has the power to identify, criticize, and gradually liberate himself from.

One of the instincts the young Lawrence would identify, come to struggle with, and attempt to suppress and deny in his own life and art is the dream of sharing identity with a beloved. In "Epipsychidion," the lover's fondest wish is that two can "become the same, . . . one / Spirit within two frames, oh! wherefore two?" [lines

573–74]. Lawrence is, to a degree, possessed of the same wish, for it is "natural" that the dream of the grandparent should become the reflex of later generations. But he is also troubled enough by the degree to which experience seems to demystify the wish to wonder if the wish itself may not be to blame for modern man's sad store of romantic experience. In "Bei Hennef," written late in 1913 during his courtship of Frieda, Lawrence hints at the two sides of his attitude towards the Romantic theme of fused identities, the theme that received its first full expression in the English tradition by Shelley. "You are the call and I am the answer," he writes, "You are the night, and I the day."

> What else? it is perfect enough.
> It is perfectly complete. . . .

> Strange, how we suffer in spite of this!

Lawrence's ambivalence towards shared identity shows up well before 1913, often in the form of an implicit question. Is the suffering of lovers trying to "complete" themselves due to the fact that they have not really been willing to forfeit their individual beings, have not yet been willing to erase the boundaries of self? Or is the very desire to be "perfectly complete[d]" by and in another, to have no secrets or even differences from the other, to blame? "If I could have put you in my heart," laments the love-bitten speaker of "The End," a poem Lawrence gave to Jessie Chambers in manuscript on the day before his mother's funeral, "If but I could have wrapped you in myself / How glad I should have been!"

> And now the chart
> Of memory unrolls again to me
> The course of our journey here, here where we part.

> And oh, that you had never, never been
> Some of your selves, my love.

Shelley had written, "I know / That Love makes all things equal: I have heard / By my own heart this joyous truth averred":

> The spirit of the worm beneath the sod
> In love and worship, blends itself with God.
> ("Epipsychidion," lines 125–29)

But the push to blend, to become equal, Lawrence half-fears, may prove to be the very force of repulsion that drives a man and woman apart. Equality implies a sameness among people that Lawrence seriously doubts; he has, after all, a few instincts that are not derived from Shelley. Eventually a god may come to resent his "equality" with the worm, and it is there that suffering and eventually "The End" of a relationship begins. In "Tease," first published in 1914 and reprinted in *Amores* (1916), Lawrence very effectively dramatizes the moment of incipient resentment by letting irritation strain his speaker's comic tone:

> I will give you all my keys,
>   You shall be my châtelaine,
> You shall enter as you please,
>   As you please shall go again.
>
> When I hear you jingling through
>   All the chambers of my soul,
> How I sit and laugh at you
>   In your close housekeeping rôle!
>
> .   .   .   .
>
> Still you are not satisfied!
>   Still you tremble faint reproach!
> Challenge me I keep aside
>   Secrets that you may not broach.
>
> Maybe yes, and maybe no;
>   Maybe there *are* secret places,
> Altars barbarous below,
>   Elsewhere halls of high disgraces.
>
> Maybe yes, and maybe no,
>   You may have it as you please;
> Since you are so keen to know
>   Everything, Miss Ill-at-ease!

As long as the Shelleyan dream of love is but a fledgling hope, hope for the future of a relationship barely begun, it has the status of prayer at the moment of utterance, that is to say, there is no reason not to believe in its possibility. It is this moment that Lawrence allows in "Mystery," a poem published in *Amores*, with "Tease." "Before / The altar" of love the speaker "cr[ies]" out to his "Most High" to "stoop / And drink" him up "Like wine that is still / In ecstasy":

Commingled wines
Of you and me
In one fulfil
The mystery.

Compared to the tersely witty "Tease," "Mystery" might seem
to be a lyrical love poem in high style. And yet even in "Mystery"
there are hints of trouble to come. Can a "Most High" and a
supplicant, a goddess and a worm, commingle and "In one fulfil /
The mystery"? Does the Shelleyan urge of radically different lovers
to become commingling flames derive ultimately from sadomaso-
chism? That is to say, is it a fiction which at once represses and
expresses the desires to drink someone up and to be drunk up, the
desires—sometimes separate, sometimes present in both indi-
viduals—to annihilate and be annihilated? One thing is clear. The
longing to blend and become equal and one in a world apart, if not
caused by a fundamentally sadomasochistic relationship, leads
gradually to feelings which could engender one. Whereas the
commingling foreseen in "Mystery" is a transubstantiating one of
precious wines, the speaker of "Repulsed," who reflects rather
than anticipates, speaks in somewhat different terms. Drunk up,
he speaks of himself as a "blank; being nothing," and says:

How we hate one another to-night, hate, she and I
To numbness and nothingness; I dead, she refusing to
   die.
The female whose venom can more than kill, can numb
   and then nullify.

The "Most High" of "Mystery" is here seen as being little short of
an evil power. The wine of communion has become the killing
venom of seduction and betrayal, and the loss of separate identity
in commingling has become blankness, nothingness, a living
death.

"Excursion Train," like "Repulsed," is one of the deservedly
acclaimed "Helen" poems that Lawrence wrote between 1909 and
1912. In it, the poet speaks with a raw immediacy paradoxically
heightened by the interior monologue form. Once again, he ex-
presses his belief that the longing for perfect commingling, having
first become a catalyst of irritation (as in "Tease"), finally develops
into an almost hateful desire to repulse the beloved. "Excursion

Train" also reveals that the turn in revulsion that follows the romantic quest for fused identity is just as inevitably followed by a return to the dream, for the dream is become our instinct, our "nature." "You hurt my heart-beat's privacy," the speaker cries, "I wish I could put you away from me; / I suffocate in this intimacy. . . ."

> How I have longed for this night in the train!
> Yet now every fibre of me cries in pain
>   To God to remove you!
>
> Though surely my soul's best dream is still
> That a new night pouring down shall swill
> Us away in an utter sleep, until
>   We are one, smooth-rounded!
> Yet closely bitten in to me
> Is this armour of stiff reluctancy,
>   And my dream is ill-founded.

Which is the dream and which is the "closely bitten" instinct: the "soul's best dream" or its opposition, "stiff reluctancy"? One seems the call, the other the answer; one the night, the other the day; one the wish, the other the fulfilment. The apparent dialectic seems ultimately to be a unity; call it dream or instinct, it is both. The longing for pure separation which follows insufferable intimacy only articulates itself as part of a larger and greater wish for that still unattained, perfect union of two in "one, smooth-rounded." Indeed, revulsion with any particular state of romantic affairs seems conceivable only as a necessary component of Romantic idealism, and thus nothing could be more Shelleyan than the dissatisfaction Lawrence feels following his failed, Shelleyan quest. It is easy to see the dream as "ill-founded" in particular but almost impossible to conceive of as being unfounded in general.

Of course Swinburne, as well as Shelley, inevitably comes to mind as we read Lawrence's early love poems, or rather, as we read the early poems in which Lawrence wrote about the impossibility of establishing a certain type of love relationship. Lawrence's figuring of Helen as a venomous serpent-woman in "Repulsed," his "dream" of an "utter sleep" that would be something like annihilation ("Excursion Train"), and indeed, whole passages of yet other *amores* are reminiscent of Swinburne. ("Nothing will ripen the bright green apples / Full of disappointment and of rain," declares the speaker of "Ballad of Another Ophelia," a poem that Lawrence sent to Harriet Monroe in 1914 and that rather obviously invokes "The Triumph of Time.") And yet in spite of Lawrence's obvious interest in Swinburne and other decadents during his early years as a poet, it is not really Swinburne that prepossesses him. Rather, the similarity between Lawrence's failed love poems and Swinburne's, like the likeness we saw between the "Hymn to Priapus" and the "Hymn to Proserpine," results from the fact that Lawrence and Swinburne both faced similar difficulties. In the case of the "Helen" poems and "The Triumph of Time," the difficulty is that of living and writing poems in a world that resists Shelley's more expansive definitions of the powers and possibilities of love.

"Lightning," a poem first published in 1911 and written at about the same time as "Tease" and "Mystery," "Repulsed" and "Excursion Train," powerfully illuminates the difficulty any modern man or woman has in finding a way of living outside the enclosures of old dreams. In so doing, the poem effectively outlines some of the troubles the poet must have in coming through one epistemology to another. The terms of the poem are more obviously sexual than those in "Mystery" or "Tease." Indeed, it might even be argued that this poem is not in any significant way about the Shelleyan dream of love, that the situation described is nothing more or less than a contest between an insistent sensualist and a Victorian prude. And yet sex, in the poem, is a willfully employed means to an end, the end being the annihilation of individuality, the swallowing up of identity. "Holding" the "clinging flesh" of a woman in a night so black that it "hid her from me, blotted out every speck," the speaker says that he

> . . . leaned in the darkness to find her lips
> 　　And claim her utterly in a kiss,
> When the lightning flew across her face
> And I saw her for the flaring space
> 　　Of a second, like snow that slips
> From a roof, inert with death, weeping "Not this! Not
> 　　this!"
>
> .　　.　　.　　.　　.　　.　　.　　.　　.　　.
>
> And I heard the thunder, and felt the rain,
> 　　And my arms fell loose, and I was dumb.

> Almost I hated her, sacrificed;
> Hated myself, and the place, and the iced
>   Rain that burnt on my rage; saying: Come
> Home, come home, the lightning has made it too plain!

It seems fair enough to say that the men who speak in Lawrence's poems—and especially in the early love poems, written with specific lovers in mind—cannot in any meaningful way be separated from the poet himself. In this case "Lightning" shows us clearly Lawrence's complex attitude towards the Shelleyan dream of claiming and being claimed. When, in the "flaring space / Of a second" the speaker sees his beloved's fear of being perfectly assimilated, even momentarily, in himself, he seems simultaneously to feel that he is being deprived of some of the thrill of lovemaking by a prude and that his beloved is something less for having been so perfectly claimed, sacrificed. She seems to be resented at once for her resistance to becoming part of him and for becoming part of him. Thematically, Lawrence's poem is as divided against itself as its speaker's consciousness is. "Lightning" does not allow us any perspective on the situation other than or larger than that offered by its speaker, who, if he is a persona, is such an unperforated one that we cannot call him that.

And yet the poem, through its intensity, does manage to reveal a problem, illustrate a dilemma, and thus, by recalling (remembering) the situation in its complexity, begin the work of recalling (silencing, removing from play, eradicating) the dream-instinct that led to the situation. The work of recalling, revealing, and thus recalling the dynamics of Shelley's dream in the sense of undreaming and eventually replacing it is extremely important to Lawrence, for if "Lightning" makes anything clear, it makes clear the fact that *with* the dream there is no love and only bad sex. The call of Shelley's vision is ultimately (and paradoxically, it might seem at first) home—home to isolation, home to an alienated self in a killing world of lonely loathing ("hated her") and self-loathing ("Hated myself"). This revelation is at once beyond anything and part of everything the speaker of "Lightning" says. It is a flash, the flash that caused the lover to recollect (the poet to write the poem), and it is the work of the essential self, that which is left over when from a man is subtracted his education, his instincts, that is to say, his conventional nature.

It was Shelley, of course, who believed so strongly in this power of what I am calling, for lack of any better term, the essential self. As any truly revolutionary spirit must, the poet of *Prometheus Unbound* believed that the powers of convention, of archaic dreams, can never become so thoroughly instinctual that *no* man will be able to see them for what they are and begin the work of dismantling them. In the first scene of his great drama of psycho-spiritual liberation, he has his tormented Prometheus call upon Jupiter to appear, saying that the forgotten "curse / Once breathed on thee I would recall." Shortly thereafter a Phantasm of Jupiter does appear and, when asked to repeat the curse, responds by saying, "Fiend, I defy thee! with a calm, fixed mind" [1.1.262–63]. Although the Phantasm of Jupiter seems to be refusing to comply with Prometheus's request, it is in fact merely repeating on command—with neither prefatory nor postscriptive comment—Prometheus's earlier curse on Jove. The scene thus suggests that the punishing gods that keep us helpless are but the mirror images, the airy "phantasms," of our weakest selves, of ourselves when we would evade responsibility for our own condition. More important, the scene suggests that man, as embodied in Prometheus, has the mysterious power to realize that his worst oppressors are his own instinctive customs, for upon seeing and hearing that the angry and punitive Phantasm of Jupiter is but the speaking image of his past self, Prometheus utters that sentence ("it doth repent me: . . . I wish no living thing to suffer pain") which is to impel him forward towards a Paradise of new beginnings. The Promethean act of "recalling" the curse thus proves symbolic. The universal protagonist's ability to remember his former act proves a symbol of man's power to transcend self in self-analysis and, by so remembering what he has always done and been, to recall his old identity in the other sense.

It may be useful to return for a moment to the figurative components of "Repulsed," "Lightning," and some other poems Lawrence wrote during the early years of his Promethean struggle with Shelley's view of love. Some of the major (and obviously related) terms would be poison, electricity, magnetism, stars, attraction and repulsion. In "Repulsed" the speaker, smothered in closeness, reveals that the "Mystery" of lover's wine has become a "venom." In "Lightning" the streak across the skies serves more than an illuminating function. It is at the same time a figure for the all-claiming love of the man; such a love, the lightning makes all too clear, is a killing jolt to individual being. "Release" turns the tables in an address by the poet to his beloved Helen. He "should have hated" her, he insists, had he known that she could "discharge" his "turgid electric ache," that she could "Drink it up . . . as lightning / Is drunk from an agonized sky by the earth." In "Kisses in the Train," probably written in 1910 about a relationship with Louise Burrows, union in love is described through the figure of magnetic force ("Like a magnet's keeper / Closing the round"). In "Lilies in the Fire," written about the same time with Helen Corke in mind, metaphorical lightning and figurative magnets become part of a larger vision of stars and blighted planets. The poet pictures his lover as a star and then says that her "brightness dims" as he "draw[s] near" and as his "free / Fire enters" her "like frost, like a cruel blight."

Lawrence, of course, is here remembering Shelley's vision of twin orbs becoming the same with one another and critically analyzing it, pointing out that as they draw close to one another the fire of one orb may become, figuratively speaking, icy frost to the other. Rather than "In one another's substance finding food," as Shelley described it, one or both human spheres may be "blighted." Many of the other images we find in Lawrence's poems on love similarly recall Shelley in such a way as to raise questions about Romantic idealism. Those of electricity and poison are part of one figure in "Epipsychidion," where Shelley uses them to speak, not of the dangers inherent in epipsychic union, but rather of the bitter shocks attendant on lesser loves. Seeking "one form resembling hers" of his vision, Shelley says he suddenly saw "There,—One whose voice was venomed melody," whose "touch was as electric poison" (lines 256–60); the temptress, needless to say, is not the true "lodestar" of the poet's "one desire" (lines 219–21). When Lawrence uses poison (in "Mystery"), electricity (in "Release" and "Lightning"), or both figures simultaneously, as he does in *The Rainbow*, to speak of the "bitter corrosive shock"[2] suffered by Romantic lovers striving for perfect union, he causes us to return to "Epipsychidion" wondering about those women whose first captivating "looks" came to pierce Shelley's "vitals," whose "honied words" eventually "betray[ed]," whose "beauty die[d]" away, and who were "not true" for long enough. He makes us wonder whether their faults and their cruelties and their ultimate repulsiveness were not entirely and inevitably the by-product of the overreacher's too-high dream, his too-personal and idealistic vision of a particular and perfect beloved, one with him in identity and meant for him eternally.

Shelley almost recognizes this possibility; "Epipsychidion" implicitly admits a relation between the "killing air" of various flawed and mortal women and the fact that the speaker is intent on finding in a "mortal form" the "shadow of" the very "idol of his thought." Shelley never denies that the revulsion felt in the presence of poisonous-seeming ladies flows from their failure to correspond with the much-sought-after ideal. But he does, nevertheless, have Emily in the poem, and she to some extent justifies all the despair and loathing and self-loathing that the speaker has suffered and will continue to suffer because of his dream. Thus, in effect, she justifies the dream itself.

In Lawrence, however, Emily disappears. Frieda, her only conceivable counterpart—the end of Lawrence's great love quest, the woman to whom he writes the whole volume *Look! We Have Come Through!* (1917), and in fact the last woman to whom he addresses any poetry—*is* the woman he is speaking to when he writes,

> You are the call and I am the answer,
> You are the wish, and I the fulfilment,
> You are the night, and I am the day. . . .

Strange, how we suffer . . . !

The absence of an Emily in Lawrence's epistemology, a world otherwise quite similar to Shelley's, amounts to an inconsistency as great as it first seems small. When Lawrence's echoes cause us to return to "Epipsychidion" doubting Emily, not only do the vamps look suspiciously like victims but the dream itself seems a venom and the quest for love, in Shelley's sense, a self-deceptive search for a solipsistic world of pure fantasy. The entire poem, indeed, begins to engender thoughts it probably could not have engendered before, becoming in the process a work that causes us at least to consider the possible drawbacks inherent in its author's own drive, longing, quest. By working carefully and patiently within Shelley's dream, switching off terms of description and skewing parallels, Lawrence has exposed the dream's most debilitating consequences and, in the process, transcended his own instincts. Once he has done so, we can no more return to "Epipsychidion" without seeing the fundamental antipathy of its currents of thought and language than we can return to *Paradise Lost*, after Blake and Shelley, without seeing Milton's obvious (but for a long time unapparent) sympathy with the devil.

It is, in fact, since Lawrence—since his poetry, fiction, world view—that "Epipsychidion" has come to be seen as a poem with a "dark" side, and even as Shelley's darkest poem. To Victorian critics, Shelley apparently *had* no dark side. Matthew Arnold saw only "luminous wings" (beating "in vain"), and even the astute Swinburne defined Shelley's poetry as a "rhapsody of thought and feeling coloured by contact with Nature."[3] The fact that to readers of our own generation Shelley's poetry sings mostly of failure and cold despair only gives credence to Gerard Genette's maddeningly provocative claim (a claim perfectly in debt to Borges) that "if it was given to me to read any page written today . . . as it would be read in the year 2000, I would know the literature of the year 2000."[4] Writers such as Lawrence are responsible for the way in which Shelley is read in our own day, and the fact that our reading differs greatly from Matthew Arnold's is proof positive that, although Lawrence worked within Shelley's vision, his Promethean self managed to call it back and alter its looks, both within his own poems and even in Shelley's.

Indeed, after steeping ourselves in Lawrence's poems and novels, we can return to find lines in "Epipsychidion" that, save for differences in diction, Lawrence might well have written, lines that, however we explain them, seem a countercurrent to the poem's main flow. "I was never attracted to that sect," Shelley writes,

> Whose doctrine is, that each one should select
> Out of the crowd a mistress or a friend,
> And all the rest, though fair and wise, commend
> To cold oblivion, though it is in the code
> Of modern morals, and the beaten road
> Which those poor slaves with weary footstep tread,
> Who travel to their home among the dead
> By the broad highway of the world, and so
> With one chained friend, perhaps a jealous foe,
> The dreariest and the longest journey go.

True Love in this differs from gold and clay,
That to divide is not to take away.
(lines 149–61)

The passage is something of an anomaly in "Epipsychidion." To be
sure, it might be argued that the all-satisfying love Shelley envi-
sions is probably the kind that would least need the dreary moral-
ity of which the poet speaks, the one that says a lover must
"select /Out of the crowd a mistress or a friend" and "commend /
To cold oblivion" all the rest. But the fact of the matter is that this is
pretty much what the poet tells us he himself has done by follow-
ing his dream. In other words, the obvious double view in Law-
rence's poetry, by calling special attention to certain lines in
Shelley, may have caused us to see a double view latent but very
much undeveloped in Shelley's poetry. Lawrence causes us to stop
and wonder if Shelley has not presented a world view complete
with shadows that, once seen, make us wonder if it is such a
different world view from the one to which it declares its opposi-
tion, that puritanical "code / Of modern morals," the "beaten
road / Which those poor slaves with weary footstep tread." The
writing of a new poem is thus often the development of an old one,
and the development of old poetry is as much an inevitable result
of recalling it in the mnemonic sense as it is a necessary step in
recalling it in the sense of calling its phenomenology back some-
what from destructive eminence.

*   *   *

For Lawrence, the destructive eminence of Shelley is generally the
tendency of Shelley's poetry to focus on that which is beyond what
is attainable in the present moment. This tendency of Shelley's to
see always in terms of the far-off is not limited, in Lawrence's
opinion, to a destructive and self-annihilating dream of love.
Rather, as the later poet tells us time and again through his own
writings, the predecessor always seems to dream of escaping the
tangles of present stuff—whatever that stuff may be. Further-
more, these tendencies, which were dreams for Shelley but have
become instinct to us all, are, in Lawrence's opinion, worth devel-
oping into something truer to the original, primitive reality that
Lawrence believes in *because* of the pains he feels when he
hearkens too much to what he will call in "Snake," his most famous
poem, "the voices" of his "human education."

One of the poems that Lawrence is fondest of recalling in his own poetic search for exiled, tactile, present reality (or rather for the reality that he as a poet is exiled from) is Shelley's "Ode to the West Wind." Working with—and giving us a new feel for—Shelley's terms, Lawrence suggests that his own poetry must nevertheless accomplish a new kind of inspiration and accomplish it, in part, by bending the Romantic poet's force in new directions.

"Not I, not I, but the wind that blows through me!" Lawrence begins his "Song of a Man Who Has Come Through," the exceptionally fine and hopeful lyric he wrote in 1914 after his marriage to Frieda:

> A fine wind is blowing the new direction of Time.
> If only I let it bear me, carry me, if only it carry me!
> If only I am sensitive, subtle, oh, delicate, a winged gift!
> If only, most lovely of all, I yield myself and am borrowed
> By the fine, fine wind that takes its course through the
>   chaos of the world
> Like a fine, an exquisite chisel, a wedge-blade inserted;
> If only I am keen and hard like the sheer tip of a wedge
> Driven by invisible blows,
> The rock will split, we shall come at the wonder, we shall
>   find the Hesperides.

Because the "new direction of Time" is borne by a wind that "takes its course through the chaos of the world," the man who wishes not to be an anachronism must let himself be borne by that same wind. The wind that has been "blowing the [old] direction," by implication, must have carried man away from the world's chaos. Its breath may well have been that of the all-too-human voices of civilization, the inspiring voices whose dreamy messages have become our very instincts.

The poet generally directs our attention to the subject of the old, exiling sources of inspiration through allusions to a particular poetic inspiration. Shelley becomes almost a metonymn for the absent subject, the less-than-fine old winds that have not carried men and women into and "through the chaos of the world / Like a fine, an exquisite chisel." Lawrence's poem, as it charts an antithetical direction, gives itself definition by calling Shelley up as thesis. This, in turn, is accomplished by working inside the predecessor's terms. Shelley had spoken of the wind's "unseen presence" as "breath." Lawrence pictures his fine wind as an unseen hammer instead: that way, his wind can seem at once harder and more effectual. Shelley's figure resides within and just beyond the surface of Lawrence's, which pictures the fine new wind's "invisible blows." Shelley had spoken of his West Wind as the "dirge"

> Of the dying year, to which this closing night
> Will be the dome of a vast sepulchre,
> Vaunted with all thy congregated might
>
> Of vapors, from whose solid atmosphere
> Black rain, And fire, and hail will burst: oh hear!
> (lines 23–28)

So Lawrence clearly at once identifies and contrasts his wind with Shelley's by making it the clarion call of a new era. It is even, perhaps, the wind that Shelley foresaw but could not yet call upon or write about:

> Thine azure sister of the Spring shall blow
>
> Her clarion o'er the dreaming earth, and fill
> (Driving sweet buds like flocks to feed in air)
> With living hues and odours plain and hill.
> (lines 9–12)

It would seem that Lawrence verifies the antithetical nature of his own poetic subject and statement by identifying it with the life-giving counterwind that Shelley only sensed by flashes of prescience. And yet, once again, the compelling power of Shelley's figures is almost eerie; the invisible force by which Lawrence is "like the sheer tip of a wedge / Driven" may seem rather different from the "azure sister" Shelley foresaw as his own wind's counterpart, and yet the earlier poet too had seen the fine new wind "Driving" its earthly subjects.

The most obvious—and important—way in which Lawrence calls Shelley up both as the old wind and as a metonym *for* those winds is by describing his new poetic role in ways that recall Shelley's. He prays for the freedom to be borne:

> If only I let it bear me, carry me, if only it carry me!
> If only I am sensitive, subtle, oh, delicate, a winged gift!
> If only, most lovely of all, I yield myself and am borrowed

> By the fine, fine wind that takes its course through the
> chaos of the world.

Shelley's wish had not sounded so different, after all:

> If I were a dead leaf thou mightest bear;
> If I were a swift cloud to fly with thee;
> A wave to pant beneath thy power, and share
>
> The impulse of thy strength, only less free
> Than thou, O uncontrollable!
> (lines 43–47)

"Oh, lift me as a wave, a leaf, a cloud!" Shelley continues. "I fall upon the thorns of life! I bleed!"

> A heavy weight of hours has chained and bowed
> One too like thee: tameless and swift, and proud.
> (lines 53–56)

Lawrence's eloquent plea to be borne in the direction of thorn and rock and chaos, to be carried along in time and flux rather than to be "chained and bowed" by "A heavy weight of hours" on one hand or to escape them on the other—this wish is given power and meaning by its familiarity with Shelley. Implicit in Lawrence's lines is the realization that the quest for a new inspiration must locate the old one or at least some representative of it and raise powerful questions about its honesty and advisability. This involves recollection, which is by necessity a resubmission to the old influence or inspiration. Lawrence seems to sense that the apprehension of the new wind and the bending of the old one are twin halves of one event: neither activity can take place without the other. The essential self's apprehension of a still unknown way depends upon an almost inexplicable feeling of dissatisfaction with the only one it has ever known, whether it be the high old way of Romantic love, the casual roadside way of Hardy's dark-eyed "gentleman," or the Shelleyan way of putting the inspired self at the center of poems.

In the first line of his "Song," Lawrence associates the new direction with the habit of singing nothing of the self. He does not even say, "I sing not of myself but of the wind that blows through myself." Rather, his first sentence—"Not I . . . but the wind that blows through me"—seeks to be impersonal to the point that it is not even a sentence. The verb "sing" or "speak," though expected, is conspicuously absent, and any guesses about the part of speech played by the personal pronoun are bound to remain hazardous. Because Lawrence alludes to an old inspiration, begs to move in a new direction, and implies that the yet untravelled way will be the way of "not I, but the wind," we, by a loose process of deduction, arrive at the understanding that Shelley and those he stands for were poets only of the I. They were singers who sang with and about their own breath, who invoked natural forces or objects (such as the wind) and even claimed to be singing of the world, but who were in fact making our world out of their dream-bearing breath. If we return to Shelley's poem after immersing outselves in Lawrence's, can we find the contradiction of which the later man's poem is a flash of comprehension? (As in his love poems, Lawrence does not fully "come through" in his "Song of a Man Who Has Come Through," except to the extent that by recognizing an epistemological contradiction one moves in a new direction, for if the central self lived fully in the old epistemology, no contradictions would be seen, or rather, they would be thought and called consistencies.)

There is indeed a certain sense in which the "Ode to the West Wind" gives evidence of a desperate confusion. One of the first things that may strike a modern reader of the poem is the way in which the poet's extremely urgent address to the wind turns on itself. That is to say, the increasing vigor of Shelley's cries and, finally, his *demands* to be lightly borne as a leaf or "wingéd seed" make him all the more a separate force, a vexed and vexing power apart, the opposite of what Lawrence knows a naturally inspired man must be when he wishes to be "sensitive, subtle, oh, delicate, a winged gift!" It might be argued that all poetic prayers for all kinds of inspiration are inevitably really commands ("Sing Heavenly Muse"), and therefore whenever a poet tells a muse he needs some motivation, he is really trying to motivate a muse, move divinity or nature, pay himself the ultimate compliment by becoming a muse's muse, and prove the veracity of the compliment by proceeding to write an inspired poem. This is especially true of Shelley and, even more, of his address and petition to the West Wind. As early as the first line there is a studied breathiness in Shelley's invocation, a breathiness which requires the reader who reads aloud to look like Aeoleus himself as he or she puffs and puffs through the line ("O wild West wind, thou breath. . ."). By the last line of this first stanza there is a loud, breathy, exclamatory repetition ("hear, oh hear!") that makes us simultaneously picture the poet as wind and as one who tells the wind what to do.

To the modern reader who looks hard at Shelley's ode, there is still more evidence that the West Wind is simultaneously a trope for the natural world and its antithesis, the self-sufficient self. That evidence is what might be called the failure of the poem. By this I mean its failure to succeed in its avowed goal of tapping awesome and seemingly eternal natural force or even of becoming the lyre of this power that "chariotest" seeds "to their dark and wintry bed," this "Wild Spirit, which art moving everywhere; / Destroyer and preserver." Immediately after commanding the wind to "hear, oh hear" his invocation in the last line of stanza 1, Shelley gives us two stanzas which could hardly be more mythopoeic, further removed from "a wood that skirts the Arno, near Florence," and a "day when that tempestuous wind, whose temperature is at once mild and animating, was collecting the vapours which pour down the autumnal rains."[5]

In the second stanza Shelley pictures the wind as one whose clouds, "Angels of rain and lightning," are "Shook from the tangled boughs of Heaven and Ocean" and spread

> On the blue surface of thine aëry surge,
> Like the bright hair uplifted from the head
>
> Of some fierce Maenad.
> (lines 17–21)

In the third stanza the poet seems to go even further from his subject, the "wild West Wind" and "breath of Autumn's being." He speaks of

> Thou who didst waken from his summer dreams
> The blue Mediterranean, where he lay,
> Lulled by the coil of his crystàlline streams,
>
> Beside a pumice isle in Baiae's bay,
> And saw in sleep old palaces and towers
> Quivering within the wave's intenser day,
>
> All overgrown with azure moss and flowers
> So sweet, the sense faints picturing them!
> (lines 29–36)

Our sense that Shelley's address to the West Wind is really a plea to the self to inspire the self, that the commanding tone the poet uses to address nature is symptomatic of the poet's mortal fear of chaotic external reality and his desire not to be driven by it but rather to drive it (and thus live and write apart from its exciting and despoiling powers), seems to be borne out by the poem that gets written, the kind of inspiration that follows the invocation. This is a lyric in which figures do not even seem to grow out of subject and setting but, rather, out of other figures. The image of the Maenad's hair is suggested by an image of clouds as hair which, in turn, seems to be generated by simultaneous images of the environment as a tree and of tree boughs as hair. The picture of "old palaces and towers" is the vision of what "The blue Mediterranean . . . saw in sleep" *before* he was "waken[ed] from his summer dreams" by wind. This is a poem in which the achievement of the state requested in the invocator's petition—in this case, identification with the wind—takes place only in conditional syntax. Immediately after the two myth-making stanzas which follow the petition at the end of stanza 1, Shelley says, in stanza 4, that *if* he were a leaf or a cloud or a wave and "share[d] / The impulse of" the wind's strength, he "would ne'er have striven / As thus with thee in prayer in my sore need."

In the fifth stanza and shortest sentence of the poem, Shelley commands:

> Be thou, Spirit fierce,
> My spirit. Be thou me . . .!

Coming to the text after Lawrence, who suggests that in times past there has been a profound dissociation of the artistic sensibility and the world's chaos, the modern reader can almost hear the stanza speak two commands. There is the one that calls out for full identification of self and world, and there is another one that D. H. Lawrence has developed, a windy message in which the poet first tells the "Spirit fierce" simply to "Be," then tells himself to "Be" himself—and to be apart from that with which he supposedly wishes to be identified. To hear this latter call is, of course, to hear Shelley verging towards the kinds of self-analysis that Lawrence will practice, to hear the kind of criticism of the dream-instinct that, Lawrence hopes, will eventually free us to move in the new direction.

The last utterance of Shelley's ode is even more interesting than the fifth stanza:

> Be through my lips to unawakened earth
>
> The trumpet of a prophecy! O Wind,
> If Winter comes, can Spring be far behind?

Why does a master of language such as Shelley end one of his most powerful poems with an eye rhyme? Convention is no adequate answer, for this is the only eye rhyme in the "Ode to the West Wind," and its position at what should be that of a trumpeting, apocalyptic call is surely puzzling. If one reads the poem as I have been suggesting it can be read, then the concluding couplet almost has the effect of turning the last stanza into a cry of despair. The poet is sinking, desperate, failing in his powers on one hand while on the other remaining utterly uninspired by the wind. It has not become him, borne him afar, empowered him. The poet, through the last stanza, ever so faintly suggests the paradox that Lawrence will find, the one that will stun Lawrence into a search for the new direction by bending Shelleyan breath. The attempt to avoid agency and to find originality through self-motivation is a route which leads to failure and, ultimately, to that state of acquiescent submission to the chaotic power of the world which is far less powerful than agency itself.

It is important to remember that Lawrence sees his own originality manifesting itself in the development of paradox, in the sensing of a profound problem in a predecessor's epistemology, and in the treacherously difficult attempt to throw it into relief. To heighten the visibility of a paradox in sensibility is, for Lawrence, the only way a man can begin to overturn values, to push off in new directions of time. That kind of heightening goes on as surely in "Song of a Man Who Has Come Through" as it does in "Lightning." It can be seen in the way the poet shows us how easy it is to do as Shelley does, that is, to confuse himself with the wind, to believe the very subject of his search is something different from what it really is. "If only, most lovely of all, I yield myself and am borrowed," he writes,

> By the fine, fine wind that takes its course through the
>   chaos of the world
> Like a fine, an exquisite chisel, a wedge-blade inserted;

> If only I am keen and hard like the sheer tip of a wedge
> Driven by invisible blows,
> The rock will split, we shall come at the wonder, we shall
> find the Hesperides.

Here is a moment of danger, a moment of being pointed in that old direction where *world* (here called wind like "an exquisite chisel, a wedge-blade") is just another name for "self" ("keen and hard like . . . a wedge / Driven"). Until the line in which Lawrence says "Driven by invisible blows," it is impossible to separate the poet from his subject by his image. But with that ninth line of the poem, the shortest and penultimate line of the stanza, we can make the separation. The line is a triumphant recall of Shelley, for it power-fully amplifies what in Shelley's poem is—even for the modern reader—a barely audible and well-hidden admission. It asserts the primacy of any cosmic force over any agent; it declares that the existence of any chisel is inevitable evidence for the hammer, however invisible that greater reality or force may be to one yet lost in summer dreams of self. Once that line has been written, once that assertion has been made, Lawrence can conclude the ten-line stanza with trumpeting prophecy:

> The rock will split, we shall come at the wonder, we shall
> find the Hesperides.

That the line is an assertion is fitting, of course, since the opening out of Shelley's poem took the form of a question. Lawrence sees himself as the Spring Shelley hoped would follow Winter, the coming true of Shelley's prophecy of his own influence. But what Lawrence foresees or prophesies is not an inspired or influenced new poet or even new direction but, rather, the very world itself— the wonder—the place he has never seen but the existence of which his central self or soul passionately believes in.

The word "Hesperides" is, of course, maddening, its tone treacherous. Is it a joke? Or could a final allusion to myth and the Romantic Tennyson amount to a retraction Lawrence offers Shelley, the poet who dreamed of a dreaming Mediterranean and fierce Maenads? Is the word a moment of doubt, doubt that the rock of our grandparents' dreams can ever truly be split, or doubt that, even if it can, the wonder come by will be anything like the one that Lawrence believes in? Certainly, doubts of this kind pervade the other poems by Lawrence which converse with Shelley's ode. There are quite a few of these, and although space permits a lengthy discussion only of the "Song of a Man Who Has Come Through," it may be worth noting that a lyric like "Craving for Spring," a poem published in the same volume as "Song," is every bit as interested in recalling Shelley but a good bit less certain that the project is imminently feasible.

Lawrence addresses spring (rather than the wind) in a decidedly Shelleyan mode, perhaps so that he can agree with the need to be borne into a new era and at the same time minimize the importance of inspiration in the sense of breath or voice:

> Ah come, come quickly, spring!
> Come and lift us towards our culmination, we myriads;
> we who have never flowered, like patient cactuses.
> Come and lift us to our end, to blossom, bring us to our
>   summer,
> we who are winter-weary in the winter of the world.

Elsewhere in the poem Lawrence seems wittily to call upon Shelley, only to end his stanza by telling us that Shelley is not really what he meant at all. The passage in "Ode to the West Wind" that Lawrence directs us towards is this one:

> Drive my dead thoughts over the universe
> Like withered leaves to quicken a new birth!
> And, by the incantation of this verse,
>
> Scatter, as from an unextinguished hearth
> Ashes and sparks, my words among mankind!
> (lines 63–67)

Lawrence writes:

> I wish it were spring
> cunningly blowing on the fallen sparks, odds and ends of
>   the old, scattered fire,
> and kindling shapely little conflagrations
> curious long-legged foals, and wide-eared calves, and
>   naked sparrow-bubs.
> I wish that spring
> would start the thundering traffic of feet
> new feet on the earth, beating with impatience.

The "fallen sparks, odds and ends of the old scattered fire" that Lawrence wishes would be kindled into new conflagrations do not turn out to be Shelleyan "words" and "thoughts," what the elder poet referred to as the "sparks" he wished to be "Scatter[ed]." They are not ideas at all. Rather, they are the sperm of winter becoming the summer's thundering traffic of feet.

The idea of a purely biological reawakening is probably offered with Whitman as much in mind as Shelley. In one of his most sensual effusions, entitled "From Pent Up Aching Rivers" (1860), Whitman hymns the reproductive power of the world in spring, "Singing the song of procreation, / Singing the need of superb children," chanting

> Of the smell of apples and lemons, of the pairing of birds,
> Of the wet of woods, of the lapping of waves.
> (lines 5–6, 17–18)

Read with Whitman in mind, the end of "Craving for Spring" seems a doubtful proclamation of competence in being free of old ashes, of the old, idealistic, Shelleyan fires. The last line of Lawrence's poem, indeed, seems to hint at the author's deep doubts that he can see the world in its pristine sensuality. "If you catch a whiff of violets from the darkness of the shadow of man," the poet says,

> it will be spring in the world,
> it will be spring in the world of the living;
> wonderment organising itself, heralding itself with the
>   violets,
> stirring of new seasons.
>
> Ah, do not let me die on the brink of such anticipation!
> Worse, let me not deceive myself.

Lawrence, if he is here doubting his own personal and poetic liberation, his readiness to come at the world's physical wonder, is certainly unlike his bardic American predecessor. That does not mean, however, that Whitman offers the kind of significant challenge to Lawrence of the first lustre that Hardy sometimes poses and that Shelley consistently provides throughout the early years of the poet's development. Lawrence senses—and shows he senses—that Whitman does not really sing the world's rough chaos so much as he deceives himself while performing a late version of the Shelleyan song of self. Through the title of the "Song of a Man Who Has Come Through" and the line that begins "Not I, not I, but the wind" and never leads to the verb "sing," Lawrence directs us towards Whitman only to have us see how different his own poetic enterprise is. The American Romantic seeks to utter the words of the collective self that he believes to be the sum of the world's reality. He writes a poem entitled "Spontaneous Me, Nature" and begins another lyric with the words:

> One's-Self I sing, a simple, separate person,
> Yet utter the word Democratic, the word En-Masse.
> ("One's-Self I Sing," lines 1–2)

Lawrence seeks a distinctness, a liberty, from men that will cause the self to be entirely effaced in pure apprehension of "the rock" of the world.

Whether or not Lawrence finds that distinction, that liberty, in his 1914 "Song" is as debatable as is the success of his struggle with his Shelleyan "instinct." But I believe that he thinks he does, for the poem does not communicate anywhere near the depth of doubt communicated by the phrase "deceive myself" at the very end of an otherwise ebullient "Craving for Spring." The word "Hesperides" may imply self-deception, but only barely, and anyway it is not placed at the end of the "Song." Rather, the word "Hesperides" immediately precedes an ending that may be heard speaking with a measure of self-confidence:

> Oh, for the wonder that bubbles into my soul,
> I would be a good fountain, a good well-head,
> Would blur no whisper, spoil no expression.
>
> What is the knocking?
> What is the knocking at the door in the night?
> It is somebody wants to do us harm.
>
> No, no, it is the three strange angels.
> Admit them, admit them.

The first three of these eight lines are least troublesome; they confirm the reading of the poem that believes Lawrence seeks to be only the agent of creation's wonder, to become its human (but undistorting) voice. The lines that follow, though, introduce angels that are somewhat harder to interpret. A highly speculative reading might see them as those presiding angels of the past (Shelley, perhaps Whitman and Tennyson) who have been re-called in the double sense and rendered not only harmless but useful. The strange angels of Lawrence's wonder-ful ending may perhaps be better interpreted as beings akin to "the angel of reality" who, speaking in Wallace Stevens' "Angel Surrounded by Paysans" without "wing" or "tepid aureole," says:

> I am one of you and being one of you
> Is being and knowing what I am and know.

> Yet I am the necessary angel of earth,
> Since, in my sight, you see the earth again,

> Cleared of its stiff and stubborn, man-locked set.

*   *   *

The ambivalence towards the Shelleyan dream that can be found in the poems Lawrence wrote between 1906 and 1917, the am-bivalence that we detect in the speaker's attitude in "Lightning" or in the last line of "Craving for Spring" or in the temptation, however fleeting, to use the chisel image to define both wind and self in "Song of a Man Who Has Come Through," is scarcely to be found in the poems that Lawrence wrote after publishing his 1917 volume. Many of these later works were brought out in 1923, in *Birds, Beasts and Flowers*; most of them use rather comfortably Shelley's poem "To a Skylark"; and all of them offer an excellent example of what Shelley meant to Lawrence after he had come through his first lustre.

The poem Lawrence wrote in Florence, in 1921, on the "Bat" never precisely echoes the poem "To a Skylark." Indeed, it wants always to call the swallow the bat's opposite. And yet it is surely a fascinating and worthy companion poem to one of Shelley's greater Italian lyrics. Shelley imagines his aviary subject singing its way upward "In the golden lightning / Of the sunken sun," away "From the earth" from which it "springest" and toward "Heaven, or near it." Lawrence's picture of himself "sitting on this terrace, / When the sun from the west . . . / Departs" and watching "serrated wings against the sky," wings "Like . . . a black glove" when thrown up against "the light, / And falling back," recalls Shelley's antithetically. For Lawrence's subject (of which he, like and unlike Shelley, could say "Bird thou never wert") is opposite to

Shelley's in every way. Unlike the bird that melts like a star of Heaven in the broad daylight, the bats are seen "sewing the shadows together." Unlike the lark that goes on ascending and ascending into the unseen, as if giving the lie to gravity, the bat's true mode is descent; bats are, Lawrence reminds us, creatures that even "hang . . . themselves . . . upside down" to sleep.

In "Bat," but perhaps more so in its textual neighbor, "Man and Bat," Lawrence emphasizes these downward (and inward) proclivities ("grinning in their sleep") in order to make the creature symbolic of the demon within. Bats are made to represent the little bit of uneducable self, the dark, primitive, grossly creaturely essence which even Lawrence, because he has heard the idealistic voices like everyone else, occasionally fears, abhors, and wishes to exorcise. The poet describes his attempt to get a bat "*out from my room!*" The room, however, occasionally seems to take on dimensions of the self. "I would not let him rest," Lawrence says, "Not one instant . . . cling like a blot with his breast to the wall / In an obscure corner":

> He *could* not go out. . . .
> It was the light of day which he could not enter,
> Any more than I could enter the white-hot door of a blast
>   furnace.

Lawrence, as if with Shelley in mind, comes to identify with a nonbird seeking shelter from the bright light of heaven that would always turn, in "quick parabola," back from the transcendental quest for the "intense lamp . . . / In the white down clear."

"Bat," "Man and Bat," and "To a Skylark" come together convincingly in "St. Matthew," one of the four poems on "Evangelistic Beasts" that Lawrence published, together with the poems on bats, in *Birds, Beasts and Flowers*. Shelley's role in "St. Matthew" is clearer than it is in "Bat," for whereas in the latter poem the swallow was the bat's antitype, in "St. Matthew" Lawrence specifically identifies the skylark with the ascent from dark reality. As does "Man and Bat," the poem speaks of a man's coming to terms with his own imperfectible nature; its speaker accepts the fact that the dark blood-consciousness has its undeniable place in human life. "St. Matthew" is a monologue in which the gospel writer, who was traditionally portrayed in Christian iconography as a winged man, uses the figures of lark and bat to portray himself as someone pulled in both directions, away from the earth and towards it, out of the dark denizens of the earthy blood-self and back into them with a joyous vengeance.

"I have been lifted up," the speaker reminds his Shelleyan Christ. "But even Thou, Son of Man, canst not quaff out the dregs of terrestrial manhood!" Consequently, as "evening" comes, Matthew explains, "I must leave off my wings of the spirit" and put on "Membraned, blood-veined wings" that "thread and thrill and flicker ever downward / To the dark zenith of Thine antipodes":

> Afterwards, afterwards
> Morning comes, and I shake the dews of night from the
>   wings of my spirit
> And mount like a lark, Beloved.
>
> But remember, Saviour,
> That my heart which like a lark at heaven's gate singing,
>   hovers morning-bright to Thee,
> Throws still the dark blood back and forth
> In the avenues where the bat hangs sleeping,
>   upside-down
> And to me undeniable, Jesus.

Lawrence's Matthew, to be sure, presents himself as having a Shelleyan side. But his recognition and acceptance of his inevitable, "terrestrial manhood" is without ambivalence, even confident-sounding.

In yet another bold poem about a winged creature as unlike a skylark as it can be, Lawrence asks, "Turkey-cock, turkey-cock / Are you the bird of the next dawn?" In spite of the evening setting of Shelley's poem, we can't help suspecting that the Romantic poet's blithe Spirit is among the present morning singers. The first paragraphs Lawrence had written in 1919 by way of introducing the American edition of *New Poems*, moreover, add some credibility to our suspicion:

It seems when we hear a skylark singing as if sound were running forward into the future, running so fast and utterly without consideration, straight on into futurity. And when we hear a nightingale, we hear the pause and the rich, piercing rhythm of recollection, the perfected past. The lark may sound sad, but with the lovely lapsing sadness that is almost a swoon of hope. The nightingale's triumph is a paean, but a death paean.

So it is with poetry. Poetry is, as a rule, either the voice of the far future, exquisite and ethereal, or it is the voice of the past, rich, magnificent. . . .

With us it is the same. Our birds sing on the horizons. They sing out of the blue, beyond us, or out of the quenched night. They sing at dawn and sunset. . . . Our poets sit by the gateways, some by the east, some by the west. As we arrive and as we go out our hearts surge with response. But whilst we are in the midst of life, we do not hear them.

The poetry of the beginning and the poetry of the end must have that exquisite finality, perfection which belongs to all that is far off. It is in the realm of all that is perfect. It is of the nature of all that is complete and consummate. This completeness, this consummateness, the finality and the perfection are conveyed in exquisite form: the perfect symmetry, the rhythm which returns upon itself like a dance where the hands link and loosen and link for the supreme moment of the end. Perfected bygone moments, perfected moments in the glimmering futurity, these are the treasured gem-like lyrics of Shelley and Keats.[6]

Shelley and Keats are poets of the skylark and nightingale (and of the finality, perfection, and exquisite form the birds symbolize). They are also characterized by Lawrence *as* skylarks and nightingale; they "sing on the horizons, . . . out of the blue, beyond us, . . . at dawn and sunset." When Lawrence refers, in "Turkey-Cock," to the bird of dawn, he probably refers both to the skylark and to its Romantic hymnist. When he foresees the new day of the sensual, strutting turkey-cock, he foresees an era in which, rather than being obsessed with perfection and futurity and all that is far off— exquisite but in life unattainable—man will live and desire to live fully "in the midst of life." Lawrence also, by implication, foresees a poetry and poet that can take even the turkey-cock as subject.

A close examination of the poem confirms the hypothesis that "Turkey-Cock" is yet another poem about birds that Lawrence wrote with the skylark poet in mind. Shelley's bird had been virtually invisible ("Bird thou never wert," "we hardly see—we feel that it is there") and bodiless ("Thou art unseen" and "Like an unembodied joy"). It was known, rather, by its vocal artistry ("yet I hear thy shrill delight," "In profuse strains of unpremeditated art,"

"Like a poet hidden / In the light of thought, / Singing hymns unbidden"). Lawrence specifically avoids identifying with his object. To do so would cause his turkey to become a figure for himself or for poets in general. (Here the desire to avoid all reflexivity, all songs of self, threatens to become a joke.) Indeed, Lawrence writes three pages on the cock without mentioning sound or voice. Lawrence's thoroughly grounded, un-skylark is no hidden poet singing but rather an all-too-visible, all-too-embodied joy:

> Your sort of gorgeousness,
> Dark and lustrous
> And skinny repulsive
> And poppy-glossy,
> Is the gorgeousness that evokes my most puzzled
> admiration.
>
> .   .   .   .   .   .
>
> Your wattles are the colour of steel-slag which has been
> red-hot
> And is going cold,
> Cooling to a powdery, pale-oxydised sky-blue.

The anti-Shelleyan physicality or bestiality of the cock virtually leaps from the evocative lines of this work, many of which afford an instructive comparison between the figurative languages used by the two poets. Shelley's similes direct the reader's mind towards the ideal or the abstract, either towards a faerieland vision of nature ("Like a glow-worm golden / In a dell of dew," "Like a rose embowered / In its own green leaves") or towards an idealized human realm ("Like a Poet hidden / In the light of thought," "Like a high-born maiden / In a palace tower"). And always Shelley reminds us that no simile can truly characterize the bird, which is divine, for "What thou art we know not." Lawrence's striking similes, on the other hand, point in the opposite direction ("Your wattles are the colour of steel-slag"), referring the turkey to "obscenely" bestial forms and finding its hot earthiness almost literal by comparison:

> The vulture is bald, so is the condor, obscenely,
> But only you have thrown this amazing mantilla of
> oxidised sky-blue
> And hot red over you.

> This queer dross shawl of blue and vermillion,
> Whereas the peacock has a diadem.

Lawrence's figurative language is thus about as different as it can be from that of "To a Skylark." It tries to tell us, in Shelley's words, "What is most like thee" and then balks, not at comparing a bird to a high-born maiden but at comparing a bright-colored bird with a brighter one.

Shelley's skylark seems to stand as the symbol of what Shelley often wishes he could be. He never can know what the greater, transcendent poet speaks of, but he can imagine that if he could understand the bird's "sweet thoughts" he would learn "ignorance of pain":

> With thy clear keen joyance
>   Languor cannot be:
> Shadow of annoyance
>   Never came near thee:
> Thou lovest—but ne'er knew love's sad satiety.

The turkey-cock, on the other hand, escapes knowledge of love's sad satiety by virtue of the fact that he is a supersexual force, an insatiable being. The turkey wattles are "The over-drip of a great passion." Lawrence speaks of the bird's "super-sensual arrogance," and the effect of almost every one of the poem's amazing descriptions is that we see the cock's entire body as an erection:

> You contract yourself,
> You arch yourself as an archer's bow
> Which quivers indrawn as you clench your spine
> Until your veiled head almost touches backward
> To the root-rising of your erected tail.

As for transcendental powers, the turkey has none. Far from seeking escape, or representing escape, from those fearful contraries that Shelley speaks of in his lyric (joyance and annoyance, desire and satiety, sleep and death, before and after, laughter and pain, sweetness and sadness, what is and what cannot be), the turkey-cock lives in and almost seems to embody a chaos of contradictions. Lawrence speaks of an ugliness and ostentation that can only be called "raw contradictoriness." He sees in the arch of the ruffling fowl's back

> a declaration of such tension in will
> As time has not dared to avouch, nor eternity been able
>   to unbend
> Do what it may.

Thus if the bird can be said to live free of earthly care, it does so as differently from Shelley's skylark as can be imagined.

Lawrence's recurrent use of "To a Skylark" in these poems written during the twenties is fairly general and rather comfortable when compared to the difficult struggle with Shelley that is evident in such earlier lyrics as "Song of a Man Who Has Come Through." The various poems on birds offer arresting images of poetic objects, but they are not difficult, liberating acts of understanding a precursor. Rather, they are what the poet writes after he has settled in his mind what was wrong with the precursor, after he has left behind one stage of his life and poetic development for another.

It is in the relatively early essays, the *Study of Thomas Hardy* (1914) and the introduction to the American edition of *New Poems* (1920), that Lawrence actually discovers the painful paradox in "To a Skylark" that has given it a destructive eminence and thus a power to confuse and divide his own later sensibility. If great, original work is the act of sensing a contradiction or conflict in a predecessor's sensibility, then the *Study of Thomas Hardy* effects a more crucial development of Shelley's lyric than do "Bat" or "Turkey-Cock" or "St. Matthew," for it is in this essay that Lawrence discovers what the Promethean part of Shelley was trying to say and liberates himself by making that statement his own. The introduction—later called "Poetry of the Present"—benefits greatly from discoveries made five years earlier. Nonetheless, it fruitfully continues the work of recalling "To a Skylark" begun in the Hardy *Study*.

It is necessary to admit, before discussing the introduction as a product of Lawrence's first lustre, that the essay was written after 1917. Thus it technically falls in what I have circumscribed and called the second lustre. My cut-off dates, however, are necessarily arbitrary; Lawrence wrote numerous poems that are more properly of a piece with earlier works than they are good examples of the state of his art at the time they were composed. Poetic careers, like species, have their throwbacks, and Lawrence himself believed his introduction to fall in just such a throwback category. He ends the piece with these words: "All this should have come as a preface to *Look! We Have Come Through!* But is it not better to publish a preface long after the book it belongs to has appeared? For then the reader will have had his fair chance with the book, alone."[7]

In the introduction Lawrence associates the skylark with its most famous poet and makes both into symbols of the search for "perfection," "completion," "consummateness," "finality," the "exquisite," "symmetry," the "supreme moment of the end," and the "gem-like." Having done this, he goes on to write a manifesto on what poetry must become by way of contrast:

> But there is another kind of poetry: the poetry of that which is at hand: the immediate present. In the immediate present there is no perfection, no consummation, nothing finished. . . . If you tell me about the lotus, tell me of nothing changeless and eternal. Tell me of the mystery of the inexhaustible, forever-unfolding creative spark. Tell me of the incarnate disclosure of the flux, mutation in blossom, laughter and decay perfectly open in their transit, nude in their movement before us.
>
> Let me feel the mud and the heavens in my lotus. Let me feel the heavy, silting, sucking mud, the spinning of sky winds. Let me feel them both in purest contact, the nakedness of sucking weight, nakedly passing radiance. Give me nothing fixed, set, static. Don't give me the infinite or the eternal: nothing of infinity, nothing of eternity. Give me the still, white seething, the incandescence and the coldness of the incarnate moment: the moment, the quick of all change and haste and opposition: the moment, the immediate present, the Now. . . .
>
> There is poetry of this immediate present, instant poetry, as well as poetry of the infinite past and the infinite future. The seething poetry of the incarnate Now is supreme, beyond even the everlasting gems of the before and after. In its quivering momentaneity it surpasses the crystalline, pearl-hard jewels, the poems of the eternities. Do not ask for the qualities of the unfading timeless gems. Ask for the whiteness which is the seethe of mud, ask for the incipient putrescence which is the skies falling, ask for that never-pausing, never-ceasing life itself.
> ("Poetry of the Present," pp. 182–83)

This entire passage on the poetry of the present is written with the nightingale and the skylark, Keats and Shelley, in mind. It probably speaks out, subliminally, against Wordsworth too, who in his "Essay, Supplementary to the 'Preface'" (1815) praised that "creative or abstracting" poetic "imagination . . . which is at once a history of the remote past and a prophetic enunciation of the remotest future."[8] Nevertheless, it seems fair to say that "Poetry of the Present" is directed more against Shelley than Wordsworth or Keats. More against Shelley because it is "To a Skylark" and not the "Preface" or the "Ode to a Nightingale" that keeps informing Lawrence's defense of his poetry. "We look before and after, / And pine for what is not," Shelley had written, not implying we should enjoy that chaos of contraries we call the present but, Lawrence would say, wishing that we could stand, even for a moment, out of time in a world of "the fixed, set, static, . . . infinite . . . eternal." "The seething poetry of the incarnate Now," Lawrence has told us by way of contrast, "is supreme, beyond even the everlasting gems of the before and after," the "pearl-hard jewels, the poems of the eternities." Lawrence goes on, in his introduction, to praise the restlessness of Whitman's poetry. Echoes of "To a Skylark" would suggest that it is Shelley, not Wordsworth or Keats, that Lawrence sees as Whitman's antitype:

This is the unrestful, ungraspable poetry of the sheer present, poetry whose very permanency lies in its wind-like transit. Whitman's is the best poetry of this kind. Without beginning and without end, without any base and pediment, it sweeps past forever, like a wind that is forever in passage, and unchainable. Whitman truly looked before and after. But he did not sigh for what is not. The clue to all his utterance lies in the sheer appreciation of the instant moment, life surging itself into utterance at its very well-head. Eternity is only an abstraction from the actual present. Infinity is only a great reservoir of recollection, or a reservoir of aspiration: man-made. . . . The quick of the universe is the *pulsating, carnal self*, mysterious and palpable. So it is always. ("Poetry of the Present," p. 183)

As Thomas Hardy had done exactly thirty years earlier in his poem, "Shelley's Skylark," Lawrence tries to define the terms of his own poetry by writing simultaneously about Shelley's unseen bird and real birds, which were also, Lawrence would have us believe, unseen by Shelley. Very near the end of "Poetry of the Present," Lawrence writes:

> The bird is on the wing in the winds, flexible to every breath, a living spark in the storm, its very flickering depending upon its supreme mutability and power of change. Whence such a bird came: whither it goes: from what solid earth it rose up, and upon what solid earth it will close its wings and settle, this is not the question. This is a question of before and after. Now, *now*, the bird is on the wing. . . .
>
> The ideal—what is the ideal? A figment. An abstraction. A static abstraction, . . . a crystallized aspiration. ("Poetry of the Present," p. 185)

When Lawrence says that questions about "whence such a bird came" and "whither it goes" are questions "of before and after," he has in mind the questions Shelley asked about the unseen bird in lieu of describing a visible one "on the wing in the winds, flexible to every breath, a living spark in the storm." Of the bird Shelley would have us believe was not just a spark in the storm but a veritable "cloud of fire," Shelley asked:

> What objects are the fountains
>   Of thy happy strain?
> What fields, or waves, or mountains?
>   What shapes of sky or plain?
> What love of thine own kind? what ignorance of pain?

In Shelley's important essay entitled "A Defence of Poetry," written in 1821, one year after "To a Skylark," we find him again picturing the great poet as an unseen presence inhabiting a realm that more common men can only wonder about. The situation described in "To a Skylark"—that of a poet marveling at a lark and wondering about the "Shapes" known to the unseen singer—is thus transferred from the figurative to a more nearly literal plane, where Shelley can talk about the way in which men marvel at the poet and wonder about the unknown, ideal space he must inhabit. Poetry "acts in a divine and unapprehended manner," Shelley writes, "and it is reserved for future generations to contemplate and measure the mighty cause and effect in all the strength and splendour of their union."

Even in modern times, no living poet ever arrived at the fulness of his fame; the jury which sits in judgement upon a poet, belonging as he does to all time, must be composed of his peers: it must be impanelled by Time from the selectest of the wise of many generations. *A poet is a nightingale, who sits in darkness and sings to cheer its own solitude with sweet sounds; his auditors are as men entranced by the melody of an unseen musician, who feel they are moved and softened, yet know not whence or why.* The poems of Homer . . . were the delight of infant Greece; they were the elements of that social system which is the column upon which all succeeding civilizations reposed. Homer embodied the ideal perfection of his age in human character; nor can we doubt that those who read his verses were awakened to an ambition of becoming like to Achilles, Hector, and Ulysses: the truth and beauty of friendship, patriotism, and perservering devotion to an object, were unveiled to the depths in these immortal creations: the sentiments of the auditors must have been refined and enlarged by a sympathy with such great and lovely impersonations, until from admiring they imitated, and from imitation they identified themselves with the objects of their admiration. Nor let it be objected, that these characters are remote from moral perfection. (Italics mine)[9]

The image of the auditor in the above passage, the auditor who *feels* he is moved and softened "by the melody of an unseen musician . . . yet know[s] not whence or why," exactly parallels that employed in "To a Skylark." There the listener can only ask unanswered questions about whence and why, before and after, of a bird that "we feel . . . is there" in spite of the fact that it remains "unseen."

I have quoted more of Shelley's prose in the passage above than is necessary to demonstrate that the thematics of the "Defence" parallel those of "To a Skylark." What we can begin to see in the passage above, in fact, is that Shelley's "Defence of Poetry" stands behind much of Lawrence's prose criticism, especially his essay, "Poetry of the Present." When Lawrence characterizes one of the voices of the old poetry as that of the nightingale, and when he says that the nightingale sings "out of the quenched night," he draws upon Shelley's prose. And he barely expands on Shelley when he proceeds by characterizing Homer as both a nightingale and skylark poet. After telling us that the skylark would sing of a perfectible future, the nightingale of a "perfected past," and that poets, "as a rule," are like one or the other, Lawrence proceeds from the image of the nightingale with these words:

> When the Greeks heard the *Iliad* and the *Odyssey*, they heard their own past calling in their hearts, as men far inland sometimes hear the sea and fall weak with powerful, wonderful regret, nostalgia; or else their own future rippled its time-beats through their blood, as they followed the painful, glamorous progress of the Ithacan. This was Homer to the Greeks: their Past, splendid with battles won and death achieved, and their Future, the magic wandering of Ulysses through the unknown.
>
> With us it is the same. Our birds sing on the horizons . . . at dawn and sunset. . . . But whilst we are in the midst of life, we do not hear them. ("Poetry of the Present," p. 181)

Lawrence, as we have learned, goes on to say that Keats and Shelley, in more recent times, managed each to perform half of the Homeric task. Shelley would no doubt have accepted the compliment happily (even if it meant admitting that Keats was his poetic complement). What Shelley could never have accepted, though, is Lawrence's claim about the essential ineffectuality of the nightingale poet, the skylark poet, and apparently, even of that rare, marvelous, Homeric hybrid. Shelley believed the poetic ideals of his "nightingale," Homer, to be at once perfect (Shelley speaks of both the "ideal perfection" and the "moral perfection" to be found in Homer) and efficacious. "The sentiments of the auditors must have been refined and enlarged by a sympathy with such great and lovely impersonations," Shelley writes, "until from admiring they imitated, and from imitation they identified themselves with the objects of their admiration." Shelley and Lawrence agree on one thing: that Homer was, in Lawrence's terms, nightingale and skylark, poet of the perfected past and an equally perfectible future. Lawrence, however, would deny that the realm of the perfect ever existed or ever will or could exist in present reality except in literature—of a certain type. Shelley believes the Greek auditors learned of, imitated, and finally "identified . . . with" (by which Shelley would seem to mean "attained") "moral perfection." Lawrence—who argues that the Greeks heard Homer "as men far inland sometimes hear the sea"—counters that modern men, "whilst [they] are in the midst of life," do not even hear the "poets of perfection."

Earlier in this chapter I generalized by saying that for Lawrence the destructive eminence of Shelley is the tendency of his poetry to focus on that which is unattainable in the present moment. It would be equally fair (if equally reductive) to say that Lawrence sees Shelley's "Defence" as having attained a similarly destructive eminence and that the later writer's prose intends to begin the work of calling Shelley's back. The earlier poet, after stating his belief that the characters in Homer are the embodiments of moral perfection ("edifying patterns for general imitation"), defends his claim by anticipating the objection that a Hector wears the armor and even the vices of a real man. "A poet," Shelley writes, "considers the vices of his contemporaries as a temporary dress in which his creations must be arrayed, and which covers without concealing the eternal proportions of their beauty. An epic or dramatic personage is understood to wear them around his soul, as he may the ancient armour or modern uniform around his body." But, Shelley concludes, the important thing to remember is that when such a figure emanates from the mind and spirit of a great poet, "a majestic form and graceful motions will express themselves through the most barbarous and tasteless costume. Few poets of the highest class have chosen to exhibit the beauty of their conceptions in its naked truth and splendour; and it is doubtful whether the alloy of costume, habit, &c., be not necessary to temper this planetary music for mortal ears."[10]

Lawrence's theoretical perspective is in diametrical opposition to Shelley's. Whereas for Shelley the proper subjects of art are ideal and the contexts through which they are presented are but "barbarous costume," a "temporary dress . . . which covers without concealing them," for Lawrence context is all. In the "Preface" to the 1928 edition of *Collected Poems*, he writes:

> It seems to me that no poetry, not even the best, should be judged as if it existed in the absolute, in the vacuum of the absolute. Even the best poetry . . . needs the penumbra of its own time and place . . . to make it full and whole. If we knew a little more of Shakespeare's self and circumstance how much

more complete the Sonnets would be to us, how their strange, torn edges would be softened and merged into a whole body![11]

Shelley had said that "no living poet" can ever be fully appreciated until his own age has passed and the jury of "peers" enmeshed in the contexts out of which the poet fashions superficial raiments has given way to "the selectest of the wise of many generations."[12]

Where Shelley focuses on the "eternal proportions" of art's subjects, Lawrence asks to be given "nothing fixed, set, static, . . . infinite or . . . eternal." And although the two poets can agree that naked splendor is poetry's *raison d'être*, Lawrence is radically revising Shelley's terms. Shelley's "naked . . . splendour" is the "form" and "truth" and "conception" that lie beyond the "barbarous and tasteless costume" which "poets of the highest class" use to "exhibit" their ideas and "temper . . . planetary music for mortal ears." Lawrence proposes a different view of poetry when he cries: "Let me feel the heavy, silting, sucking mud, the spinning of sky winds. Let me feel them both in purest contact, the nakedness of sucking weight, nakedly passing radiance. . . . Give me the still, white seething, the incandescence and the coldness of the incarnate moment." He transforms what for Shelley would have been merely natural hues into a "white seething," a nakedness "passing radiance," an "incandescence" that Shelley would have seen, no doubt, as part of the "dome of many-colored glass" that "stains the white radiance of eternity" ("Adonais," lines 462–63).

Poetry, for Shelley, "lifts the veil from the hidden beauty of the world, and makes familiar objects seem as if they were not familiar," for it finds always the "exalted content" of things. It reveals and thus, in Shelley's view, is itself "the perfect and consummate surface and bloom of all things, it is as the odour and the colour of the rose to the texture and the elements which compose it, as the form and splendour of unfaded beauty to the secrets of anatomy and corruption." The pleasure poetry gives, in Shelley's view, is correspondingly higher than the pleasure that can be given by familiar objects—even roses. For "there are two kinds of pleasure," he tells us, "one durable, universal and permanent; the other transitory and particular." Poets are, by definition, "those who produce and preserve" the "pleasure in this highest sense."[13]

Lawrence, in "Poetry of the Present," has allowed Shelley's definition to stand, as it were, for the poetry of the past. Shelley says poetry is "perfect and consummate": Lawrence speaks of a "consummateness and perfection" in the old poetry. Shelley writes, "It is as the odour and the colour of the rose to the texture and the elements which compose it"; Lawrence counters by ignoring the analogical nature of Shelley's statement and saying simply that "another kind of poetry" would view odour and colour in a different way. "The perfect rose is only a running flame, emerging and flowing off, and never in any sense at rest, static, finished" ("Poetry of the Present," p. 182). The flower, no matter how idealized, "still has its roots in . . . manure," Lawrence reminds us, "and in [its] perfume hovers . . . the faint strange scent of earth, the under-earth, . . . the black . . . corrosive humus. Else the scent would be just sickly sweet."[14] The poetry of the present recognizes no "consummate . . . bloom": the "water lily heaves herself from the flood, looks round, gleams, and is gone." Shelley insists that poetry doesn't concern itself with "anatomy and corruption," and Lawrence responds by saying, "Tell me of the . . . *pulsating, carnal self,*" of "the incarnate disclosure of the flux, mutation in blossom, laughter and decay perfectly open in their transit, nude in their movement before us" ("Poetry of the Present," pp. 183, 182).

"Free verse," that "insurgent naked throb of the instant moment," is something that Whitman practiced but could not put to fullest use, owing to his tendency to sing more often of an inner order and a human network of associations than of the chaos of a world in flux. Whitman, of course, wrote lines that perfectly anticipate Lawrence's "Introduction." He speaks of "the corpse" and says:

> I think you are good manure, but that does not offend me,
> I smell the white roses sweet-scented and growing,
> I reach to the leafy lips, I reach to the polished breasts of
>   melons.

But Whitman writes these lines in the forty-ninth meditation of "Song of Myself" (1855), the meditation immediately preceding the one in which he speaks of something in the world and says, "There is that in me—I do not know what it is—but I know it is in me." Lawrence sees himself as developing Whitmanian free verse through the recall of Shelley, that is, through the development of a poetry that will be totally involved in time, in physical objects, and thus in the realm of contexts which, by being utterly impersonal, are neither spiritual nor intellectual.

In Shelley's view, poetic language is powerful because of its "relation to thoughts alone," whereas the more "physical" pigments and paper and strings and wood and wind and light involved in other artistic media interact and thus "enfeeble" communication, "interpose between conception and expression," "limit" the power of the "hieroglyph." But Lawrence relishes an art form "instantaneous like plasm" in which the media and their objects all, in Shelley's proto-Lawrentian words (that is to say, in a language Lawrence developed), "have relations among each other."[15] In poetry "There must be the rapid momentaneous association of things," Lawrence writes, "which meet and pass on the forever incalculable journey of creation: everything left in its own rapid, fluid relationship with the rest of things" ("Poetry of the Present," p. 183). "Much has been written about free verse," he goes on to say,

> But all that can be said, first and last, is that free verse is, or should be, direct utterance from the instant, whole man. It is the soul and the mind and the body surging at once, nothing left out. They speak all together. There is some confusion, some discord. But the confusion and discord only belong to the reality as noise belongs to the plunge of water. . . . The utterance is like a spasm, naked contact with all influences at once. (Ibid., pp. 184–85)

Free verse thus restores relation by reuniting the mind with physical things through their words. Through the spontaneous language of free verse, the soul, mind, and body can truly be surging at once.

The first and most famous paragraph of Shelley's "Defence," of course, expends at least as much energy in making distinctions between such things as Lawrence's introduction expends in trying to fuse them in unity. "Reason is to the imagination as the instrument to the agent, as the body to the spirit, as the shadow to the substance," Shelley writes, implicitly setting up a value system in which bodies are but the instruments of greater agents, shadowy umbrages of a difference called the soul substantial. The same basic world view—and the same terminology—hold sway in "Epipsychidion," where the lover cries out,

Beloved! O too soon adored, by me!
For in the fields of immortality
My spirit should at first have worshipped thine,
A divine presence in a place divine;
Or should have moved beside it on this earth,
A shadow of that substance, from its birth.
(lines 132–37)

Upon reading "The Wild Common," the first poem to appear in
Collected Poems, a volume Lawrence claims to have arranged, "as
far as possible, in chronological order,"[16] we realize that Lawrence
is, from the beginning of his career as a poet, trying to return to a
pre-idealistic view of things by using but recombining Shelley's
terms; soul becomes shadow vis-à-vis body, the only true
substance:

But how splendid it is to be substance, here!
My shadow is neither here nor there; but I, I am royally
here!
.   .   .   .

Over my skin in the sunshine, the warm, clinging air
Flushed with the songs of seven larks singing at once,
goes kissing me glad.
.   .   .   .

Oh but the water loves me and folds me,
Plays with me, sways me, lifts me and sinks me,
murmurs: Oh marvellous stuff!
No longer shadow! —and it holds me
Close, and it rolls me, enfolds me, touches me, as
if never it could touch me enough.

When Lawrence says, at the end of the poem, "All that is right, all
that is good, all that is God takes substance," he is attempting to
return us to the world where man lived fishlike. That is, he lived a
marvelous, deliciously lovely life in which, because all the ele-
mental stuff that enwombed him was outside and beyond knowl-
edge and understanding, all the element was mystery. He would
return us to the meaning that, he will argue much later in *Apoc-
alypse,* "the Greeks meant by the word god." He would achieve
that state, long forgotten to Western consciousness, in which
"everything was *theos*; . . . whatever struck you was god,"

whether "a pool of water" or the "chill of the water as you touched it."[17] And he is attempting to move us into such an epistemology by recalling Shelley's.

"The Wild Common" still seems to be on Lawrence's mind in 1919 as he writes down his critical views in "Poetry of the Present." When he writes in that essay of the wonderful poetic plasm in which soul and substance, indeed "all influences at once," speak together, he says: "There is some confusion, some discord. But the confusion and the discord only belong to the reality as noise belongs to the plunge of water. . . . The utterance is like a spasm, naked contact with all influences at once." This might seem to suggest that Lawrence thinks "The Wild Common" is close to being free verse, since it is a poem about a "naked lad" immersing himself with a plunge not only in water but also in the colors of may-blobs and gorse bushes, the sounds of insects and rabbits and lark songs.

"The Wild Common" is, however, a rather puzzling work. Although it does provide the general reader a lively vision of things in which the divinity of mere substance, *theos*, can be appreciated, it presents the student of transitional poetry with more questions than answers. Take Lawrence's sensual immersion in the "songs of seven larks singing at once." If his poem is in no way a quest for Shelleyan goals ("truth," "ideal," "form," "universals," "exalted content"), then what are we to make of the number seven? The physical world may be mysterious, but the number seven has traditionally suggested a more-than-physical mystery.

We could see the number as a compromise, a compromise similar to the use of a formality like regular rhyme in a poem full of rough diction and conversational rhythms. And there is, to be sure, another way of viewing the number that sees it as evidence, not of a tendency towards epistemological and aesthetic relapse, but of something quite the opposite. It could conceivably be argued, for instance, that if the poet had not truly "come through," he would most likely shy away from using the number seven in a poem that seeks to describe the lush world of substance even if seven was, in fact, the number of things smelled, seen, or heard. The use of seven might thus be seen, not as proof that the poet is still a metaphysician, but rather as confirmation of the fact that he is not; seven is merely a number, a way of describing, appropriate in all poetic contexts so long as it truthfully records experience.

We can similarly explain away the fact that skylarks make the "seven-fold" songs enjoyed by the poet of "The Wild Common." We could say that if skylarks are what the poet heard, then skylarks are what he should say he heard; only a poet still dominated by the Shelleyan vision would hear larks but then say they were darkling thrushes or oven birds, since his own poem seeks to be true to simple, sensual experience.

And yet we wonder. It may be true that the poet of the present should be able to say he heard seven skylarks if he really heard seven skylarks, but our personal suspicion is probably that nobody could count more than two or three simultaneous birdsongs, or that even if seven birds could be heard singing at once, at least one would be a swallow or a thrush. We wonder if the poet is not protesting too much our bad faith and his own complete independence from it.

The allusions in "Poetry of the Present" to Shelley's prose and poetry on one hand and, on the other, to "The Wild Common," a poem which makes use both of Shelley's prose (shadow vs. substance) and poetry (heard but apparently unseen skylarks)— these allusions in concert are extremely helpful to our understanding of how Lawrence accomplishes what he accomplishes in "Poetry of the Present." By suggesting "The Wild Common" as *exemplum* Lawrence has reminded the contextual reader of the difficulties he or she had with that very early poem. He thus sharpens, no doubt inadvertently, our awareness of ambivalences in the essay itself. For instance, the careful reader becomes sensitive to a tension not unlike that in "The Wild Common" when he or she reads; "The living plasm vibrates unspeakably, it inhales the future, it exhales the past, it is the quick of both, and yet it is neither." Is such a living plasm ultimately unlike that skylark which, because of its freedom from temporal constraints, need not "look before and after" and "pine for what is not"? What contains both past and future while being neither of those things save for the eternal? And isn't the poetry Lawrence would usher in supposed to be utterly unconcerned with all but the present moment? Or consider the following sentence from "Poetry of the Present": "The perfect rose is only a running flame, emerging and flowing off, and never in any sense at rest, static, finished. Herein lies its transcendent loveliness" (p. 182). The use of the word "perfect" to describe a state of roughness (in the sense of "never [being] finished") and mutability ("only a running flame") is curious enough to make us suspect some ambivalence on Lawrence's part. The use of the word "transcendent" to conclude this supposed celebration of the physical in all its transience almost confirms us in our doubt. What does Lawrence mean by saying, "We have seen the invisible," after saying that "A water-lily heaves herself from the flood, looks round, gleams, and is gone"? He goes on to describe the "invisible" that the observer has seen by saying: "tell me of nothing changeless or eternal. Tell me of the mystery of the inexhaustible, forever unfolding creative spark." Here Lawrence is doubly provocative. He seems to elevate, curiously, flux to the status of a First Principle, an "invisible . . . mystery." He also tells us of something "forever unfolding" right after asking us to tell him "of nothing changeless," as if unaware that a reader might be surprised at the juxtaposition.

An even more subtle difficulty with this introduction to the American edition of *New Poems* is with the evident polish that has been applied to the surface of the prose. Below is requoted a passage that with every reading seems more surprising, not only in its rather odd alliances of imagery (cold and incarnate, still and seething, white and the immediate moment) but also in the lyricism of its style:

> Let me feel the mud and the heavens in my lotus. Let me feel the heavy, silting, sucking mud, the spinning of sky winds. Let me feel them both in purest contact, the nakedness of sucking weight, nakedly passing radiance. Give me nothing fixed, set, static. Don't give me the infinite or the eternal: nothing of infinity, nothing of eternity. Give me the still, white seething, the incandescence and the coldness of the incarnate moment: the moment, the quick of all change and haste and opposition: the moment, the immediate present, the Now.

Earlier, Lawrence had deprecated the "treasured gem-like lyric[ism]" of Shelley, and in spite of the fact that one person's impression of what is "gem-like" probably differs significantly from another's, still, many readers of the passage surely sense some kind of tension between subject (mud, seething) and style. The latter, paradoxically, seems wonderfully described by that earlier passage in which Lawrence speaks of "the perfect symme-try" of the poetry of the past, "the rhythm which returns upon itself like a dance where the hands link and loosen and link for the supreme moment of the end" ("Poetry of the Present," p. 182).

"Poetry of the Present" is not the only piece of prose that betrays the difficulty Lawrence had in simultaneously remembering and writing against Shelley. In the *Study of Thomas Hardy*—the essay written in 1914 which Lawrence says in one letter is "about anything but Thomas Hardy" and in another calls "a sort of Story of My Heart" (*Collected Letters*, pp. 290, 298)—Lawrence struggles more arduously with his Romantic predecessor by way of writing about his aging contemporary, for the Bard of Dorsetshire, the ostensible subject of the *Study*, is often depicted as possessing Shelleyan deficiencies—and talents. Indeed, towards the end of the essay it almost seems as if Hardy, the Victorian literary parent who was old enough to be Lawrence's grandfather, has been used as a stand-in for the departed Romantic, the literary grandparent.

The *Study*, like other of Lawrence's essays, poems, and even novels, becomes quickly embroiled in contradiction. Its author deplores the repressive, constricting world of "Law" (which, he will eventually argue, Hardy always subscribed to), and then he deplores the women's movement for combatting one tight, "cabbage" system of law with another. Next, he calls for "a parliament of men and women for the careful . . . unmaking of all laws."[18] Against a vision of parliaments, laws, and subsequent wars, he opposes the "impressive," "influential," "individual," "extravagant being." He cites Dido as his example, calling her "like a poppy, a self in flower." The final aim of every living being, he writes, "is the full achievement of itself. . . . Not the fruit . . . but the flower is the culmination" (*Hardy*, pp. 402–3). But when he comes to the subject of World War I, his view of that catastrophe is as odd as his view of women's liberation. On one hand, he sees it as the type of thing that results from man's obsession with a collective identity; he attacks it and calls for its end. On the other, he cannot repress his feeling that the war is in some ways a "war for freedom of the bonds of our own cowardice and sluggish greed of security and well-being" (ibid., p. 407).

When we arrive at Thomas Hardy, the object of Lawrence's critical attentions in the book, ultimate views are not that much easier to come by. The famous blanket criticism of Hardy that Lawrence has given the world is, of course, that his elder's works always have to become the tragedies of those who, more or less pioneers, have died in the wilderness. . . . This is the theme of novel after novel: remain quite within the convention, and you are good, safe, and happy in the long run . . . : or, on the other hand, be passionate, individual, wilful, you will find the security of the convention a walled prison, you will escape, and you will die, either of your own lack of strength to bear the isolation and the exposure, or by direct revenge from the community. (Ibid., p. 411)

But can Lawrence's sensibility be as diametrically opposed to Hardy's as it would seem to be in the passage quoted above? Surely no writer would bother reading more than a few poems or chapters by a precursor so alien to his tastes and beliefs. And if he did, we would hardly expect him to write a "study"—and call it the "Story of My Heart."

The fact is that Lawrence has found in Hardy part of the world view, or part of his definition of the world view, that he believes to be fundamentally anti-Hardyan, anti-Law. As much as he dislikes the conventions, walled prisons, and communities in which Hardy's "pioneers" or "passionate, individual, wilful" characters die, he is overwhelmingly impressed by his predecessor's passionate, individual, willful pioneers. So much so that he almost seems to think the development and propagation of such selves in flower could be his own role in splitting the rock, bringing us to the wonder, finding the Hesperides. The Hardy characters that Lawrence admires are those like Elfride Swancourt (of *A Pair of Blue Eyes*), Sergeant Troy, Farmer Boldwood, Eustacia Vye, Wildeve, Michael Henchard, Dr. Fitzpiers, and Felice Charmond (the latter two are in *The Woodlanders*). These are the men and women who, in Lawrence's words, "are always bursting suddenly out of bud and taking a wild flight into flower, always shooting suddenly out of a tight convention . . . into something quite madly personal." It is characters such as these—most of whom end up mad or dead— whom Lawrence calls "people each with a real, vital, potential self" that "suddenly bursts the shell of manner and convention and commonplace opinion, and acts independently, absurdly, without mental knowledge or acquiescence" [Hardy, p. 410].

Lawrence's mixed feelings towards Thomas Hardy become even more difficult to sort out the more we reflect on the Hardy corpus. Perhaps a character like Michael Henchard could be called

"quite madly personal" in some complimentary sense of
that phrase, but Farmer Boldwood seems more accurately
described as a pathetic man, eccentric only because of the sad gap
between the world his fancy projects and the one in which
stronger individuals come to flower. Troy's willful, individual per-
sonality is that of the entirely selfish, mustachioed villain of melo-
drama; Wildeve seems but an ineffectual fancy man; and the only
thing "madly personal" about Dr. Fitzpiers is that he buys people's
brains to look into because he is, as Hardy says early on in *The
Woodlanders*, a "Transcendentalist," a "Romantic" and therefore
primarily a "Faustian."[19]

The power of Lawrence's rhetoric about the necessity of being
passionate, individual, and willful is undercut not only by the
examples he cites (and fails to cite) in Hardy's fiction. It would also
seem to be jeopardized by the fact that the more Lawrence defines
the kind of individual he so highly values, the more perfectly
Shelleyan that kind of individual seems. He began by speaking of
Dido and of those Hardyan eccentrics who are, according to Law-
rence, equally "extravagant being[s]" as characters who always
burst into flower and never worry about producing fruit. The
flower is perhaps Shelley's favorite image; he speaks in the "De-
fence" of the "plant [which] must spring again from its seed, or it
will produce no flower," of the "consummate . . . bloom of all
things," and of the "odor and color of the rose." Moreover, when
Lawrence goes on to define further those characters of "Love" (as
opposed to "Law"), his characterization becomes considerably
more allusive and attributable. In such men and women, Lawrence
writes,

> There is always excess, a brimming-over. At spring-time a bird
> brims over with blue and yellow, . . . a lark flies up like heady
> wine, with song. . . . When is a man a man? When he is alight
> with life . . . he is a bird eternally in song. He has excess con-
> stantly on his hands, almost every day. It is not with him a case of
> seasons, spring and autumn and winter. And happy man if his
> excess come out in blue and gold and singing. . . . [All] creatures
> are like fountains . . . when they leap their highest. (*Hardy*,
> p. 421)

Knowing what we do of Lawrence's view of "To a Skylark"—
that it epitomizes Shelley's doomed search for the invisible and the

unavailable—it seems odd that he would use the "lark . . . alight" as his emblem of vital being. But he does more than that. The blue and gold color scheme of Lawrence's world of excess would seem to derive from Shelley ("The blue deep thou wingest, / . . . and soaring ever singest / In the golden lightning / Of the sunken sun"). Lawrence's man "alight with life" like a "bird . . . in song" shares with Shelley's singing "cloud of fire" an immunity to "seasons, spring and autumn and winter." Even Lawrence's notions of "excess" itself (and the images of overflowing, of fountains, with which he communicates it) appear to have their source in Shelley:

> All the earth and air
>   With thy voice is loud,
> As, when night is bare,
>   From one lonely cloud
> The moon rains out her beams, and heaven is overflowed.
>
> .   .   .   .
>
> Like a high-born maiden
>   In a palace tower,
> Soothing her love-laden
>   Soul in secret hour
> With music sweet as love, which overflows her bower.
>
> .   .   .   .
>
> Like a rose embowered
>   In its own green leaves,
> By warm winds deflowered,
>   Till the scent it gives
> Makes faint with too much sweet those heavy-winged thieves.

The skylark is, of course, Shelley's type of the best poet, and in "A Defence of Poetry" Shelley uses the image of the overflowing self, the fountain, specifically to describe what the supreme individual produces, namely, the poem. "All high poetry is infinite," he writes; "it is as the first acorn, which contained all oaks potentially":

> Veil after veil may be undrawn, and the inmost naked beauty of the meaning never exposed. A great poem is a fountain ever

overflowing with the waters of wisdom and delight; and after one person and one age has exhausted all its divine affluence which their particular relations enable them to share, another and yet another succeeds, and new relations are ever developed, the source of an unforeseen and an unconceived delight.[20]

The poet himself, Shelley says in the same essay, may not have foreseen or conceived of the future that his poems delight so miraculously. It is "not that I assert," he writes, "poets to be prophets in the gross sense of the word. . . . A poet participates in the eternal, the infinite, and the one; as far as relates to his conceptions, time and place and number are not." Nevertheless, he remarks, "poets are the hierophants of an unapprehended inspiration; the mirrors of the gigantic shadows which futurity casts upon the present; the words which express what they understand not; the trumpets which sing to battle, and feel not what they inspire; the influence which is moved not, but moves." A poet's "thoughts are the germs of the flower and the fruit of latest time." Without even knowing he does so as he writes, he "beholds the future in the present."[21]

Lawrence's definition of the self in flower, the being in excess, is of course in some ways opposed to Shelley's definition of the poet. Shelley spoke of the man whose "thoughts are the germs of the flower and the fruit of latest time," but for Lawrence thought and even consciousness itself have little to do with truly extravagant being, self-achievement, "the flower to be striven for."

> The bringing of life into human consciousness is not an aim in itself, it is only a necessary condition of the progress of life itself. Man is himself the vivid body of life, rolling glimmering against the void. In his fullest living he does not know what he does; his mind, his consciousness, unacquaint, hovers behind, full of extraneous gleams and glances, and altogether devoid of knowledge. Altogether devoid of knowledge and conscious motive is he when he is heaving into uncreated space, when he is actually living, becoming himself. (*Hardy*, p. 431)

Still, Shelley did not say the poet was motivated to knowledge or that consciousness was his aim. In many ways Lawrence's account of the man whose consciousness hovers behind, full of gleams and glances, could describe Shelley's poet, too, who was the "hierophant" of "unapprehended inspiration," whose "words . . . express what they understand not." Shelley's poet, looked at one way, could seem a true Lawrentian self-without-consciousness. He participates in "the infinite and the one; as far as relates to his conceptions, time and place and number are not." Lawrence even entertains a conception of the extravagant self as a kind of voyager into the future that is somewhat similar to Shelley's view of the poet as one who somehow beholds, without consciously knowing, "the future in the present." Lawrence says the "mind . . . hovers behind" the "man . . . rolling glimmering against the void," "heaving into uncreated space"; and when he continues by describing this "void" as "the future," his terms recall precisely Shelley's passage, even the part about the poet whose "thoughts are the germs of the flower and the fruit of latest time." Of the "potential self" that, like Dido or Hardy's more eccentric characters, keeps "shooting . . . into something quite madly personal," Lawrence writes:

> This is the fall into the future, like a waterfall that tumbles over the edge of the known world into the unknown . . . .
>
> It is so arranged that the very act which carries us out into the unknown shall probably deposit seed for security to be left behind. But the act . . . is not for the depositing of the seed. It is for leaping off into the unknown, as from a cliff's edge, like Sappho into the sea. (Ibid., p. 441)

As I have implied but never stated outright, Lawrence develops a myth about "Love" and "Law" in his Hardy study in which "Love," loosely translated, means something like spiritual or imaginative will or aspiration and "Law" something like (self-) repression, restriction, limitation, or restraint. Part of the myth of Love and Law is the opposition of male and female. The male, in Lawrence's scheme, has only a little to do with sexuality in the obvious sense: that is to say, a woman could be primarily "male" in her being (as Hardy's Eustacia Vye is, according to Lawrence). "Male" is Lawrence's word for the will to abstraction, transcendence, and all that is beyond the quotidian. The "male" and "Love" by no means perfectly overlap, but they do seem to have more than a little to do with one another; it is the male that is always straining against the tight, hardbound world of Law (which includes, of course, both natural and man-made constrictions).

The female, by way of contrast, represents in Lawrence's mythology the realm of the quotidian, the necessary, the body, the physical (and thus in certain areas overlaps with the principle of Law).

After seeing the degree to which Lawrence's description of the self "leaping off into the unknown" is indebted to Shelley's "skylark" and "Poet," we cannot be surprised to learn that Shelley is, for Lawrence, the epitome of maleness. "In what we call happy natures," in "the lazy, contented" person, Lawrence writes, "there is a fairly equable balance . . . . Such a man . . . does not suffer the torture of desire of a more male being." The "pure male," on the other hand, "is himself almost an abstraction, almost bodiless, like Shelley . . . . In the ordinary sense, Shelley never lived. He transcended life. But we do not want to transcend life, since we are of life."

> Why should Shelley say of the skylark:
>   "Hail to thee, blithe Spirit!—bird thou never wert!—"? Why should he insist on the bodilessness of beauty, when we cannot know of any save embodied beauty? Who would wish that the skylark were not a bird, but a spirit? . . .
>   I can think of no being in the world so transcendently male as Shelley. He is phenomenal. The rest of us have bodies which contain the male and the female. If we were so singled out as Shelley, we should not belong to life, as he did not belong to life. But it were impious to wish to be like the angels. So long as mankind exists it must exist in the body, and so long must each body pertain both to the male and the female.
>   In the degree of pure maleness below Shelley are Plato and Raphael and Wordsworth, then Goethe and Milton and Dante, then Michelangelo, then Shakespeare, then Tolstoi, then St. Paul.
>   A man who is well balanced between male and female, in his own nature, is, as a rule, happy, easy to mate, easy to satisfy, and content to exist. It is only a disproportion, or a dissatisfaction, which makes the man struggle into articulation. (*Hardy,* pp. 459–60)

Lawrence keeps saying that "we do not wish to transcend life, since we are life." He insists that we should all wish to "contain the male and the female" and thus be "easy to mate, easy to satisfy, and content to exist." But can he mean it when the alternative is to be in company with Paul, Shakespeare, Michelangelo, Dante, Milton, Goethe, Wordsworth, and Shelley? Even if we can momentarily convince ourselves that Lawrence is trying to explode our intellectual-idealist value system by presenting the columns of Western civilization in a negative light, we can hardly forget the fact that this entire essay has been in praise of extravagant being. The silent, hard-working Hardy characters who were or learned to be easy to satisfy, content to exist, were the characters Lawrence scorned. The Gabriel Oaks were the ones who learned that to be "good" and to bide your time "quite within the convention" is to end up "safe and happy." Also, in the passage criticizing the "maleness" of Shelley, Lawrence seems incontrovertibly opposed to the principle of articulation: only dissatisfaction "makes the man struggle into articulation." This is surely an odd position for a poet to take, and it would seem to give the lie to Lawrence's statement that "the rest of us . . . contain the male and the female." Finally, there is simply no getting around the fact that earlier in the essay Shelley's singing skylark had been Lawrence's figure for the self reaching its own full achievement. "A lark flies up like heady wine, with song," he had written. "When is a man a man? When he is alight with life . . . he is a bird eternally in song." Either Lawrence is confused about whether he thinks it desirable to be "male," or he is uncertain about what he thinks of Shelley, or both.

In "Poetry of the Present" we saw an ambivalence towards Shelley that seems to be ultimately inextricable from the simultaneous ambivalence towards the world and the art through which it is depicted. In the *Study of Thomas Hardy* exactly the same situation exists, only the crucial uncertainty about Shelley is subsumed in, or altered to look like, or shared with, an ambivalence towards another writer. I think the last alternative is most likely. In the *Study of Thomas Hardy*, Hardy is the Shelleyan figure for just about all but those six or seven pages in which Shelley becomes the Hardyan subject. By that I mean that Lawrence shows thoroughly mixed feelings about Hardy which are symptomatic of his attitudes towards the world at large. Lawrence's *own* heart was divided; his attitudes toward the world were mixed and even hopelessly opposed. Lawrence, after all, is confused because the most powerful voices of his education spoke out of self-division. Put another way, Lawrence's instincts are bound to be as confused as were the dreams of his grandparents. Because Lawrence's epistemology is consequently full of ambivalences, it is hardly surprising that he exhibits inconsistent attitudes towards his predecessors.

The fact remains, nonetheless, that Lawrence can sometimes sense and demonstrate the destructive and self-destructive oppositions and repressions out of which his precursors wrote. These realizations and demonstrations, however occasional, are evidence of some movement on his part out of the old modes of consciousness. The precise analysis of the dreams of the grandparents is the liberating act of self-analysis that points the way to the future. The way to the future, in turn, is to recall the past, to force it to withdraw from destructive eminence by remembering in it those always repressed or counteracted primitive "flashes" that could "light the way" into the new direction of time.

Lawrence's double view of Shelley in some parts of the *Study* and his similarly bifocal view of Hardy in others has already been made apparent. In the final pages of the work, however, Lawrence returns to each subject, this time to make his comparison of the two explicit. Of Shelley's poetry he says:

It is most wonderful, . . . this sense of conflict contained within a reconciliation:

> Hail to thee, blithe Spirit!
>   Bird thou never wert,
> That from Heaven, or near it,
>   Pourest thy full heart
> In profuse strains of unpremeditated art.

Shelley wishes to say the skylark is a pure, untrammelled spirit, a pure motion. But the very "Bird thou never wert" admits that the skylark *is* in very fact a bird, a concrete, momentary thing. If the line ran, "Bird thou never art," that would spoil it all. Shelley wishes to say, the song is poured out of heaven: but "or near it," he admits. . . . And the last line is the tumbling sound of a lark's singing. . . .

The very adherence to rhyme and regular rhythm is a concession to the Law, a concession to the body, to the being and requirements of the body. They are an admission of the living, positive inertia which is . . . other than the pure will. . . .

> In this consummation, they are the resistance and response of
> the Bride in the arms of the Bridegroom. (*Hardy*, p. 478)

Here Lawrence's mixed feelings about Shelley are subordinated to
an analysis of their determinants, namely, Shelley's mixed feelings
or, as Lawrence would have it, "sense of conflict contained within
a reconciliation." The analysis is thus sharper and more honest
than many in the *Study;* Shelley is not presented as all spirit, all
Love, all male, as he was earlier when Lawrence was venting his
decidedly negative attitudes towards the precursor. There was, in
fact, in Shelley a powerful will to recognize and celebrate "the
being and requirements of the body" and its "living, positive
inertia." That will—existing but dormant in most of the voices of
Western civilization since Homer—is frustrated in Shelley, but
frustrated to the point that its presence is notable. It is Shelley's
will to celebrate "the body" and its "living positive inertia" that
Lawrence must recall and develop in his own poetry, as he will in a
few years in splendidly sensual lyrics on fruits:

> Look how black, how blue-black, how globed in
>   Egyptian darkness
> Dropping among his leaves, hangs the dark grape!
> ("Grapes")
>
> I am thinking . . . of the peach before I ate it.
>
> Why so velvety, why so voluptuous heavy?
> Why hanging with such inordinate weight?
> Why so indented?
> ("Peach")
>
> I love to suck you out from your skins
> So brown and soft and coming suave,
> So morbid, as the Italians say.
>
> What a rare, powerful, reminiscent flavour
> Comes out of your falling through the stages of decay:
> Stream within stream.
> ("Medlars and Sorb-Apples")

If Shelley felt a strange pull "other than" that of "pure will,"
Lawrence has surely described that pull, that body, that powerful
inertia, in these passages from *Birds, Beasts and Flowers* (1923).

Returning to "The Wild Common" again for a moment, we can complicate in a revealing way our discovery that Lawrence was moving us into the future by recalling an ancient vision of *theos*, of a divinely physical world, and that he was recalling (in the sense of remembering) the lost vision by recalling (in the sense of removing from play and power) Shelley's more recent one. What can be seen now is that the Greek vision of "substance" exists in Shelley's, lying undeveloped in but coloring subtly the shadowy Shelleyan landscape. We might similarly complicate our reading of the "Hymn to Priapus" by wondering if the at once erotic and spiritual love that Lawrence signifies by the Greek God is not to some extent recognized by the poems of Shelley, Swinburne, and Hardy. Indeed, we might even be so speculative as to say that it is only through Shelley and his Victorian followers that Greek is known to Lawrence. This is not to say that Lawrence never read a work of Greek but, rather, to say that if he had never done so, he would still have known its world view because he had heard about it, subliminally, from the *sotto voce* of Shelley's words of instruction.

In *Apocalypse,* written shortly before Lawrence's death and published in 1931, Lawrence spends much of his time attacking John of Patmos. The author of the Revelation—exactly like Shelley, Lenin, and St. Francis, according to Lawrence—"cr[ies] *anathema!* to the natural proud self of power, and tr[ies] deliberately to destroy all might and all lordship."[22] And yet Lawrence also admits, here and there in his book, that "there are flashes throughout the first part of the Apocalypse of true cosmic worship." These flashes of a pagan, not Christian, vision Lawrence likes; they put modern man in touch with a "lordly and splendid" vision of a world he otherwise could not know. "These flashes" that "can hardly be attributed to John of Patmos" but rather to an "older cosmic vision"[23] are what Lawrence seeks to brighten in his own work called *Apocalypse,* just as the vision of a divinely sensual world that Lawrence sees flashes of in Shelley's poetry is the vision he would broaden and deepen in his mature poetry.

And yet Lawrence, however much he may draw out Shelley's appreciation of the physical, the inertia of the body, is not really developed Shelley. Rather he is developed Hardy, who developed Shelley by recalling Swinburne.[24] Immediately after the passage in which Lawrence finds in Shelley a countered will to relate to the physical, he begins talking about Swinburne's "concession to the body, so that the poetry becomes almost a sensation." That is not to say that Lawrence thinks Swinburne has already completed his own task, for Swinburne's sensuality is found to be the obviously defensive pose of a being almost too male, too prone to transcendence and abstraction, to live. Swinburne, Lawrence says, "sings the Supreme Law to gain rebalance in himself, for he hovers always on the edge of death, of Not-Being, he is always out of reach of the Law, bodiless, in the faintness of Love that has triumphed and denied the Law" [*Hardy*, pp. 478–79]. Then, by way of an equally short encounter with Tolstoi, Lawrence comes to Hardy and finds much "the same cry." There is, as there was in Swinburne and Shelley, both the metaphysical "curse upon the birth in the flesh" (Jude's final act) and the powerful "adherence to the flesh" that is responsible, in Lawrence's opinion, for the unique power of Hardy's fiction: "His feeling, his instinct, his sensuous understanding is, however, apart from his metaphysic, very great and deep, deeper than that, perhaps, of any other English novelist. Putting aside his metaphysic, which must always obtrude when he thinks of people, and turning to the earth, to landscape, then he is true to himself" (ibid, pp. 480–81).

Lawrence, perhaps because he is a strong voice of my own education, seems to me to be exactly right both about Hardy's sensual side and about that other, more "male" side of him that kept the sensuality always, if barely, in check. Perhaps the most interesting work of Hardy's for corroborating Lawrence's view is the poem entitled "Shelley's Skylark," for it shows not only the two sides of Hardy, but also the embryonic understanding of Shelley that was to be developed further by Lawrence's mind and language. The poem, written between Pisa and Lucca, begins by saying that "Somewhere afield here something lies / In earth's oblivious eyeless trust," the "lark that Shelley heard," the remains of that which "moved a poet to prophecies— / A pinch of unseen, unguarded dust, . . ."

> Though it only lived like another bird,
> And knew not its immortality:
>
> Lived its meek life; then, one day, fell —
> A little ball of feather and bone;
> And how it perished, when piped farewell,
> And where it wastes, are alike unknown.

> Maybe it rests in the loam I view,
> Maybe it throbs in the myrtle green,
> Maybe it sleeps in the coming hue
> Of a grape on the slopes of yon inland scene.

Here is surely an example of that "sensual understanding" that is greater in Hardy than in any English novelist that preceded him, if by "sensual understanding" we mean, like Lawrence, the "recognition" of the "requirements of the body" and its "inertia." The irony in the line that says that the skylark "knew not its immortality" is one that Lawrence has caused to seem, from our perspective, perfectly proto-Lawrentian. Still more powerful—and equally Lawrentian—is the translation and development of a Shelleyan term like "immortality" into a vision of a bird that need never look "before and after" as it decays gloriously in rich loam, throbs in a myrtle's green, and purples a grape on Italian slopes.

In the first stanza, when Hardy speaks of the dust of Shelley's subject as being "unseen, unguarded," he seems to be doing two things. On one hand, he is saying that although the bird is not safe within the walls of some churchyard open to public visitation, dust it was and to dust it has long since returned. This is the side of Hardy that sees everything in terms of the body, of the physical and its decay. The poet is being macabre and even grotesque in his treatment of Shelley's skylark as nothing but a seventy-year-old corpse in order to make the claim that his own epistemology is not metaphysical and that Shelley's epistemology, which was, is as dead to modern poetry as is the "ball of feather and bone" that was the precursor's true and only source of inspiration. This side of Hardy is elaborated in the stanza that follows, the one that speaks of the "dust of the lark that Shelley heard / And made immortal" even "Though it only lived like another bird." Although Hardy admits that in some sense the lark is immortal, he limits the admission severely in several ways. First, he uses the word "though" to underline the fact that other than the one implicit in organic cyclicality, the only immortality the bird has is a poetic one. If Shelley had not come along, its fate would have been the same as that of "any other" fowl. Secondly, he writes with a looseness of syntax which allows the reader to think that Shelley may have "made immortal" the "dust of the lark." Immortal dust, a figurative oxymoron, has the effect both of maintaining the slightly macabre humor of the poem and, more important, of quietly reasserting the fact that the flesh is all there is to write about, that a poet can write about it as if it is Something Else, but not without his work becoming itself a kind of oxymoron, an absurd contradiction of its own inevitable subject.

On the other hand, Hardy's first stanza also makes a strange pun in the words "unseen, unguarded," words that remind us, and not critically, of Shelley's claim, "Bird thou never wert." The lark, Shelley had told us, was a presence but an invisible one. Hardy's pun says that, for the poet writing at the end of the century the Romantics ushered in, the "blithe Spirit" of Shelley's "extasy" must remain unseen, unregarded—doubly invisible. Such a pun almost serves as a revelation of Hardy's other side, for it could be seen not only as praise of Shelley's greater spirituality but also as evidence of Hardy's belief in his precursor's feeling that the sky-lark was "heavenly." If the bird was invisible, then how much more invisible must be the bones it never had. Why look for the living among the dead?

Both sides of Hardy—the physical and the metaphysical, female and male, "Law" and "Love"—can be seen in the poem's final two stanzas:

> Go and find it, faeries, go and find
> That tiny pinch of priceless dust,
> And bring a casket silver-lined,
> And framed of gold that gems encrust;
>
> And we will lay it safe therein,
> And consecrate it to endless time;
> For it inspired a bard to win
> Ecstatic heights in thought and rhyme.

To say that the bird does exist as dust is again to emphasize that what Shelley "*made* immortal" was nothing but feather and bone. And yet the invocation to faeries is odd. If we hear it spoken without considerable irony, we may be left wondering why Hardy ends up this little ode on merely organic immortality talking with unseen, immortal, winged presences. If, on the other hand, we hear the invocation spoken tongue-in-cheek by a hard-boiled post-Romantic, we may be moved to ask the following question: if the quest for any organic remains of Shelley's subject is fit only for nonexistent faeries, how exactly does that contradict Shelley's claim that his subject was not a bird at all? Finally, Hardy's language, in this movement, is in many ways similar to that polished, gemlike prose Lawrence gives us in "Poetry of the Present" when he keeps talking about mere nature in flux through terms like "radiance," "incandescence," "whiteness." Hardy may begin the penultimate stanza by affecting a precious tone ("Go and find it, faeries"), but by the third line of the stanza there seems to be no affectation intended. Thomas Hardy, poet of the body, its energy, and its decay, seems to end his poem by speaking in mellifluous whispers about a "casket silver-lined, / And framed of gold that gems encrust," for his attitude towards the "bard" that won "Ecstatic heights in thought" is close to elegiac, far from scornful.

Lawrence, who proves his enchantment with Hardy through the very act of writing the lengthy *Study*, obviously gets a good measure of his own divided sensibility from his predecessor. Not only is Lawrence's ambivalence toward the physical and the metaphysical, the flesh and the spirit, a reminiscent one, but so is his attitude towards Shelley, whose words helped to plant the seeds of profound sensuality, spirituality, and conflict in Hardy's sensibility. We cannot prove that Lawrence's fixation, in his prose, on "To a Skylark" is due to the fact that Hardy chose that particular ode as the focal point of his most explicit poetic encounter with Shelley. But we can, I think, suspect that Hardy's "Shelley's Skylark" is behind the passage in which Lawrence says Shelley wanted to treat the bird both as a heavenly spirit and as just another living bird. And Hardy's interaction with Shelley may even have something to do with the fact that when Lawrence wants to deny the validity of the poetry of eternity in "Poetry of the Present," he often says something like, "The bird is on the wing in the winds . . . , its very flickering depending on its supreme mutability. . . . Whence such a bird came: whither it goes . . . is not the question."

What we have seen is that in 1914, while writing the *Study of Thomas Hardy*, Lawrence's central self saw, and set forth, and analyzed a profound tension or paradox in Hardy's sensibility, an original act that led him to realize perhaps for the first time the dynamics of Shelley's earlier and partially determining world view. Hardy proved Lawrence's key to Shelley. Perhaps because Hardy had taken "To a Skylark" to be quintessentially Shelleyan,

Lawrence comes to use the poem as a term in his own indebted but significantly developed view of Shelley's problematical power. Once Lawrence, led by Hardy and by his own exposure of Hardy's developed Shelleyan sensibility, has settled into his view and his terminology, he can further articulate as his own the "sensuality" or "femaleness" or "physicality" of Shelley's vision simply by writing rather obviously if pointedly (in "Bat" or "Turkey-Cock" or "St. Matthew") against "To a Skylark." For Lawrence "To a Skylark" is no longer really a complex poem by Shelley but, rather, what Hardy had begun to make it, a trope for that abstracting and, in Lawrence's opinion, death-dealing aspect of Shelley that must be recalled from Western consciousness.

Second Lustre: 1917–1923 Poetic Objects

Chapter Three

Proper and Vulgar

In his at once amusing and instructive essay entitled "The Unemployed Magician," Karl Shapiro imagines himself talking with the god of letters. Late in the conversation, a few moments before the deity has revealed Himself in recognizable human form, He makes the statement that "the highest compliment that can be paid the poet" is "for a man to travel thousands of miles to a strange land, to stand in a certain spot and say: So this is where Thomas Hardy got his hair cut." Shapiro accepts the divine word on the subject, but he is not willing to accept without argument another of the god's pronouncements, namely, that when poets found they "couldn't compete with religion" they "invented Myth" as a ploy to put themselves "back on the map." Shapiro is moved to disagree. "But myth is everything to us," he shouts:

> The beliefs and legends of every age are re-formed in our poems to give them new life and to give life its meaning for those who would live not only as human animals. It is metaphysic in its purest form. It is the very protoplasm of poetry.
>
> You sound like Shelley, the god said. (He made a move as if to stand up.) . . .
>
> I started to protest but it was too late. . . . I shook hands with the god, who smiled and winked at the attendant. As the door closed quickly behind me I managed one more glimpse over my shoulder. The man in the chair—I still can't believe it—was D. H. Lawrence.[1]

Shapiro seems to be identifying, however indirectly, Shelley and Hardy as poets who meant a great deal to Lawrence and his work.

He seems to think that the debts to Hardy were ones Lawrence felt more comfortable about. Shapiro certainly knows—as is evident from the comments he makes on Whitman elsewhere in the piece —that Lawrence had many models, many mentors, and therefore that the literary contexts of his poetry are various and complicated. Those mentors changed, or at least their relative importance to the poet and his poems changed, over the years of Lawrence's development; the author of forty-seven poems published together in 1923 on birds, beasts, flowers, and other poetic objects has by and large come through his difficult struggle with Hardy, with Shelley, and with the latter poet's once-eminent idealism.

Lawrence is not, of course, the only poet who has come through into an altered sensibility. The history of Victorian and modern poetry is to a great extent the history of men and women who have, at least once in their careers, undergone a radical change in poetic outlook and style. Nor is Lawrence the only one of these poets who was devoted early on to Shelley and whose youthful devotion was an integral part of the faith that had to be painfully cast off. Swinburne's early volumes, *Atalanta in Calydon* (1865) and *Poems and Ballads* (1866), are tortured by their author's simultaneous desire and inability to believe in God on one hand and, on the other, in the Romantic and social possibilities that Shelley had at least envisioned. Robert Browning, after writing the idealistic, Shelleyan *pastiche* that is "Pauline," turned towards the view that divinity is always embodied in the "rose-mesh" of the flesh,[2] a view he came to express in the rough, casual, conversational diction of poems like "The Bishop Orders His Tomb in Saint Praxed's Church."

Not all poets since Shelley have evolved in the direction of the "wheel of life / With shapes and colors rife"[3] and towards a poetic diction that, on the surface at least, appears to be loose if not quite frenzied. T. S. Eliot and W. H. Auden underwent conversions of a more traditional sort; they went through crises of sensibility suffered in the face of a world in which "dreadful martyrdom must run its course / Anyhow in a corner, some untidy spot / Where dogs go on with their doggy life,"[4] but their crises were resolved in favor of Christian dogma and the relatively traditional, formal diction of *Four Quartets* and *The Sea and the Mirror*. Nevertheless, it is probably fair to say that most poets of the past century have emerged from whatever center of indifference they once found themselves in to embrace, not a creed, but rather the realm of the physical, the world, the body. "Away the dreams that but deceive," Matthew Arnold declares in his pivotal "Stanzas in Memory of the Author of 'Obermann,'" "I in the world must live." Rilke's search for God as mystery (in *Das Stunden-Buch*, 1905) gives way in the *Duino Elegies* to the decision "not to interpret roses," to behold as "With all its eyes the creature-world beholds / The open."[5] Yeats, who in 1893 published *The Rose*, a volume with Shelleyan verities much in evidence, in his *Last Poems* (1936) seeks those images

> That constitute the wild
> The lion and the virgin,
> The harlot and the child.[6]

And Swinburne, who in the "Prelude" to his second-lustre *Songs Before Sunrise* (1871) tells the story of someone very much like himself, suddenly asks: "what has he whose will sees clear / To do with doubt and faith and fear?" The answer comes in the form of action:

> Then he stood up, and trod to dust
> Fear and desire, mistrust and trust,
>   And dreams of bitter sleep and sweet,
>   And bound for sandals on his feet
> Knowledge and patience of what must
>   And what things may be, in the heat
> And cold of years that rot and rust
>   And alter; and his spirit's meat
> Was freedom, and his staff was wrought
> Of strength, and his cloak was woven of thought.[7]

The reader who moves from *Look! We Have Come Through!* (1917) to *Birds, Beasts and Flowers* (1923), Lawrence's next volume of new poems,[8] confronts a poet who has accomplished the radical transition that he only boasts he has made in his earlier troubled volume about the struggle for emergence. The reader also confronts a poet who seeks, in Swinburne's words, fresh "knowledge" of "what must / and . . . may be" in the "heat / And cold of years that rot and rust / And alter." Lawrence had once called Swinburne the poet whose work continually "adhere[s] to the body, to the Rose, to the Flesh, the physical in everything." Yet this description applies even more properly to Lawrence, who, as he successfully turns from his quest for Shelleyan "Mystery" to consider the essential physical properties of a cypress and a tortoise and rotten medlars "brown and soft and coming suave," becomes "almost a sensation and not an experience or a consummation" (*Hardy*, pp. 478–79).

It is hardly surprising that, when the poet shifts his focus from the poetic loves to the poetic objects of the fleshly world, poets such as Wordsworth, Coleridge, and Keats begin to provide more challenging and useful contexts than does Shelley. They are poets who, more than Shelley and most others in the English tradition, value the sensual world as poetic subject. They are also poets who discover, as Lawrence discovers in the best poems in *Birds, Beasts and Flowers*, that the unmediated perception of the sensual world is made all but impossible by language, what Lawrence will come to call the "accursed voices" of his "education." Finally, it is Wordsworth, Coleridge, and Keats who have an impact on Lawrence's second lustre because they see Milton almost as the embodiment of the obstructive force of education. For Milton is to the second major period of Lawrence's poetic development what Shelley was to the first: the parent from whom other influential predecessors sprang and the author of the language which must be doubly recalled if, in the words of the "Song of a Man Who Has Come Through," the poet is to "come at the wonder" of the original world, the physical garden of earthly delights that poets of perfection have literally and figuratively overlooked.

Lawrence's emergence into an epistemology whose end is, not God, but the rough chaos of the world is an emergence with numerous literary-historical precedents. It would be wrong to infer, however, that the poet altered his purposes to conform to poetic development à la mode. In the preceding chapter I have argued that the love battles Lawrence fought with Shelley's poetry and his similarly tumultuous relationships with certain women were the textual and personal strands of a single, complicated web of experience, or, to recur to my earlier metaphor, the separate crosscurrents of influence that make up a larger condition of interfluence between life and art. Similarly, the turn to the world and the body in the second lustre of his career had as much to do with the changing facts of his experience as it had to do with his changing tastes in old poems or with the example set by literary models.

Between 1914, the year Lawrence all but completed the *Look!* volume, and 1920, the year he wrote the earliest of the poems to appear in *Birds, Beasts and Flowers*, Lawrence had married. Marriage—specifically, marriage to Frieda—had a significant part in the poet's changing view of the world and how it should be represented. In 1914, the year of his marriage, Lawrence wrote: "To love, you have to learn to understand the other. . . . It is damnably difficult and painful, but it is the only thing which endures . . . . I don't feel a changed man, but I suppose I am one" (*Collected Letters*, pp. 285, 287). The relation of marriage, as much as any other single literary or nonliterary experience in Lawrence's life, turned the poet's view outward, away from dreams and feelings and towards the uncomprehended otherness of the world. "I believe there is no getting of a vision," Lawrence came to believe,

> before we get our sex right. . . . Because life tends to take two streams, the male and the female, and only some female influence (not necessarily woman, but most obviously woman) can fertilise the soul of a man to vision or being. Then the vision we're after, I don't know what it is—but it . . . contains awe and dread and submission, not pride or sensuous egotism and assertion. . . . We want to realise the tremendous *non-human* quality of life—it is wonderful (*Collected Letters*, p. 291).

Lawrence writes to Bertrand Russell, a year after marrying Frieda, that "any man who takes a woman is up against the unknown" and that it is through a mature, male-female relation that "the shell . . . of life" "gets broken." He specifically identifies E. M. Forster's limitation as an artist with that writer's inability to come to know a woman, to love a woman as something other than a self-manifestation. It "is sensationalism," the poet argues, almost as if he had his old, Shelleyan self in mind, "to go to a woman" only to better know oneself. "Love is, that I go to a woman to know myself, and . . . to go further, to explore in to the unknown, which is the woman, [to] venture . . . upon the coasts of the unknown" (ibid., pp. 318–20).

Struggling to know the unknown as flora and fauna seems to have been, for Lawrence, very much a part of coming to know a woman in the relation of marriage. During those traumatic war years, the early years of marriage in which Lawrence and Frieda lived isolated in cottages in Cornwall, not at liberty to move about because of his antiwar sentiments and her family connections, the poet wrote often in letters of the "original world" that, along with his Eve, he was struggling to explore and come to know. "We have lived a few days on the seashore, with the wave banging up at us," he tells Lady Cynthia Asquith. "It is a great thing to realise that the original world is still there—perfectly clean and pure, many white advancing foams, and only the gulls swinging between the sky and the shore; and in the wind the yellow sea poppies fluttering very hard, like yellow gleams in the wind, and the windy flourish of seed-horns" (ibid., p. 358). There is "another world," a "rarer reality," the poet writes in 1916 after the *Look!* volume had been completed and was being readied for the printers. It is "a world with thin, clear air and untouched skies, that have not been looked at nor covered with smoke" (ibid., p. 410).

Frieda's role in Lawrence's relation to this natural world outside the self, this primeval fact of the Cornwall landscape, is not always implied, but when it is, its importance can hardly be overlooked. "What we want is the fulfilment of our desires, down to the deepest and most spiritual desire," Lawrence writes to Catherine Carswell from Cornwall: "The body is immediate, the spirit is beyond: first the leaves and then the flower: but the plant is an integral whole. . . . And I shall find my deepest desire to be a wish for pure, unadulterated relationship with the universe, for truth in being. My pure relationship with one woman is marriage, physical and spiritual" (ibid., p. 467).

At this point two objections might be raised. One would have it that the war itself motivated Lawrence's extreme concentration on his marriage and an unadulterated relation with the nonhuman universe. ("It was a beautiful day here today," the poet writes in one of his most descriptive letters from Cornwall to Lady Ottoline Morrell. "What does it matter about that seething scrimmage of mankind in Europe?" [ibid., p. 424]). Another objection might be that all of the letters written before 1917 fall within what I have called Lawrence's first poetic lustre.

The war no doubt was one of those contexts within which any discussion of Lawrence's changing sensibility must be defined. Many of Lawrence's best attempts to get to know flowers, fruits, and the feminine were written in an explosion-torn villa in San Gervasio that had been lent to Lawrence by a friend who had moved up to Fiesole, while the war was still going on, to get away from an ammunition dump.[9] Nevertheless, the fact remains that these poems were written after the armistice and after the issuance of passports that allowed Lawrence and Frieda to leave a country that they had been unwelcome in but unable to leave for several years. In Cornwall, while the war raged, Lawrence had revised *Women in Love* and begun what is perhaps his worst novel, *Aaron's Rod*, but he had written only those few new (and unexceptional) poems that he published in 1919 in his tiny volume entitled *Bay*. The war, therefore, seems to have refocused Lawrence's poetry only after its horrors had subsided; while it was still being waged, the conflict so narrowed the artist's field of vision that it virtually closed it off.

In response to the arguable position that the poet's coming to grips with marriage took place during what I have defined as the first poetic lustre and not the second, I would once again stress that even the best attempts to locate the watershed years of a poet's career are bound to miscategorize those inevitable writings that come piping into an author's canon like children from another time. (If the "Introduction" to *New Poems* (1919) can, in Lawrence's words, "belong to" a 1917 volume, then letters written between 1915 and 1917 can surely herald the second lustre.) And again, the fact that Lawrence wrote only nine poems between 1914 and 1917[10] and only thirteen more (published in *Bay*) between 1917 and 1920[11] suggests that the letters written in Cornwall amount in some ways to poem substitutes; they surely had no little bearing, therefore, on the poems that Lawrence was later to write.

Certainly, the letters from Cornwall bear less resemblance to the talky, often very personal letters Lawrence wrote between 1908 and 1915 than they do to the letters written after 1919, letters which very often consist of beautiful, pared-down descriptions of landscapes, animals, and people that Lawrence saw in their animal-like simplicity and unself-consciousness. "I like the Italians deeply," Lawrence says in the first letter he writes after arriving in Fontana Vecchia, the Sicilian house that became the nearest thing to a home he and Frieda were to have during the period he worked on *Birds, Beasts and Flowers*. "I like the Italians deeply; and the

sun shines, the rocks glimmer, the sea is unfolded like fresh petals.
I am better here than in England" (*Collected Letters*, p. 623).

Lawrence liked Sicily in particular; "I like [it] so much better
than Capri," he wrote to Fritz Krenkow in 1920.

> It is so green and living, with the young wheat soft under the
> almond trees and the olives. The almond blossom of Sicily is over
> now . . . but the peach is in blossom. —We have quite a lovely
> villa on the green slope high above the sea, looking east over the
> blueness, with the hills and the snowy, shallow crest of Calabria
> on the left across the sea, where the straits begin to close in. . . .
>
> There are people here—many English. I . . . don't want to
> know too many, it is too distracting. Fortunately I have begun to
> work again. Most foreigners leave, end of May.
>
> Etna is a lovely mountain—deep hooded with snow—such a
> beautiful long slope right from the sea. (Ibid., p. 624)

One of the reasons Lawrence loved Sicily was because he con-
sidered it one of the least European places in Europe. Its land-
scapes represented to him the edge of the unknown that was the
physical universe and therefore, along with his wife, the thing he
desired "unadulterated relationship with." He speaks of "Sicily
unknown to me . . . in the Mediterranean dawn" shortly after his
arrival in Taormina, a "peaceful and still" and "sappy" place.[12]

When Lawrence left Sicily, as he did several times during his
two-year sojourn there, it was because he had come to feel that the
place was the far edge of Europe instead of the nearest frontier of
the earth's unknown body. "I like it much the best of any place in
Italy: and adore Fontana Vecchia. But my heart and my soul are
broken, in Europe."[13] "Where does one go?" Lawrence asks at
such a time, when plotting a nine-month hiatus in his life as a
Sicilian. The answer, in January of 1921, proved to be "Sardinia,
which is like nowhere, . . . which has no history, no race, no
offering. . . . It lies outside civilization." Sardinia has never been
"landed" by the "net of European civilization," Lawrence writes in
Sea and Sardinia (1921), "and the net is getting tattered."[14]

To Lawrence's mind, the beauty of the two islands, Sicily and
Sardinia, was the beauty of the physical body, and even the rough
spots in the landscape he saw in terms of anatomy. "Steep, craggy,
wild," he writes in *Sea and Sardinia*, "the land goes up to its points
and precipices, a tangle of heights. But all jammed on top of one

another. And in old landscapes, as in old people, the flesh wears away, and the bones become prominent. Rock sticks up fantastic- ally."[15]

As for the people, they are like the landscape. They are physical contours to be experienced not for their feelings, personalities, or souls, but in the way that beautiful birds or animals or stretches of scenery are experienced. Lawrence tends to represent the island- ers, moreover, by the women, as he does when he describes a train ride he took with Frieda from Messina to Palermo:

> Enter more passengers. An enormously large woman with an extraordinarily handsome face: an extraordinarily large man, quite young: and a diminutive servant, a little girl child of about thirteen, with a beautiful face. —But the Juno—it is she who takes my breath away. She is quite young, in her thirties still. She has . . . a pure brow with level dark brows, large, dark, bridling eyes, a straight nose, a chiselled mouth. . . . She sends one's heart straight back to pagan days. . . . She wears a black toque with sticking up wings, and a black rabbit fur spread on her shoulders. She edges her way in carefully: and once seated, is terrified to rise to her feet. She sits with that motionlessness of her type, closed lips, face muted and expressionless. And she expects me to admire her, I can see that. She expects me to pay homage to her beauty: just to that: not homage to herself, but to her as a *bel pezzo*.[16]

The description of the Sicilian woman could be said to be the work of a chauvinist seeing all women as mere pieces, as sex objects. So to describe Lawrence and his attitude, however, is to miss the respect he affords both the woman's independence from himself and the genuine mystery of her individuality, not her mere feminine mystique. It is, I would argue, the same respect that Lawrence tries to afford the entire world during his second poetic lustre, a respect that will turn his poetry into a struggle to know nature by seeing nature as an embodied mystery, as in itself it really is, rather than by relying on old superstitions and anthro- pocentric formulae that ultimately belittle the world.

The association Lawrence makes between "coming up against" a woman and dealing faithfully with the body of nature may have first occurred to him in Cornwall, while he was rewriting *Women in Love*. In the chapter entitled "In the Train," Rupert Birkin says,

"I want the finality of love."

"The finality of love," repeated Gerald. And he waited for a moment.

"Just one woman?" he added. The evening light, flooding yellow along the fields, lit up Birkin's face. . . .

"Yes, one woman. . . ."

"And you mean if there isn't the woman, there's nothing?" said Gerald.

"Pretty well that—seeing that there's no God."

"Then we're hard put to it," said Gerald. And he turned to look out of the window at the flying, golden landscape.

By the time Lawrence publishes *The Plumed Serpent* in 1926 the association barely made in *Women in Love* has assumed a literalness that is paradoxically confusing and certainly not flattering, either to women or to Lawrence. The following passage, which describes the ceremonial marriage of Kate Leslie and Cipriano, is to be found in the chapter entitled "Marriage by Quetzalcoatl."

"This woman is the earth to me—say that, Cipriano," said Ramón, kneeling on one knee and laying his hand flat on the earth.

Cipriano kneeled and laid his hand on the earth.

"This woman is the earth to me," he said.

In *Birds, Beasts and Flowers*, Lawrence does not make the earth the mere adjunct to discussions of love, as he does in his early love poems and is still doing, to some extent, in his excursion train chapter of *Women in Love*. With the exception of one or two poems, the lyrics of the second lustre do not say that "woman is the earth to me," either, as Cipriano does. Instead, marriage remains a powerful but unstated analogy in *Birds, Beasts and Flowers*. The world is to be loved rather than abused and left behind like the dancing partner of the "Hymn to Priapus." It is not, however, to be "loved" in the all-consuming way that Lawrence loved his mother and that he himself deemed "unnatural." It is to be loved, not to the degree that it reflects the outward and inward conditions of the life of its observer, but rather for its difference.

*   *   *

It was on the beautiful piece of Sicilian countryside that stretches down from Fontana Vecchia to the beaches below Taormina that Lawrence met a snake and began his struggle to commence an "unadulterated relationship" with the "non-human universe." The struggle to deal with a snake purely on its own terms, like Lawrence's all-too-human struggle to deal with a woman as the other that will never be fully comprehended, is a struggle that Lawrence, in Gerald Crich's words, "is hard put" to win. That is not to say that "Snake" fails as a poem, any more than it is to say that the Lawrences' marriage failed as a marriage. Instead, great poetry might be generally defined as a fortunate fall, the result of unique and interesting if failed attempts to leave the baggage of all cultural presupposition behind and to confront the naked world nakedly. It is the failure to jettison contexts that makes great poems speak where they might otherwise remain silent, much as it is the failure to treat a husband or wife as someone fully separate from oneself that makes a marriage more than a convenient living arrangement.

"Snake," surely one of the great poems in the English language, has been interpreted so often that another critical analysis might seem superfluous, and yet the extant readings offer half-views of the poem's meaning, half-views that a contextual approach can revealingly complement. Keith Sagar has said that in "Snake" Lawrence "records . . . the creative meeting of poet and phenomena."[17] But surely any poem, no matter how abstract, solipsistic, or hallucinatory, could be called the "creative meeting" of poet and world. Graham Hough similarly hedges his bets by saying that in his "nature poetry" Lawrence "breaks sharply" with "tradition" by making an "energetic . . . attempt to penetrate into the beings of natural objects, to show what they are in themselves, not how they can sustain our moral nature. . . . Of course it is radically subjective; who can know what it is . . . one meets when one meets a snake?"[18] To their views I would add that it is because Lawrence's *Birds, Beasts and Flowers* poems also record a unique meeting of a poet and tradition that the meeting of poet and phenomena seems so "subjective" to Hough, so "creative" to Sagar, so original to both.

Similarly, I seek not to argue with but rather to complicate the many interpretations of "Snake" that focus on its sexual motifs.[19] To read the poem as being about the way voices of the dead continually come between us and the enjoyment of the other, the physical world that may exist beyond the fictions in which we live, is not to deny the reading which says that the poem is about a man's failed attempt to get in contact with his own primitive sexual being, his blood-consciousness. Rather, these two interpretations interlock, just as do the two sides of Lawrence, the one that believes in the primacy of the physical, the other in the primacy of the linguistic.

Having said all this, it may be best to begin by admitting that provocative sexual innuendo crawls out of every crack and fissure of this work, as it does out of so many of the poems in the *Birds, Beasts and Flowers* volume. There is the "yellow-brown slackness" of the "slack long body" of the snake, the snake that with "crowned" head moves in, out of, and between a wet-bottomed "trough" and an "earth-lipped fissure" in the "burning bowels of the earth." (It is a "horrid . . . hole" from which the speaker of the poem recoils in fear.) And there are less explicit images and metaphors that are nonetheless sexual in their implication. We hear of the smoking heat, of the speaker's quest for relief "in pyjamas," and of voices of education that, like Freudian advocates of delayed gratification, seem to cry out against the snake and its quick and easy access. The "peaceful, pacified" look of the reptile upon withdrawing from the trough—the snake looked "*as one* who has drunken" (italics mine)—is yet another detail that, together with some general allusions to temptation in Paradise, allows us to believe that the poem is about sex.

The temptation into sexual life, however, was not the temptation described by Genesis or by *Paradise Lost*, and it is not the only temptation depicted by "Snake." The temptation that this reading will focus on, one that Lawrence resists and then seems to succumb to through his very act of resistance, is the temptation to approach the world outside of oneself not personally, not originally, but through the knowledge imparted by the language of other men, through the nagging voices of education.

"Snake" is the evidence of a struggle to be obedient only to the voice of one's inner being. It is evidence, finally, of the poet's acquiescence in the feeling that, since his language is a learned one, his perceptions can never be fresh; fruit of the corrupting tree has been eaten before any scene can be viewed, before any poem about a snake can be begun. Lawrence, even as he struggles to view a place, to respond to its inhabitant, and to write an original poem about both, realizes that other men have been on the scene before him. His own relationship with the world, he fears, can hardly be that "unadulterated relationship with the universe" that is his "deepest desire" so long as he is the result of an earlier intercourse with reality, his vision and his epistemology engendered by a larger-looming language.

The poet of "Snake" wants to come up against the earth, the female, but when he wakes up and descends "the steps" that lead to her refreshments, he suddenly realizes that he "must wait, must stand and wait, for there he was at the trough before me."

> Someone was before me at my water-trough,
> And I, like a second comer, waiting.

The snake, the first comer, described also as a "god," a "king in exile," and "a guest" from the "underworld," is like a father, returned from the dead to remind the son of his derivations. The poet can only feel that the earth is not to be his in "pure, unmediated relation," for what he witnesses while he waits at the stone trough and then watches the god and king return to his home beyond the "earth-lipped fissure" is like a ritual re-enactment of the cycle of life and death that antedated and indeed produced him. The speaker's mixed feelings of respect ("I felt so honoured") and revulsion ("horror . . . / Overcame me") are the feelings of a man who voyeuristically witnesses his father's two deaths: the symbolic intercourse with the mother that gave the child his being and the "withdrawing into that horrid black hole" of death that forced the son into the position of dependent independence. A second comer, he has to deal with the world as if he were an Adam, as if the world that is in fact like a mother to him were really like his wife, his Eve.

I am not speaking of the snake as symbol of Lawrence's biological father, any more than I am suggesting that the earth is a trope for the poet's beloved mother. By the time of the second poetic lustre, Lawrence's love for his mother and his dread of his father have been "purified" or transformed by the poet's highly creative consciousness. They have become analogies through which Lawrence understands the terrible difficulty of entering into poetic marriage with the original world of objects in nature. No poet is himself an original; indeed, the way in which he sees that which is the end of all his desire has been conditioned by a patriarchal education.

What I am suggesting is that at one level of the poem's discourse the snake serves, not as a living example of the earth Lawrence wants to come to know and love in its mysterious otherness, but rather as an analogy for that past that led up to and made Lawrence what he is. It suggests the source of the highly interpretive "education" that would insist on possessing the poet's very being by telling him the meaning of all he sees—"black snakes are innocent, the gold are venomous"—and by advising him on how to respond to the world, once it has been so seen and interpreted: "If you were a man / You would take a stick and break him now." The snake signifies the world view Lawrence inherits, the tree of tradition, history, religion, literature, and other forms of human "knowledge" that are always tempting him to be unoriginal, urging him to become the product (by accepting the fact that he is the product) of all that has been known and said before his conception.

The snake thus, like a Freudian dream condensation, serves a remarkable double function. On one hand, it calls to mind a learned epistemology, a maze of contexts into which all of us are born. On the other, however, it suggests by analogy the female absence, the "original world" that Lawrence wrote of from Cornwall, the "rarer reality that has not been looked at" for a long time. To see and present a snake as unadulterated texture, color, and form would be to resurrect a natural, living object via patricide, to return it to our world by killing off the system of myth that cozens us to be blind to our sensual Paradise. This system tempts us automatically to accept the "fact" that certain things imply certain ideas because men have thought so and told us so in that past from which we derive. To present a snake without presupposition and free of all such ideas would be to do in a limited and more believable way what Don Ramon Carrasco seeks to do in *The Plumed Serpent* (1926). He tries to conjure up "the snake of the world" which, though "the rocks" are its "scales" and though the "lake[s] lie . . . between" its "folds," remains invisible to mankind.

To a few of "the peons" who witness Ramon's rite, "it seemed . . . as if really they saw a snake of brilliant gold and living blackness softly coiled around Ramón's ankle and knee, and resting its head in his fingers, licking his palm with forked tongue."[20] But

Lawrence makes it clear from what Ramon says that to the conjurer himself the elusive earth-snake remains just beyond the realm of the visible. Lawrence, too, in "Snake," fails at revealing the snake that our education blinds us to. The necessary patricide is not committed—indeed, as we shall see later, cannot be committed—by "Snake;" it is the physical snake, rather, that is excluded from the world of the poem. As a result of Lawrence's volley of sticks and words it "convulse[s] in undignified haste" into the dark, and the poet is left with "something to expiate; / A pettiness" that must be, in part, that paternal voice of education which cannot be ignored, the second-hand "knowledge" that constantly reasserts its priority over men and the world through which they blindly move.

Amid talk of tradition, language, a Paradise, blindness, and sight, it is hard to resist seeing Milton as one tenor of the snake's vehicle, as a metaphoric vehicle to the tenor of the educating past. *Paradise Lost*, certainly, is a tree of knowledge, an act of visionary blindness, a serpent that deceived and continues to deceive us. Milton is unquestionably one of the storytelling elders who condemned us, through a manipulation of signs, to a life of keeping our distance from snakes even as we attack evil with our tongues.

Leslie Brisman, writing in the *Georgia Review*, has said that "for the belated poet," all attempts to "recapture Paradise" are fated to become, ultimately, "the attempt to recapture *Paradise Lost*."[21] Lawrence seems to know this, for his own struggle to confront in innocence a simple snake not only fails to land him in a personal Eden but also fails to lead him back to the unfallen world of Genesis. Why is this so? First, because Milton stands between the English poets and Genesis in time; it is difficult for a writer to approach the world of Genesis except by way of *Paradise Lost*. Second, because Milton powerfully influenced the Romantic tradition from which a post-Romantic writer springs. Finally, because Milton, far more than the author's of the Genesis J account in which the charming, anthropomorphic Hebrew folktale first appears, made the story of our original parents into an ideograph. He made a complex, symbolic, metaphysical system out of a story in which the serpent, though cursed by God above all other beasts of the field, is not even identified as Satan.

Precisely at the same time that Milton's Satan entered the sleeping body of the serpent with his own distorted logic, Milton invaded the sleeping form of the natural reptile with Western man's conception of Supreme Evil. Thus the poet quenched our orbs to the reality of a creature with whom we share our planet. He drove the serpent into exile, or rather, he drove us into exile from the purely physical world in which mere snakes exist, thus making primordial contact all but impossible. One of the ways in which Lawrence subtly suggests this fact is by setting his poetic attempt to get to know a snake, on one plane at least, in Milton's Paradise. He thus implies that in writing *Paradise Lost* Milton to some degree shaped the way we see things outside us and the way we look for unmediated experience. In Milton's epic, Paradise is described as a rural "mound" of trees making "loftiest shade," a "verduous wall" of "Fir and branching Palm" rising in "ranks," "Shade above shade," and allowing the "gentle gales" to make off with the "balmy spoils" of their "Odors . . . spicy" and "odiferous . . . perfumes" (4.134–63). In Lawrence's short, powerful epic about an heroic but failed effort to escape Milton's so-called Paradise, the poet seeks his confrontation with raw nature "In the deep, strange-scented shade of the great dark carob-tree," a shade surrounded by a broken but still effective bank of a wall. Thus, before Lawrence even tells us that he is "a second comer" to a no longer virgin scene, we suspect this may be so.

Harold Bloom has written of poetry that it is often "at work imagining its own origin."[22] Through "Snake," which pictures a father figure returned from the dead who symbolically copulates with the "bowels of the earth," Lawrence imagines that he and the world he lives in and depicts must be in no small part the product of Milton's earlier, mental intercourse with some earlier, relatively physical reality. Because Milton's mind has invaded nature with the notion that it is now fallen from grace, later men perceive a world battered, raped, and swollen by Milton's ideas. And because of what they see, they are often provoked to abuse it further. When the voices of Lawrence's education finally "overc[o]me" him, when he picks "up a clumsy log" and throws it, he implicitly revises an old cliché with Milton very much in mind. Sticks and stones seldom break bones, but words can hurt, even kill.

The difficulty involved in seeing anew, let alone in becoming patriarch to a new poetic line, is expressed in "Snake" by awareness of a previous work of literature and by the poet's admission that he is no apocalyptic second coming but merely a second comer. The fact that Lawrence does not succeed fully in realizing what he had called, in a letter, "the tremendous *non-human* quality of life" is also apparent in the way in which he tries to accept the snake that the voices of education would have him reject. The poet's struggle against a system of education corrupted largely by its insistence upon assigning ideas to objects is compromised by his own anthropocentric projections. From the moment he "sees" the snake at a distance (it may be to Lawrence's credit that he never uses the word *serpent*), he feels compelled to call it a "he." This snake doesn't even begin life in the poem primarily as a reptile. "He" is seen from the start as a male; then, quickly, as a large mammal which just may be engaged in some simple thoughts as he inspects the poet with a meaningful, if vaguely meaningful, look; then, immediately following, as a higher being—not just a male mammal—"mus[ing] a moment" if not quite brooding over chaos.

Lawrence goes on, as if to make a revolutionary break with the perceptions and poems of the past, by asking, "must I confess how I liked him, / How glad I was he had come like a guest in quiet?" Like a man breaking into new realms of understanding, he can't help wondering whether it was "perversity, that I longed to talk to him," whether it was "humility, to feel so honoured," honoured "still more / That he should seek my hospitality / From out the dark door of the secret earth?" It is clear by now, however, that the poet's attempt at original behavior and language is compromised by the fact that he is not really "up against the unknown," in the words of his letter to Bertrand Russell on love. He is not taking a new look at a snake, enjoying what he sees, and telling us about it. Or, at least, he is doing so only *after* he has, in the blink of an eye, reformed it mentally and set it in a scene whose props are old ideas —ideas about divine guests and honored, hospitable human hosts, about perversity and humility, conversation and confession, the light of the world and the "dark door" to another realm. Not unlike the Romantic lover who in his "pride and . . . egotism" is unable "to love a woman as something other than a self-manifestation," the poet is attracted to a snake that he has made over into nothing more or less than a manifestation of the Western self.

As the address progresses, Lawrence makes the snake into "a god, unseeing." Just as the phrase "king in exile" suggests indirectly the poet's estrangement from a purely sensual world at the same time that it personifies the snake, so the depiction of a creature as a blind god refers, through a similar kind of indirection, to the myopia of the visionary who projects ideas—even icono-clastic ones—upon the chaos of the phenomenal world. Matthew Arnold had objected, long before Lawrence, to the tendency of writers since Byron to overlook the world by "promiscuously adopt[ing]" its shapes and forms for mere symbols of their own private, poetic ideas.[23] Lawrence manages promiscuous conversa-tion neither with actuality nor, it would seem, with his own ideas. The shape he describes comes to him not from the relative cool-ness of the actual earth behind the poet's house but, rather, from the heat of the volcanic underworld, seen and never touched; and that through which this hot, thirsty form of the subterranean fire is "seen" is the vision—Miltonic but Dantean as well—of a fiery Inferno. Both predecessors describe the heat of hell through de-scriptive allusions to the "fuell'd entrails" of Mount Etna.[24] Law-rence's snake is

> earth-brown, earth-golden from the burning
> > bowels of the earth
> On the day of Sicilian July, with Etna smoking.

Lawrence has been properly educated to see the Sicilian mountain near which the snake lives as an emblem of hell, as is obvious from a reading of *Sea and Sardinia*, where he speaks of the mountain's "terrible dynamic exhalations" and "demon magnetism." Lying "under heaven" and "rolling . . . orange-coloured smoke" and "rose-red flame," Etna exists beyond the safeness of our world, beyond "the dividing line." It "bre[aks] the souls" of all who visit it; it "makes a storm in the living plasm"; it drives "men mad." It "is She one must flee from," he concludes. "One must go: and at once."[25]

That which the would-be radical "likes," then, that which "honors" him by its presence, that which the poet sees and would seek, in spite of Western morality, to call regal and godlike, brave and heroic, is not the cold-blooded snake, the loveless and lively brute with a slack, long body. The snake that the poet likes does not even signify the amoral sexual life. It is, rather, what Lawrence has called "the great corruptive principle,"[26] what Kate Leslie, in *The Plumed Serpent*, will have her "soul . . . alert[ed]" by, a snake resting its head on its "fold, like the devil himself."[27] The snake of "Snake" is, as Sandra Gilbert has pointed out, "the Satanic snake" which, "like Blake's vision of Milton's Satan," is "not evil but good."[28] Thus Lawrence's act of rebellion amounts to an attempt to like the proud adversary, the demon "king" of the "underworld," and even to crown the mighty enemy a modern hero.

Milton has Lawrence in chains even Samson could not break. (By Milton I mean the poet of *Paradise Lost* and the Milton fashioned by Blake, Wordsworth, Shelley, and others. Lawrence can know the original only by way of the dependents; that is part and parcel of what "Snake" is about.) If he is revulsed by the snake, then he pays tribute to what Milton has made of it. If, on the other hand, he honors the exiled king as his hero, his prince, his better god, well, Milton set that precedent too. In fact, it is precisely at the pivotal moment when Satan possesses the serpent that he is both the great old Adversary of the early books and the horrible dissembler of the later ones. Even a third option open to Lawrence—of treating the snake neither as new hero nor old enemy but, rather, as a comrade and brother, a fellow foster child of meadow, grove, and stream—is doomed to redundancy. No sooner does the poet regret the "vulgar" and "mean act" of assaulting the innocent, no sooner does he "despise [him]self and the voices of [his] accursed human education," than, he says,

> I thought of the albatross,
> And I wished he would come back, my snake.

Keith Sagar, who is usually an extremely perceptive reader of Lawrence's poetry, sees no irony in these lines. He correctly reminds us, in *The Art of D. H. Lawrence*, that Coleridge's Ancient Mariner anticipated Lawrence's expiation of a gratuitous act of violence against an innocent natural creature. The Mariner expiated his "pettiness," of course, by coming arduously to accept his own brotherhood with all creatures, particularly with coiling, twining sea snakes:

> They coiled and swam; and every track
> Was a flash of golden fire.
>
> O happy living things! no tongue
> Their beauty might declare:
> A spring of love gushed from my heart,

> And I blessed them unaware.
> (lines 280–85)

Sagar goes on to suggest that Lawrence's recollection of the albatross marks his return to natural, unconventional behavior. He defends his view by arguing for the unconventionality of the Mariner's act. "Instead of reacting conventionally (snakes are slimy and disgusting), he allows his spontaneous feelings of love and acceptance to find expression."[29]

What Sagar overlooks is that Lawrence, in speaking of the albatross, is *not* expressing original, spontaneous, unconventional feelings. Rather, his great originality is in subtly and ironically showing us the ways in which certain voices of education assert their primacy even as others are despised. By creating an interfluence of texts from Genesis to Coleridge's *Rime* within the same poem, Lawrence deftly illustrates the way in which anticonventional acts recapitulate other conventions, in this case the anti-Biblical and anti-Miltonic conventions of Romanticism. When Lawrence, just after sharing his thought about the albatross, goes on to call the snake "my snake," he is still elaborating on the world view of Milton's Romantic heirs. It is they who have taught us imaginatively to possess reality, to see all of nature as our own, that is, as being continuous with us and the confirmation of our imaginative life. Indeed, the "pettiness" that Lawrence feels the need to "expiate" in the poem's last lines may not be the less-than-blessed act of throwing a log at a snake but rather the fact that both to do so and then to feel sorry afterwards he has to think of hell, the garden, and the albatross.

The line in which Lawrence's mind goes out to the murdered sea bird, moreover, is not the only one in which he thinks of Coleridge. Nor is the reference to "Etna smoking" Lawrence's only re-vision of a literary hell. He is seeing and reacting as he has been taught by *Paradise Lost* and Coleridge's *Rime*, for instance, when he speaks of seeing, that hot "July" day, the serpent "writhed like lightning" while "I stared with fascination . . . in the intense still noon." The fallen legions of Milton's epic, awaiting Satan's news of his conquest of earth, are transformed into "swarming" serpents of "horrid shape" and "forked tongue." They are thus but one figurative step from writhing lightning. "Parch'd with scalding thirst," they "roll" their way across hell's hot surface to trees bearing "fair

Fruit" which, upon being "Chew'd," prove "bitter ashes" (10.504–70). The ancient Mariner's early vision of "slimy things" that "did crawl . . . / Upon the slimy sea" takes place in no less an inferno, "in a hot and coppy sky" under "the bloody Sun, at noon." Coleridge's fiery lake, like Lawrence's desert noon, is, in Lawrence's later words, "intense still"—the air has "nor breath nor motion" and the mariner's boat lies "as idle as a painted ship upon a painted ocean" (lines 111–26.)

Even Lawrence's thirst (thirst is, after all, the fact of life which first brings about the confrontation with the serpent) seems too poetically redundant to allow for unmediated perception of an object. Not unlike Milton's snakes with their innumerable dust-dry fruits, Coleridge's Mariner has "Water, water, every where, / Nor any drop to drink." So, for a long while at least, he says,

> With throats unslaked, with black lips baked,
> We could nor laugh nor wail;
> Through utter drought all dumb we stood!
> (lines 157–59)

Lawrence has a pitcher and a trough, but unlike Coleridge's Mariner, who later drank whole buckets of sweetest dew, he never quenches his thirst in his poem. That is because someone else has been at the trough before him and because the trough, as we see it, is nearly dry. Even the snake, his predecessor, "rested his throat upon the stone bottom." The fact that Lawrence takes no drink in "Snake" may be symbolic of the poetic inarticulateness which, he feels, must be his punishment for succumbing to the irresistible temptation to see the world through other men's language. The ancient Mariner stood perfectly "dumb" "Through utter drought." Because Lawrence's perceptions are at once structured by and revealed through Coleridge's more (but far from) original glimpses and discussions of a world of thirst and drought, snakes and albatrosses, horror and eventual sympathy, he suffers his own kind of drought and, in his own provocatively talkative way, stands dumb with ashes of old fires in his mouth.

Coleridge, like Milton, exacts a double payment from his second comers, for just as Lawrence must prove his derivation from Milton whether he attacks or sympathizes with a king in exile, so Lawrence's various attempts at liberating himself from Romantic language and epistemology are also doubly doomed from the start, a fact which the poet implicitly recognizes when he says, near the end of the poem, "I wished he would come back, my snake." For if Lawrence were to bring the snake back—that is, reverse the snake's reversion to the underworld of the past, wrest the snake from the dead-man's grip of his predecessors and by so doing possess it entirely as his own unencumbered subject—he would run counter to his purpose and thus undo his own revolt. That is because Lawrence's only hope to be absolutely and entirely different from the paternal poets is not to possess the snake at all, not to make the snake "mine," not to destroy the serpent by projecting on it any of his own ideas, anxieties, fears, guilts, hopes, or thoughts whatsoever. So, Lawrence admits, by possessing the snake I fail at wresting him—and myself— from my predecessors, but by leaving the snake utterly unen- cumbered by the emotional and intellectual forms of my own individual mind, that is, by refusing to be a Romantic or Coleridgean poet, I necessarily fail to make the creature "my snake." The nearest thing Lawrence can achieve to self-libera- tion is a reversal of Coleridge's *Rime*: he atones for violence against a snake by thinking kindly of an albatross. However successful the poem as a whole may be, this victory is surely more pathetic than profound; more precisely, it is through the pathetic admission of defeat that Lawrence succeeds in making his radical and original claim about the double bind of Romantic epistemology.

Not all the predecessors who prove to be influences in "Snake" turn out to be albatrosses. Some precursors and their poems suggest ways for Lawrence to express a problem without complicating it in the process. Swinburne's "Hymn to Proser- pine" provided a language with which Lawrence could form- ulate, in "Hymn to Priapus," his inability to leave the past behind; it did so without intensifying the fear of future in the way that Hardy's "dancing" poems seemed to do. *Macbeth*, a play that Lawrence tells us was one of the four most influential works he ever read (the other three, he says, were Words- worth's Immortality Ode, Keats's "Ode to a Nightingale," and the Nonconformist *Hymnbook*),[30] provides a means of expressing ambivalence towards tradition and power. Unlike *Paradise Lost* and Coleridge's *Rime*, however, it does not become itself a trope for that debilitating, paternal tradition.

That Shakespeare's play is rife with serpent imagery is almost predictable. (Lady Macbeth is once compared to an "innocent flower" with a "serpent under't" [1.5.64].) There is more, however, than snake (or king, or crown) imagery in *Macbeth*, to speak of the play's importance to Lawrence. Lady Macbeth, upon being greeted by the visiting king as his "honour'd hostess," agrees that the "honours" are "deep and broad, wherewith / Your Majesty loads our house" (1.6.17–18). Of course, she is only pretending, but Macbeth actually *does* feel deeply honored—so much so that he begins to waver in his murderous resolution. "He hath honour'd me," he says to his wife (1.7.32);

> He's here in double trust:
> First, as I am his kinsman and his subject,
> Strong both against the deed; then, as his host,
> Who should against his murtherer shut the door.
> (1.7.12–15).

Lady Macbeth is dumbstruck by what she sees as her husband's newfound fear. "Would'st thou," she nags him, "live a coward in thine own esteem?" She exhorts him to say he would rather murder Duncan and says—recalling the time when he first unveiled his murderous plan—

> When you durst do it, then you were a man;
> And, to be more than what you were, you would
> Be so much more the man.
> (1.7.41–51)

Following Shakespeare, Lawrence sets his story of an eventual, unnatural violence within the contexts of an honoring guest–honored host situation. Like *Macbeth*, "Snake" thus intensifies the reprehensibility of an act that is already against a "kinsman," an inmate of this active universe. "He's here," Lawrence might well have said of his own honoring visitant, "in a double trust." The trust is violated because of the effectiveness of voices, and the voices within speak straight from Lady Macbeth's mouth. Her line "When you durst do it, then you were a man" speaks to as well as from her husband's psyche, just as do Lawrence's voices of education when they urge him, "If you were a man, you would break him." Shakespeare's murdered guest, moreover, anticipates

Lawrence's nearly murdered one by being not only a king but also (and almost inseparably) a paternal figure. Lady Macbeth explicitly compares King Duncan to a "father as he slept," and she says that "had he not resembled" her father, she would have killed him herself (2.2.12–13).

Macbeth (together with *Paradise Lost*) thus provides Lawrence with a way of speaking of tradition, power, and fruitless acts of insurrection. Keats's *Lamia*—that beautiful, exotic narrative in which a serpent is transformed into a woman by a god and then is loved by and lost to a mortal man—is equally important to "Snake," for it informs the poem's treatment of the themes of imagination, metamorphosis, and loss. A brief recollection of *Lamia* may be useful here, since the details of the story Keats tells about Corinth, Hermes, Lycius, and Apollonius—although superficially very different from those of the short Sicilian chronicle—are useful in establishing the importance of the Romantic text.

The "gordian shape" of the "dazzling" lamia, or snake, seemed "Some demon's mistress, or the demon's self" until she "breath'd upon" the eyes of Hermes and delivered to him the wood-nymph he desired (*Lamia*, 1.47–56, 124). She was thereupon rewarded by a "convulsion" which, "as the lava ravishes the mead," "undrest" her "Of all her sapphires, greens and amethyst" and left her looking like an irresistible woman (1.154–61). Waiting by a roadside in Corinth, she next used song to invade the innocent mind, "shut up in mysteries" and "wrapp'd like his mantle," of Lycius, a young man who consequently fell in love with her to the vague displeasure of a city whose citizens "Mutter'd" like men in "a dream" (1.241–42, 350–53). "Enthroned" in a splendrous world, Lycius proposed marriage to his disguised lamia, and all went well for the mismatched couple until the wedding banquet, a magnificent feast to which everyone in Corinth was invited as an honored guest. The feast took place amidst "haunting music" in a "glowing banquet room ... mimicking" a watery "glade / Of palm and plantain" and lit by a "stream of lamps" flowing across a "marble plain." It was here, at this banquet, that the "cold" and "ruthless" eye of Apollonius saw through the human disguise to the snake that lay thereunder. He revealed the lamia's reality, and the long-deluded Lycius immediately died (2.17, 121–50, 230–82).

The superficial details as well as the more general concerns of the text can be seen finding their way into Lawrence's poem. Like

Keats's gordian deceiver, Lawrence's reptile appears as "dazzling" as a precious stone; it is one of those bright, "earth-golden," venomous snakes that, unlike the "black" ones, are never "innocent." The false, imaginatively fabricated latter-day garden in Keats's poem stands behind Lawrence's still more recent oasis. It is dry and parched, for it is watered only by lamps which stream across a marble plain. (Lawrence's gordian shape rests his throat upon stone in the intense, still light of noon.) Keats's subject "seem'd . . . the demon's self"; Lawrence's snake "seemed to me" a "king" of the "underworld." The "enthroned" snake of *Lamia* was metamorphosed into a person while she "writh'd about" in a "convulsion" of "phosphor and sharp sparks," a lightning-like seizure which, as "the lava ravishes the mead," "undrest" her of her "gems." The snake of Lawrence's "Snake" is similarly ravished—that is, is "undrest" of its reality—through the magical metamorphosis of traditional personifications. The invasion of the brute by Lawrence and his educated, "musing" humanity (which would be deity) takes place in a stanza that all but speaks of ravishing lava: "Snake" mentions "the burning bowels of the earth" and Mount Etna "smoking." After the illusion-breaking projection of the log, the bejewelled king of demon turns back into a reptile while Lawrence tells us that it "convulsed in undignified haste" and "Writhed like lightning." The words recall, almost accurately, the lamia that "writh'd about" in a "convulsion" of "sharp sparks."

Many more parallels remain; only a few can be recounted. The modern poet, like Lycius, is in love, not with a serpent, but with what a serpent has become. Keats, that is to say, is analogous to Hermes. Like Lycius, Lawrence is a second comer who would possess something that is neither what it seems nor his to possess. It is an apparition; it has been "made" what it is by someone else.

Lamia anticipates the interwoven motifs of sight, blindness, and dream which run throughout "Snake." Keats's snake is at once an agent of blindness and a catalyst of imagination and of dreams; she fabricates Hermes's wood-nymph by breathing on his eyes and inducing a dream, for "Real are the dreams of Gods." Later, when she appeals to a visionary "wrapp'd," "shut up," in "mysteries," she induces a dream which "closes" his "eyelids" to reality more tightly than ever before. Indeed, she causes the citizens of Corinth to "mutter" like men who "talk in a dream," everyone, that

is, save the one man whose "ruthless" sight cannot be "pierce[d],"
the man whose vision and whose language cannot be influenced
by the snake. But Lamia is a victim as well as a deceiver, a dreamer
as well as an enchantress, blind as well as blinding. She may
imprison men in a world of imagination, but she too, Keats tells us
explicitly, has been a "dreamer" in a "prison-house," a lover of a
world she can never fully enter (2.281–82; 1.203).

The confrontation between Lawrence and serpent, like that
between Lycius and his beloved, takes place in a dream world of
imagination considerably distant from the usual stuff of reality.
The snake, Lawrence says, "lifted his head, dreamily," or, later,
"Proceeded" very "slowly, as if thrice adream." The poet, of
course, is doing here exactly what he was doing in those earlier
lines in which he admitted his own blindness ("unseeing") and
separation from the physical world ("exile") by projecting them
onto the snake. (It may even be that his view of himself as "thrice
adream" is the loose calculation of a wishful thinker, since *Mac-
beth, Paradise Lost, The Rime of the Ancient Mariner,* and *Lamia*
all stand between the poet and the sensual reality of his object.) As
for there being two lamias in *Lamia,*—one a tyrant, the other a
victim; one evil, the other sympathetic—so there are two snakes in
"Snake." There is the snake which is a Lord of the Underworld,
King in Exile, Knowledge, Deception, Satan, Evil. And there is the
snake whose disappearance can be attributed to the aforemen-
tioned snake. This is the serpent that lives in the only paradise
man could ever have, the physical creature unseen by the poet
tempted if not fated always to view reality through an ever-thick-
ening lens of moral, intellectual, and imaginative projections.

Finally there is the problem of Apollonius. The suddenly hurled
log that breaks the reverie in "Snake," causes the god and king
suddenly to be seen as an "undignified" beast, and drives the
living into the "black hole" of the dead is roughly analogous to the
deadly, demystifying eye of the old Corinthian sage. Indeed, the
"Apollonian" act in "Snake," that of hurling the log, turns out to be
as complex as is Keats's use of Apollo's name to characterize a man
who destroys an imaginative world. The act of hurling the log is
one that ultimately derives from art; if writers since Genesis had
not used poetic language to transform the snake, then the pro-
jectile would never have been thrown. But the log, which is
superficially a symbol of art, is a symbol of dead art, art become the

antithesis of imaginative, original being. Like Keats's old sage, whose name suggests reason and science as well as poetry, the log is a destructive "cold philosophy" (*Lamia*, 2.230).

The arrival at this understanding of Lawrence's projectile suggests that there may be yet another romantic poet somewhere behind "Snake." The notion that writers beginning with the author(s) of Genesis have transformed the snake strongly recalls Blake's vision of *The Marriage of Heaven and Hell.* "The ancient Poets," Blake writes in the caption to the eleventh plate,

> animated all sensible objects with Gods or Geniuses, calling them by the names and adorning them with the properties of wood, rivers, mountains, lakes, cities, nations, and whatever their enlarged and numerous senses could perceive. . . .
>
> Thus men forgot that all deities reside in the human breast.[31]

Blake does not himself strive, as Lawrence strives in "Snake" to little avail, to strip the object world of all the names and geniuses that the poets have projected upon it. Indeed, the first principle of Blake's "b" treatise on the subject, "THERE is NO Natural Religion," is that "man's perceptions are not bounded by organs of perception. He perceives more than sense (tho' ever so acute) can discover."[32] Nevertheless, Blake would more than agree with Lawrence that some boundaries inscribed around human perception have widened consciousness, while others have, unfortunately, pinched it. If we read the inscription under plate 14 of *The Marriage of Heaven in Hell* with Lawrence in mind, we can almost picture a poet who has lost a chance with one of the inhabitants of the rarer reality, the infinite world of uncomprehended otherness around him, because earlier poets have condemned him to a cavern that narrows his vision and makes him petty: "If the doors of perception were cleansed every thing would appear to man as it is," Blake says. "For man has closed himself up till he sees all things thro' narrow chinks of his cavern."[33]

*   *   *

Lawrence's interest in Coleridge, Keats, and even Blake during that period in which he takes his relation to the nonhuman universe as the subject of his poetry is hardly surprising. It is no more surprising than that he was most interested in Shelley, Swinburne, and Hardy during those earlier years in which his subjects were ideal love, impossible love, and longed-for pleasures turning to pain. Nor should we be puzzled over the fact that Lawrence became discouraged with his ability to appreciate and show us the wonder of the world that he had so strongly hoped he could show just after meeting Frieda ("Song of a Man Who Has Come Through") and that he still felt he could "realise" in 1916, in Cornwall. Blake, Coleridge, and Keats often write implicitly of the difficulty, even the impossibility, of getting free of certain old myths and of knowing the "wonder" directly. And the Edenic myth, in both its original and revised, Miltonic version, often seems to be at once the trope for the unspoiled world and the most serious obstacle standing between the Romantic mind and its longed-for consummation with the elements.

Coleridge's *Rime of the Ancient Mariner* implies its sense of the difficulty of original conception through its narrative form. A Wedding Guest hears a tale from a Mariner. The Wedding Guest is not, however, the narrator of the tale as we hear it, a fact which would suggest that any reader of the poem is, in the words of "Snake," "thrice adream." The relationship between the Mariner and the Wedding Guest is that of an elderly father or grandfather and a son who has no choice but to listen to his elder's tale. The Mariner is an "ancient" man with a "skinny hand" who often seems but a "grey-beard loon" to his listener. But the listener, in spite of his derision and fear, is so transfixed by the teller that he "listens like a three years' child" (lines 1, 9–15). (The Wedding Guest seems to feel much the same mixture of revulsion and fascination in the presence of the uninvited guest, the Ancient Mariner, that Lawrence will later feel as he "stand[s]" and "stare[s]" and feels "afraid" and yet "honoured" by his "first comer," the snake who is like a father returned from an underworld of life-in-death.) Whether the childlike listener would escape the elder's *Rime* or not, "the Mariner hath his will" and the "child . . . cannot choose but hear" (lines 15–18). He seems fated to be "stunned," to be made "of sense forlorn" by the paternal teller. He is destined to be made the "sadder" and "wiser man" who will rise "the morrow morn" when "The Mariner . . . whose beard with age is hoar, / Is gone" (lines 618–25).

The nightmarish, grandfatherly yarn that becomes instinctive wisdom or a body of knowledge to the younger generation, moreover, is a tale about a "hellish thing" that takes place in a darkness visible called a "dismal sheen." It is the story of a man conversant with God but plagued by fiends, a man whose act of irreverence turns the sea into a "wave aflame" wherein "death fires danced" and on which snakes "did crawl with legs" (lines 171, 117–28, 171). What the Mariner describes may be the primary event of his personal past, but it more often than not reminds us of the old story of the Primary Event. Because dead bards provide many of the terms of the Mariner's tale, his scene is recognizably artificial (his "painted ship" plies a "painted ocean").

Keats, too, tells a tale that is in no small part the story of the Fall. *Lamia* is a rhyme about hot imagination and cool reason, about deception and a death which results, about ecstatic, forbidden experience, about dreams and visions, blindness and sight. There is a God who can have things mere mortals can't, a man who awakens in "amaze, / To see" a lovely woman he wants to wed, a stream-fed garden of "several large" and many "slighter trees," a banquet complete with "honored guests," and, of course, a "demon . . . serpent" that would claim a place in a world for which it was not created (2.124–40; 1.322–24).

Keats says, some time after Lycius' "fall" for the "soft voice" of the disguised snake,

> For all this came a ruin: side by side
> They were enthroned, in the even tide,
> Upon a couch, near to a curtaining
> Whose airy texture, from a golden string,
> Floated into the room, and let appear
> Unveil'd the summer heaven, blue and clear,
> Betwixt two marble shafts:—there they reposed.
> (2.10–29)

As deeply as Lycius is lost in the delicious illusion that Lamia brings, it seems unlikely that he enjoys glimpses of any "summer heaven, blue and clear" and entirely external to the illusion. The poet suggests through his imagery that life outside is something framed by (and thus not a frame around) the larger, not smaller, artistic or poetic illusion, whether it be Miltonic or otherwise. The "real" sky, in other words, can only be seen "Betwixt . . . marble shafts" and "curtains" that "Float" between perceiver and world, looking like nothing so much as those curtains controlled by "a golden string" that frame the illusory world that an audience sees on a stage. The fear that we exclude a reality outside the inner sanctum where we receive and revise the fictional songs of love we inherit, Keats would seem to suspect, may intimate the existence of that world, but it may just be part of the illusion. The window in the inner sanctum that appears to open out upon reality may in fact be only a proscenium arch separating parts of the same theater, a theater surrounded only by nothingness.

Lawrence creates a similarly uncertain dialectic through the concept of voice; "Snake" would seem to claim throughout that it grows out of a tension between noble, true, realistic, and "original" voices within (analogous to the voice of Adam's God) and the tempting, corrupting voices of "knowledge" or "education" (analogous to Satan's intrusive, foreign voice). But on closer examination the voices within are at times uncomfortably similar to the voices without:

> The voice of my education said to me
> He must be killed. . . .
>
> And voices in me said, If you were a man
> You would take a stick and break him now.

Lawrence's claim that he has personal voices within sounds more than suspect, and it is my conviction that the poet intended it to. Indeed, to my mind, "Snake" reserves its claim to bold originality precisely by combining and developing Coleridgean and Keatsian contexts to raise a demystifying or "deconstructive" question about the myth of personality. The phrase "if you were a man" means not "if you were your own, freethinking person" but rather, in Keith Sagar's words, "if you had the same, stereotyped, civilized responses as everyone else."[34] If Sagar is right to so interpret "man"—and I believe that he is—then Lawrence uses the phrase to suggest in advance that the jaculation of the clumsy log may not be the outcome of a dialectic of outer and inner voices but, rather, an event fated by a perfectly conventional language without and a language within which are one and the same.

In the love poems of the first lustre, Lawrence sometimes showed his awareness of the fact that revulsion with any particular state of romantic intimacy may only be an expression of a lingering idealism. And yet the lover, in the general view of the Lawrence who wrote the "Hymn to Priapus," is not deluded in believing that there is a world of love beyond the walls of the Romantic dream-instinct and thus a chance that he or she may eventually come through to a love that is "faithful and faithless together" to old definition. The poet of "Snake," although he hedges cynicism implicitly by experiencing his doubt as revelation, nonetheless seems more cynical about man's ability to act or speak except in accordance with the dictates of old voices.

To be sure, Lawrence can "confess how [he] liked" a serpent. But he is really only telling us *that* he liked the snake; he "must" but he seems to have no words to "confess how [he] liked him." Thus an ungrammatical colloquialism attempts to cover for failure to say something through some original "voice within." When he finally does attempt to explain "how," he can only refer us to a previous text by thinking "of the albatross," thus implicitly retelling in a word an old, old story. Once again, the voice within turns out to be the voice without, the voice of an old tale-teller who is external to, even if he has been internalized by, the so-called speaker. The so-called blue of reality unconfined by the palace inured in illusion seems only to be a play within a play, for to describe it Lawrence must see it through the proscenium arch of an ancient rime.

For Blake that arch of ancient poetry, those narrow doors of perception, could be cleansed or, rather, replaced by others fashioned by a Poetic Genius capable of widening man's vision. But Blake accepts the premise of Judeo-Christian culture which says that "reality" is always informed by some vision, some story. "We of Israel taught that the Poetic Genius (as you now call it) was the first principle . . . of human perception," Ezekiel tells the speaker of *The Marriage of Heaven and Hell* over dinner with Isaiah.[35] One of Blake's authorative-sounding devils declares that "man has no body distinct from his soul," and as for the bodies outside the human soul, "the forms of all things" are "Angel & Spirit & Demon" and derive from the human soul, according to Blake's poem entitled "All Religions Are One."[36] Lawrence, through a poem such as "Snake," may fear that Blake is right that the only way to see beyond our painted scenery to the "thin clear air and untouched skies that have not been looked at nor covered with smoke" is to knock the scenery down and paint grander vistas. But he passionately hopes otherwise.

*   *   *

The prosodic style of "Snake" is by and large the casual style
that Lawrence forged in the process of coming through. There
are some four-beat lines that recall Hardy, if at a distance ("And
stooped and drank a little more"), there are semi-Swinburnian
hexameters ("And flickered his two-forked tongue from his lips,
and mused a moment"), and there are many conversational-
sounding hybrids ("Someone was before me at my water-
trough"). But there are other lines with a difference:

> He lifted his head from his drinking, as cattle do,
> And looked at me vaguely, as drinking cattle do,
> And flickered his two-forked tongue from his lips, and
>   mused a moment,
> And stooped and drank a little more,
> Being earth-brown, earth-golden from the burning
>   bowels of the earth
> On the day of Sicilian July, with Etna smoking.

As Graham Hough has noticed, sometimes this "rhythm trem-
bles on the verge of regular iambic pentameter for a line or two,
then relapses into a looser conversational run."[37] Hough goes on
to suggest, however, that the regular pentameter is analogous
to the poet's "Orphic" powers of "apprehension" and the
"looser" lines to the "accursed" human "voices," whereas to my
way of thinking the very opposite connections must be made.
The nearly regular pentameter of "looked at me vaguely, as
drinking cattle do" suggests traditional prosody *and* the tradi-
tional poetic way of (un)seeing an object; the "loose" and
"casual" phrase, "flickered his two-forked tongue from his lips"
(a phrase echoing the untraditional sounds of Swinburne and of
Hardy's Wessex ballads), comes closer to singing the truth of a
snake.

It is nearly impossible to identify any one voice of Lawrence's
poetic education as the cause for his "verging" towards "reg-
ular" poetry, but the grammar of "Snake" may allow for some
educated speculation. "Snake" is first and foremost a poem of
the "I":

> And immediately I regretted it.
> I thought how paltry, how vulgar, what a mean act!

> I despised myself and the voices of my accursed human
> education.
>
> And I thought of the albatross,
> And I wished he would come back, my snake.

Whitman, who did not often write in blank verse, may come first to
mind as a context here, but the grammar of "Snake" is ultimately
not the grammar of the Whitmanian "I," which writes catalogues
of experience in lines so long and sentences so irregular that they
seem the product of a wider intercourse with reality than any one
man could actually have. Rather, the "I" of "Snake" is one recalling
a singular experience with a simple object and predicating a moral
attitude on that one experience. It is more nearly the "I" of the
boat- and egg-stealing episodes of the first book of *The Prelude* by
Wordsworth. It is even more nearly the "I" that governs the
loosely traditional pentameter of Wordsworth's "Resolution and
Independence," a poem recalling a day on which the poet awoke,
took a walk, and instead of seeing a snake,

> Beside a pool bare to the eye of heaven,
> I saw an old man before me unawares.
> (lines 54–55)

The man, although he at first seems like a foreign object—a "huge
stone," an inanimate thing "endued with sense," and an armor-
plated "sea-beast crawled forth . . . to sun itself" (lines 57, 61–63)—
eventually becomes the poet's image of human resilience.

Wordsworth, whose presence can be felt mainly if not exclu-
sively in the rhythms and grammar of "Snake," was in fact the
most influential of the Romantic predecessors to whom Lawrence
turned during his second major poetic lustre. Along with Coleridge
and Keats, Wordsworth set the precedent of turning to the natural
world in response to a slackening faith in eternal verities. No less
than Coleridge and Keats, Wordsworth became frustrated by the
degree to which Miltonic images of Nature—both Paradisiacal and
cursed—stand between the poet's mind and the demystified
world that he seeks.

In 1798, four months after publishing *Lyrical Ballads*, Words-
worth wrote fifty-six lines of poetry that he intended to include in
The Prelude. Instead, these lines were deleted from the manu-
script of the autobiographical narrative and printed in the second

edition of *Lyrical Ballads*. "Nutting" (for that became the title of these lines) recalls a day on which the poet, as a young man, set out walking through a "tangled" wilderness, came upon "A virgin scene" of trees hanging full of "tempting clusters" of hazel nuts, and "dragged to earth both branch and bough, with crash / And merciless ravage" without evident cause or premeditation. Then, equally unexpectedly, he "felt a sense of pain when [he] beheld /The silent trees, and saw the intruding sky." It is a poem that can be (and has been) interpreted as a familiar enough Wordsworthian statement about the passionate, physical, at times ravenous, intercourse of the child with nature and, consequently, about the calmer, more philosophical appreciation enjoyed by the older, sadder, and wiser poet.[38] There is another way of reading "Nutting," however, in which the work seems to have as much to do with a poet's changing attitude towards both the poetic past and his own originality as it does with his changing attitude towards the natural world.

"In the eagerness of boyish hope," Wordsworth writes,

> I left our cottage-threshold, sallying forth
> With a huge wallet o'er my shoulder slung,
> A nutting-crook in hand; and turned my steps
> Tow'rd some far-distant wood, a Figure quaint,
> Tricked out in proud disguise of cast-off weeds
> Which for that service had been husbanded,
> By exhortation of my frugal Dame—.

The frugal Dame of the poem seems as much as anything else to serve as a reminder that no father is mentioned in connection with this familial cottage in which "cast-off weeds" have "been husbanded." If we imagine for a moment that the absent father could stand out for the poetic past (the poem is a variation on the pastoral mode, after all, in which shepherds with shepherd-crooks are often poets first and foremost), then the "quaint" or "antique" clothes of "huge proportions" which "Trick . . . out" a mere child "in proud disguise" suggest the slightly comical presumptuousness of the young poet's setting forth to do his father's work and, perhaps, the inappropriateness of the medium he inherits, that is, the oversized and ill-fitting language in which he begins his quest for life and work in his own "far distant wood."

We may see the boy, then, as an adolescent poet setting forth with no interface of his own to mediate between himself and the "thorns, and brakes, and brambles" of the world. He has only the old clothes that have been "husbanded" for this important "day . . . from many singled out" when he would take up his parent's occupation. If we remember the "Preface" to *Lyrical Ballads* and that the "Poets" of the past had for centuries enjoyed and relied on an "inheritance" of old "phrases and figures of speech which from father to son have long been regarded as the common inheritance of poets,"[39] we can see that for years the poetic occupation has been nut-gathering, "sallying forth" to gather the sweetest kernels of old language and then stuffing them in one's own "huge wallet." In some sense, then, the old clothes and the nuts of the poem are subliminally analogous; the poem is at once about the defilement of the past and presumptuous self-exposure.

When he reaches the wealth of that "banquet" where all remains ripe for the plucking, the adolescent of "Nutting" can almost revel in his father's death or absence, for he feels the joy of acting "fearless of a rival," of "eye[ing]" a "dear nook / Unvisited" by a more experienced predecessor. Having "Forc[ed]" his way "Through beds and matted fern, and tangled thickets" into this "virgin scene" where "not a broken bough /Drooped with its withered leaves, ungracious sight / Of devastation," he sees, growing in the arboreal bower, "tempting clusters" of hazels. There, for one sweet moment, he stands "Breathing with such suppression of the heat as job delights in; and, with wise restraint / Voluptuous." The incongruous-seeming description of the inner nook or bower of trees as "Tall and erect" and "with tempting clusters hung" may be a repressed recognition of the fact that the "nuts" available to the unrivaled young poet in this "virgin scene" are those of his own poetic father as well as those of Nature. The description may also be seen as the result of a kind of literary transferral, since it is the young poet himself who "With sudden happiness beyond all hope" is to "sit" beneath "the trees" and begin to "play" with "flowers" and "luxuriate . . . with indifferent things," "Wasting" his "kindliness" on "stocks and stones." In either case, the luxuriant bliss of fondling delight ends when

> up I rose,
> And dragged to earth both branch and bough, with crash

> And merciless ravage: and the shady nook
> Of hazels, and the green and mossy bower,
> Deformed and sullied, patiently gave up
> Their quiet being.

Something has gone wrong. The boy-poet presumably came to gather the nuts of the past. Yet he apparently walks on empty-handed, having only managed to lay waste the groves in which nuts grew.

What kind of bower is it that Wordsworth wrecks? To speak in general terms, it is the bower of past literatures, past poems. This is not a natural oasis but, rather, the silent garden out of time (nourished by "fairy" waters that "murmur on / For ever") into which young poets journey for the seeds of their own poetic future. It recalls Spenser's Garden of Adonis, for "right in the middest of" the "thickest covert" of that impenetrable "Paradise," there was an inner "arbor" protected by the "inclination of trees" (*The Faerie Queene*, 3.6.43–44). More specifically, the bower raped so viciously by the young Wordsworth is a type of Milton's Paradise; Wordsworth, like Lawrence, is therefore at best a second comer.

Satan, after entering Eden, came to a wall inside the borders of that untrammeled realm and suddenly realized that Eden is not the inner sanctum but, rather, that "delicious Paradise / . . . Crowns" it

> with her enclosure green,
> As with a rural mound the champaign head
> Of a steep wilderness, whose hairy sides
> With thicket overgrown, grotesque and wild,
> Access deni'd.
> (4.133–37)

Satan immediately jumps over the "verduous wall," the "undergrowth / Of shrubs and tangled bushes" that Milton says were "thick entwined." Like the savage adolescent of Wordsworth's later poem, he sees a "row / Of goodliest trees laden with fairest Fruit." He enters the grove, Milton says, as a "Wolf . . . / Leaps" into "a fold," as "a Thief bent to unhoard the cash of some rich Burgher" climbs "In at the window" of a house that had seemed to be "Cross-barr'd and bolted fast." Around him is a verdant world "Water'd" by "many a rill." A "Valley spreads" her "flowery lap" with blossoms "of all hue," and "Fruits" are "Yielded" by "com-

pliant boughs" while "Flocks" are "Grazing" on the "tender herb"
(4.138–333).

Wordsworth's debts to Milton are clear enough. He follows his
elder in making a bower within a bower; he situates his dearest
nook within a virgin scene of "pathless rocks" and trammeling
underbrush. He changes the "hairy sides" of Milton's Paradise to
"matted fern" but alters the "tangled bushes" of Milton's "thicket
overgrown" only enough to make a "tangled thicket." The sexual
symbolism Wordsworth employs to describe his forced entry into
the "virgin bower" derives from the sexual metaphors Milton
employs to describe Satan's somewhat easier invasion of God's
own "virgin scene." Wordsworth's "tempting clusters" may be
nuts, but they descend from the "tempting fruit" of Paradise.
Milton's originals were "Yielded" by "compliant boughs"; Words-
worth's hazels "patiently gave up / Their quiet being." The
younger Wordsworth, who "sate" and "played" among the
"flowers," thus becomes a "flowery lap" within the "flowery lap"
of Milton's Paradise. As for the "fairy water-breaks" that "do
murmur on / For ever," they have as one of their sources the
"Fountain"-fed "rill" of Milton's timeless, subterranean "River
large." Even the rocks that "fleeced with moss, under the shady
trees, / Lay round me, scattered like a flock of sheep" seem like the
barely repressed presences of the "Grazing . . . / Flocks" of Mil-
ton's pastoral scene.

Satan entered Paradise in the guise of an angel come to enjoy
God's creation and praise His name. Wordsworth recalls a day on
which he entered a bower as if to gather its nuts but ended by
desecrating, not harvesting, its untouched fruits. By doing so in
this second-generation lyrical ballad through allusions to Satan's
entry into the yet unviolated Paradise, he suggests that his earlier
and more iconoclastic edition of *Lyrical Ballads* may have been an
energetic but nonetheless destructive act of Satanic bravado,
duplicity, and finally overreaching. Like Satan, the younger poet
entered the creation of one greater than himself in disguise,
wearing the clothes of a greater being; like Satan, he came to steal
what was not his and then, when he couldn't have it or wouldn't
settle for it, wrecked it for generations to come. "Nutting," by its
allusions to old poetry, can be read at once as a confession and an
act of atonement.

In many ways Lawrence sought to erase, during his *Birds,
Beasts and Flowers* lustre, the memory of all that Wordsworth

became—a careful, respectful, and respectable poet speaking of the years that bring the end of iconoclastic utterance. Lawrence would return to a poetry like that of the adolescent Wordsworth, the poetry in which Wordsworth let his personal "demon" speak. Only through such a return, Lawrence seems to feel, can poetry rid itself again of "completeness" and "consummateness" and approach a condition in which it might convey "the insurgent naked throb of the instant moment" ("Poetry of the Present," p.185).

"Figs," written in the fall of 1920, some three months after "Snake," is a poem by Lawrence which is very nearly like "Nutting." So similar are the two poems, in fact, that I suspect a specific indebtedness which need not be proven to make my point: in "Figs" Lawrence, like the poetic adolescent of Wordsworth's vintage piece, rapes the conventional bowers but then, unlike his confessional predecessor, tries to make the claim that he feels no guilt for his actions. Lawrence, rather than speaking of the need to repress the restless, ravaging demon of youth, would have us believe it is our only hope for original experience and original expression, for a poetry that goes "Nutting" not for the old chestnuts of the past but, rather, in the gardens of unmediated sensual experience.

"The proper way to eat a fig, in society," Lawrence begins by telling us,

> Is to split it in four, holding it by the stump,
> And open it, so that it is a glittering, rosy, moist, honied,
>   heavy-petalled four-petalled flower. . . .
>
> .   .   .   .
>
> But the vulgar way
> Is just to put your mouth to the crack, and take out the
>   flesh in one bite.
>
> Every fruit has its secret.

The poet is doing many things here, the least important of which is to point out the two ways of eating a fig. "The proper way to eat a fig" translates quite readily into "the proper way to look at the world," for that, really, is what is described in the first stanza—looking, not eating. "The proper way to eat a fig" is to look at the world and see something it isn't and never has been—in this case, to see the fig as an open, "rosy," "four-petalled flower." (It is also, of course, to miss the fig's true "secret," the secret of the flesh-yielding crack.) A fig, of course, has no flower, or put more accurately, the flower that it must make to produce its fruit is not externally visible. "Involved, / Inturned," the fig "flower[s] inward," makes a fruit-producing blossom that is and has always been "secret" from man's vision:

> There never was any standing aloft and unfolded on a
> > bough
> Like other flowers, in a revelation of petals;
> Silver-pink peach, venetian green glass of medlars and
> > sorb-apples,
> Shallow wine-cups on short, bulging stems
> Openly pledging heaven:
> *Here's to the thorn in flower! Here is to Utterance!*
> The brave, adventurous rosaceae.

What Lawrence means, then, by "The proper way to eat a fig" is the habit of making a mere fruit into flowers for our vision, of seeing a thing in the world as something it isn't (a "revelation" of petals standing "aloft" like so many eucharistic "wine cups," for instance). This, in turn, is the habit of making believe not only that all of nature must speak to man ("*Here's to the thorn in flower! Here is to Utterance!*") but that it must always speak clear, comforting messages of a divine presence in or above or behind its temporal forms ("Openly pledging heaven"). "The vulgar way" to eat a fig, which is Lawrence's way, stands for the more direct, tactile experience of the world enjoyed by one who is blind to all such visions. The "gentle" man, in the words of Wordsworth's very early ballad entitled "Simon Lee," must "make a tale of everything." For Lawrence that would include turning a smelly fruit with a "purple slit" into a rosy, four-petalled, heavenly Utterance. The vulgar man accepts, even revels in, the tremendous nonhuman quality of life; he puts his "mouth to the crack, and take[s] out the flesh in one bite."

The parallel I am drawing between Lawrence's "Figs" and Wordsworth's "Nutting" becomes visible when we realize that what Lawrence seems to be describing is his own rough ravishment of a virgin fruit that "society"—the rules handed down from father to son, the "voices" of our "education"—tells us to treat in a mannered, almost worshipful way. What Lawrence seems to be alluding to, through the sexual metaphors he uses to describe his very physical enjoyment of a certain fig's hithertofore undisturbed inside, is the natural lust that he, as an irrepressible male creature of the sensual world, feels for all that is female in this "womb-fibrilled" system called nature ("put your mouth to the crack," "Every fruit has its secret," "The fissure, the yoni," "Sap that smells strange on your fingers"). That, of course, is what Wordsworth seems to be describing in "Nutting": a day on which he set out to gather nuts, carefully and properly with his special "nut-ting-crook" as *per* the instructions of the parent who sent him forth, but, instead, upon spying the "tempting" fruits of a "virgin scene," attacked the "dear nook . . . with . . . merciless ravage."

Wordsworth, however, was also talking about his rape of certain idealistic conventions as they are symbolized in the literary bower (Miltonic but Spenserian as well), the artificial imitation of a pre-lapsarian world where fairy waters flow forever, "pleasure loves to pay / Tribute to ease," and the "heart" can afford to "luxuriate with indifferent things." So, too, as Lawrence tells us of his natural urge to ravish the fig, to eat to the core of the fruit without taking time to "open" it with customary delicacy, what he is really describing is a rape not so much of a fig as of custom itself. Thus, both poets seem to talk about two ways of dealing with the world when in fact they are talking at least as much about two ways of looking at tradition, one with the "wise restraint" (Wordsworth's phrase in "Nutting") that keeps us in awe of a world not our own, the other with the "vulgar" energy that restores us to touch or taste even at the cost of some old, sustaining visions. Wordsworth "drag[s]" down the timeless bower only to be "pain[ed]" by the "intruding sky"; Lawrence puts his mouth to the crack at the cost of a comforting if artificially fashioned "revelation" of "heaven." Wordsworth's destruction of the bower is described in terms of a rape that, in turn, symbolizes liberating, literary iconoclasm for which the mature Wordsworth feels rather guilty. Lawrence's undelayed self-gratification via the fig, similarly, is an act of social nonconformity which suggests his rough poetic originality, an originality for which it would seem he feels no Wordsworthian shame.

In "Figs" as in "Nutting" there is a curious symbolic hermaphro-ditism allowing that which is violated by the poet, the "virgin scene" or the still "secret" bower of the fig's "wonderful . . .

centre," to be primarily female but male at the same time. Words-worth had followed up his reference to a "nook / Unvisited" with the description of a grove "Tall and erect" and "hung" with "tempting clusters." Lawrence similarly appends to his paean to "the crack" the observation that, "As you see" this "fruit . . . standing growing, you feel at once it is symbolic: / And it seems male." Then he rushes on: "But when you come to know it better, you agree with the Romans, it is female." Wordsworth, too, had hurried on from his allusion to male anatomy with assurances that what he tore apart was "A virgin scene."

In both poems the violation of a yielding bower that, nonethe-less, almost "seems male" may speak simultaneously of the sen-sual enjoyment in poetry of female nature and the concurrent rape of paternal traditions that, in the words of Wordsworth's "Pre-face," "from father to son have long been regarded." The paternal, from Lawrence's point of view, includes Wordsworth, and Words-worth is—along with Milton and his parents from Moses to Spenser—that which Lawrence would disregard, an author of the manners he would violate in "Figs."

In his "Lines Composed a Few Miles Above Tintern Abbey," one of the latest and least untraditional of the first-edition *Lyrical Ballads,* Wordsworth speaks of being "laid asleep / In body" and of becoming "a living soul,"

> While with an eye made quiet by the power
> Of harmony, and the deep power of joy,
> We see into the life of things.
> (lines 47–49)

This primarily aphysical inspection is, of course, the kind of habit that Lawrence would break through poems such as "Figs." When we taste, we taste that physical "substance," in the words of "The Wild Common," that "marvellous stuff" that is there to be tasted. When we are laid asleep in body and seeing into the life of things, Lawrence would suggest, we tend to see that which is dictated by our intellectual, spiritual, and metaphysical wants. In the sixth book of *The Prelude*, Wordsworth is unsettled by the fact that he somehow crossed the Alps without knowing it, that the natural mountain ridge did not offer the metaphysical vantage point from which to see, as the poet had once seen from his vantage point above Tintern Abbey, that all time and space are unified by "something far more deeply interfused / Whose dwelling is the light of setting suns" ("Tintern Abbey," lines 96–97). So, during his physical descent, he ascends, in mind, to the height he had expected the Alpine ridge to provide, the place where bothersome discontinuities, whether Eastern and Western Europe or, in the words of Shelley's "Mont Blanc," "awful doubt" and "faith so mild," can be seen as mere parts of a divine wholeness. "Imagination," Wordsworth says immediately after being told by a peasant "*that we had crossed the Alps,*" "rose from" his "mind's abyss" in "strength / Of usurpation" (*The Prelude,* 6.591–600). Soon

> the sick sight
> And giddy prospect of the raving stream,
> The unfettered clouds and region of the Heavens,
> Tumult and peace, the darkness and the light—
> Were all like workings of one mind, the features
> Of the same face, blossoms upon one tree;
> Characters of the great Apocalypse,
> The types and symbols of Eternity,
> Of first, and last, and midst, and without end.
> (6.632–40)

Lawrence, in "Figs," does not quite deny the possibility that the universe is so ordered. What he does deny is the desirability of "knowing," of "seeing," such things through the mind's eye. For "with an eye made quiet" by the "soul" we would see everything in nature, even "black drizzling" rocks, as signs, as "Utterances," meant to confirm our mental hopes and speculations. To commit the physical world to such knowledge—that is, to fit it mentally into our preconceived notions of what is epistemologically "proper,"—Lawrence might claim, is to rape reality far more viciously than we do when we merely burst the "milky-sapped . . . secret" of its fruity bowers with our tongues.

Original sin, after all, was committed not when man ate a secreting fruit but, rather, when he tried to know in his mind metaphysical secrets that did not need to be known to live a life of bliss. Following that attempt came the change in—the symbolic deflowering of—nature ("cursed is the ground" in Genesis; Milton's "Earth felt the wound"), a change which as much as anything else signified the corruption of man's "knowing" vision. In his own revisionary way Lawrence is saying that the quest for metaphysical complexities amounts to error and leads to the belief of the corrupt, namely, that man and the deliciously simple elements of his world are fallen and are somehow embarrassingly less than that which they signify or could signify. Once the mind in search of metaphysical "knowledge" sets out to rape or "la[y] bare"—as opposed to simply enjoying—the world's "secrets," Lawrence tells us in "Figs," "rottenness soon sets in" to the world of man's mind:

> When Eve once knew *in her mind* that she was naked
> She quickly sewed fig-leaves, and sewed the same for the
>   man.
> She'd been naked all her days before,
> But till then, till that apple of knowledge, she hadn't
>   had the fact on her mind.

Wordsworth, humbly voyaging in great old clothes to the lovely, visionary bowers created by the great gentle minds of the past, suddenly and mindlessly wrecked the groves of man's mythical projection, symbolically exposing his naked demoniacal self in the process. But then he quickly covered up, struggling to reclothe himself and us—in poems such as "Nutting," the Intimations Ode, and *The Prelude*—with some of the traditional literary places, attitudes, and forms which have long helped poets to show that there is a "Spirit in the woods" and that all "blossoms" of all bowers offer, in Lawrence's words, a potential "revelation of petals . . . pledging heaven" or, for Wordsworth, "Characters of the great Apocalypse, / The types and symbols of Eternity." In "Figs," Lawrence would finish off Wordsworth (in both the "proper" and "vulgar" sense of the phrase) by finding poetic nakedness, the blindness to vision that once allowed for it, and the mere but marvelous physical world which gloriously "intrudes" once nakedness and the poetical blindness of perfectly physical sight have been refound. He seeks to take off the pretty "fig leaves" that poets like Spenser, Milton, and Wordsworth have "quickly sewed" in their "Imagination" to clothe the naked world by covering up our unmediated sight of it with visions. The "proper way to eat a fig," which is to begin by pretending that, deep down, it's a flower, is, as I have argued earlier, a symbol of a certain kind of misguided poetic search for some elusive "life of things," for what Milton deemed "things invisible to mortal sight" (3.55). Lawrence would be different from all poets since Eden, all of whom in their search for the invisible have obscured the visible. They have, in Lawrence's view, merely recapitulated the original, hypocritical act of artifice, that poetic result of Adam and Eve's wish, as Milton has it, to "hide / The Parts" of nature through "skill" (9.1094–1112). Lawrence would, in the words of his marriage-week letter, undertake the "damnably difficult" enterprise of "learn-[ing] to understand the other," not of obscuring it in the emotions of self-reflective revelations.

"Figs" is not the first poem in which Lawrence seeks to come "up against the unknown" in the way that husband and wife come up against each other's differences. Nor is it the first poem in which he seeks to avoid the visionary's blindness by denying the old, myth-laden traditions. Even "The Wild Common," the very early poem placed first in *Collected Poems,* sought to abandon the pursuit of metaphysical shadows. In that poem Lawrence—who was talking about the soul, the spirit, the realm of the Idea—speaks of a shadow that acts like a "dog to its master" and adds, playfully, that "I am holding his cord quite slack." Whereas for Swinburne God was "the shade cast by the soul of man,"[40] Lawrence is seeking, even during his first poetic lustre, to define the soul as the equally vacuous shadow cast by man's physical being. "What if the gorse-flowers shrivelled, and I were gone?" Lawrence asks. "What if the waters ceased?"

> What is this thing that I look down upon?
> White on the water wimples my shadow, strains like a
> dog on a string, to run on.

Shelley asked of "Mont Blanc"

> And what were thou, and earth, and stars, and sea
> If to the human mind's imaginings
> Silence and solitude were vacancy?
> (lines 142–44)

Lawrence's question—which seems, like Shelley's, to imply that without the immortal human psyche, physical reality would have no import or consequence or therefore existence—is not meant to be taken so seriously. The dogged "shadow" which seems to symbolize that which might or might not live on after death, which might or might not exist at a transcendental remove from experience, is going nowhere no matter how "loose" the "cord" is held, no matter how it might seem to "strain" to run "on" and away from its physical analogue. Indeed, Lawrence says,

> My shadow is neither here nor there; but I, I am
>   royally here!
> I am here! I am here! screams the peewit; the may-blobs
>   burst out in a laugh as they hear!
> Here! flick the rabbits. Here! pants the gorse. Here!
>   say the insects far and near.

We do not need to know that "The Wild Common" concludes with the sound of seven pealing Shelleyan skylarks to know that as a struggle to avoid the shadow of spirituality, the poem is something of an early, failed experiment. The convention of having Nature speak to man, even if like the peewit it screams only of its physical hereness, runs dangerously counter to the poem's purpose of defining the word as an unintelligent and unintelligible realm of merely sensual experience. (We saw the same convention compromising Hardy's similar purpose in "The Mother Mourns," a work in which Hardy showed his own inability to admit the death of a once-nourishing Romantic metaphysic.) The other poems Lawrence wrote during his first lustre and in which he strives not to see the world as blossoming "Utterance" are similarly compromised, though in different ways. Through "Red Moon-Rise," first published in *Love Poems* in 1913, Lawrence intends to usher in a fearful age of darkness in which "The open book of landscape" shall be interpreted "no more,"

> for the covers of darkness have shut upon
> Its figured pages, and sky and earth and all between are
>   closed in one.

"Crushed between the covers, we close our eyes," Lawrence says, for this is a "night-time" that "makes us hide our eyes." And yet, although the sensual poet claims to "drown" his "fear," claims to be utterly glad to be visionless, he couches his claim in archaic, self-consciously literate, allusive, even mystical language that betrays the lingering fear to give up "vision" (in the natural, perhaps, but especially in the supernatural sense) and become a poet of touch, taste, linguistic spasm. "I am glad," he says,

> Glad as the Magi were when they saw the brow
> Of the hot-born infant bless the folly which had

> Led them thither to peace; for now I know
> The world within worlds is a womb, whence issues all
> The shapeliness that decks us here-below.

In "The Wild Common" there is a tension between idea (the dumbness of nature) and technique (through which, even in Lawrence's poem, nature finds "Utterance"). In "Red Moon-Rise," a similar tension is created by following a physical "within" ("world within worlds is a womb") with a metaphysical "below" ("decks us here-below"). Furthermore, Lawrence sets a free and asymmetrical poetic form off against a self-consciously artificial poetic diction made up of "thither"'s and "whence"'s and sporadic rhymes, thus causing what would be an agnostic and antiromantic manifesto to take on an old-fashioned tone reminiscent of "proper" writers from Paul to Wordsworth.

"Figs," though a strong poem arresting in its rhetorical directness, is ultimately no more successful than these two relatively unconvincing lyrics of the first lustre in communicating physical reality simply, without reliance on old traditions, odes, or scriptures. Metaphors of fig leaves, nakedness, knowledge, trees of revelation, and a looking into that is really a covering up cause the poem to end up talking not so much about physical experience as about old myths. Yet Lawrence's poems of the second lustre fail to convey unmediated visions of the purely physical world in a different way—and for different reasons—from those works written before 1917. "The Wild Common," written in 1905 or 1906, reverts to God and Shelley and the convention of the pathetic fallacy for the same reason that "Red Moon-Rise" comes to include words like "Magi," "bless," and "below": Lawrence has not yet "come through" his Shelleyan belief in a stratified creation in which soul is to body as substance is to shadow. In a poem such as "Figs," however, the eventual turn to the subject of Eve sewing fig leaves does not signify a lingering half-belief in metaphysical verities and laws so much as it signifies the fact that old myths, however vacuous, stand in the way of unmediated experience. The Shelleyan, Swinburnian, and even Hardyan contexts of first-lustre poems more often than not suggest that a lingering spirituality impedes the quest for a poetry that would reveal the chaos of the world. The Biblical-to-Miltonic-to-Romantic contexts of second-lustre poems often suggest Lawrence's fear that language itself is the greatest impediment to the discovery of a poetry that would redeliver man to those coasts of the un-European unknown and even restore our marriage—that is to say our pure, unadulterated relationship—with the universe of objects. When Lawrence speaks, in "The Wild Common," of the light reflecting off a gorse bush as "Little jets of sunlight texture imitating flame" or of birds "proclaim[ing]" their "triumph . . . over the ages," he gives us good reason to be skeptical of his skepticism. By contrast, we conclude "Snake" fully believing that the poet *knows* the snake was never a threat to either his manhood or his morals and that his assault on it was therefore petty. (Nor was the snake a threat to his safety; Lawrence threw the log, he has pointedly told us, at a creature in the act of disappearing.) Indeed, the speaker's offensive is petty largely because it was occasioned by voices no longer believed in but retaining the maddening power to play tricks with a person sees, even a modern person who has fully "come through."

"Grapes," written in the same house in San Gervasio (and probably in the same month) as "Figs," is another of the poems on fruit in which Lawrence would return us, free of those petty, disruptive voices of our education, to the lost world of unadulterated experience. As in so many of the *Birds, Beasts and Flowers* poems, the poet is looking for a subject that will allow him not to see and speak of "first, and last, and midst, and without end." The grape, like the fig, is such a secretive fruit that it seems it could hardly lend itself to a visionary, poetic mode. "Many fruits come from roses," Lawrence muses, "From the rose of all roses, / From the unfolded . . . / Rose of all the world":

> What then of the vine?
> Oh, what of the tendrilled vine?
>
> Ours is the universe of the unfolded rose,
> The explicit
> The candid revelation.
>
> But long ago, oh, long ago
> Before the rose began to simper supreme . . .
> There was another world, a dusky, flowerless,
>   tendrilled world

> And creatures webbed and marshy,
> And on the margin, men soft-footed and pristine,
> Still, and sensitive, and active,
> Audile, tactile sensitiveness as of a tendril which
>   orientates and reaches out,
> Reaching out and grasping by an instinct more delicate
>   than the moon's as she feels for the tides.

At such a moment Lawrence suceeds impressively, for his poem here would seem almost to become the blind, tactile plant it takes as its subject. When his line "reaches out, / Reaching out and grasping" its object without seeing even its colors, let alone its symbolic possibilities, we know just what it is that he is trying to do. The grape is, on one hand, a "flowerless" subject which prevents visionary speculation and, on the other, a grasping model for the new poetry of simple sensation.

Here, though, the poet faces a difficulty. What he seeks to sing is a world of "tactile sensitiveness" that existed before the laserlike eyes of visionaries bathed it in visionary blindness:

> Of which world, the vine was the invisible rose,
> Before petals spread, before colour made its disturbance,
>   before eyes saw too much.
> In a green, muddy, web-foot, unutterably songless
>   world
> The vine was the rose of all roses.

But the poets who "saw too much" were singers. Song, in fact, was the medium through which they blocked off our perception of the "unutterably songless world" of experience that now lies beyond "fern-scented frontiers." So if vision, or seeing "too much," is the province of "song," then how is Lawrence going to return us to "the brink of re-remembrance"? How is he, in poetry, to help us "sip the wine" which takes us back to the world where all enjoyed "naked communion communicating" as now we "never communicate"? "Grapes," by definition, can only be just another song. That is to say, it is just another "clothed vision" preventing us from knowing the unclothed world in prelinguistic "naked communion." The process that the modern poet would seek to reverse becomes the process by which the reversal is vainly attempted. Not unlike Wordsworth before him, Lawrence seeks to write a poem which doffs an inherited poetic garb and, instead, only adds a suit to an ever-growing wardrobe.

The poet recognizes the considerable difficulties he faces, partly through self-conscious structure (he discusses the failures of the way we now communicate in the way we now communicate) and partly through irony. Hopeful claims like "we are on the brink of re-remembrance" are immediately followed by wry observations that undo the force of the credo:

> we are on the brink of re-remembrance.
> Which, I suppose, is why America has gone dry.

"The grape," Lawrence declares, "is swart, the avenues" into which it leads us are "dusky and tendrilled, subtly prehensile,"

> But we, as we start awake, clutch at our vistas
> democratic,
> boulevards, tram-cars, policemen.
> Give us our own back,
> Let us go to the soda-fountain, to get sober.

The sarcasm, in this case, does more than declare the unlikelihood that mankind may travel back down the avenues from which he has unfortunately come forth. Through his use of the pronoun "we," the poet-prophet implicates himself in the modern, sober, rationalistic scheme of things.

Where ironies do not reveal Lawrence's fear that the return to songless sensual paradise is a fond but unrealizable hope, literary allusions—general and specific—often do. For instance, Lawrence would take us back to a world of delicious, unknowing drunkenness, but to do so he ends up alluding to "Bacchus," the created idol of a people already fallen from the purity of that state. To be able to name the state "bacchanalian" is to be outside it; to be truly bacchanalian would be to be unable to know or name it as an observable condition of being. Thus the state which the poet would return us to is "prehensile," but the language or song with which he would return us is already comprehensive. No name from Greek mythology can return us to a real world of sensation, for, as he finally admits in his poem, "Bacchus is a dream's dream." By invoking the word and the mental image it connotes, a poet refers to another poet's fanciful, symbolic construct.

"Grapes," like "Figs," is in a sense both an attempt to represent a real world in direct, nonfigurative language and a revelation of the difficulty, even the impossibility, of that enterprise. To represent a real world through a new poetic mode, the poet must call attention to the difference of his subject through the difference of his rendering. And to do that is to turn grapes and figs quickly into "Grapes" and "Figs"—figures of a proper mode of being and a proper (if Bacchanalian) mode of expressing being. That amounts to denying the propriety of symbolic language in symbolic language, a fact Lawrence makes clear through his choice of symbols that are neither new nor being used to represent new things. I have mentioned the way in which a general allusion, such as the reference to the figure of Bacchus, preempts the possibility of a return to the dusky, preconscious or at least pre–self-conscious world for which we *literati* have no better word. Lawrence's use of figs or grapes (or even roses) as "Symbols," as he expresses it in a one-work line in "Figs," of a forgotton world (or a world of revelation we should hope to forget) is equally a "dream."

The fig, as John Freccero has recently pointed out, "stands [in literary history] for a tradition of textual anteriority that extends backwards in time to the Logos."[41] He defends his claim amply, citing examples such as the conversion of Augustine, which took place under a fig tree when Augustine looked into the Bible because two men had been converted by looking into a book in which someone else had been converted upon hearing the gospel read. Freccero also cites the example of Nathaniel, who was seen by Christ under a fig tree and was soon thereafter converted, not by Christ himself, but by Philip, one of Christ's converts. The fig is also, of course, the biblical symbol (adapted by Milton in *Paradise Lost*) of that knowledge of evil prompting man to secrecy, to the kind of hypocrisy and deception and self-deception characteristic of Satanic consciousness. At points, Lawrence would seem to want us to believe that his "Fig" is not plucked from the groves of Milton's recultivated Paradise, that it does not signify textual anteriority, and that he, therefore, is not just another bookish convert. He would make his claim, first of all, by having us believe that his fig tree is notable primarily for its diversely ruminated fruit, whereas the "Tree whose broad smooth Leaves" Eve "together sew'd" was "The Figtree, not that kind for Fruit renown'd,"

> But such as at this day to *Indians* known
> In *Malabar* or *Decan* spreads her Arms
> Branching so broad and long.
> (9. 1101–4)

Secondly, Lawrence seems to want us to think that his fig, besides being "that kind for fruit renown'd" is not a symbol of what Milton calls "guilt and dreaded shame" (9.1114) but, rather, of "male" or "female" sexual essence incarnate, of the "wonderful . . . conductivity" by which we experience "the centre" of our physical being.

But Lawrence knows, I think, that we will accept these claims with no small measure of skepticism. We have already seen that in a poem which must declare the fraudulence of certain revelations in order to celebrate the secrecy of certain sensual truths, the fig quickly and inevitably turns from a fresh symbol of unfallen nature into a time-worn symbol of shame, secrecy, and knowledge, as surely as the fig fruit, having "kept her secret long enough," "explodes, and you see through the fissure the scarlet,"

> Like a wound, the exposure of her secret, on the open day.
> Like a prostitute, the bursten fig, making a show of her
> secret.

Once the fig has turned, moreover, it is only a matter of time before the poem's focus must shift from the secretive fruit to the ensecreting leaves. By the time Lawrence has Eve sewing fig leaves, by the time a poem about sucking a naked crack has become a poem about revelation, guilt, and knowledge, Lawrence's "secret" has "burst," which is to say that his knowledge has been carefully and purposefully exposed. He can no more be an Adamic innocent than any other modern poet. Like all poems, "Figs" is another well-woven suit of clothes, another fruit from the same old tree. Its originality lies in the fact that it has been opened up and ruminated differently.

One of those differences inheres in the poem's concern with the identity of modern woman. Midway through the work the "enclosedness" of the fig fruit is described as a "Mohammedan woman"; three stanzas later the "bursten" fig is a brazen whore advertising her wares to the world. By this point the fig is hardly a

fig as Lawrence had first defined it ("Symbol" of "The flower-
ing . . . inward"), so it is little wonder that the poem turns its
attention from women as a way of talking about the fig to
women as tenor, as signified, as subject:

> The year is fallen over-ripe,
> The year of our women. . . .
> And rottenness soon sets in.
>
> .   .   .   .   .   .
>
> Now, the secret
> Becomes an affirmation through moist, scarlet lips
> That laugh at the Lord's indignation.
>
> *What then, good Lord!* cry the women,
> *We have kept our secret long enough.* . . .
> *Let us burst into affirmation.*

As Sandra Gilbert has commented, "Lawrence seems far more
interested in the notion that women are like figs than in the
idea that figs are like women."[42]

I would suggest, speculatively, that Lawrence knows that he
is and that however sincere the unfortunate antifeminist
rhetoric may be, the poet is showing us that its appearance in
the text is not so much a departure from the old fig myth as it
is an inevitable and inextricable by-product of the poem's turn
to that traditional, mythical treatment of the fig. In the quota-
tion above, I have left a stanza out. The omitted passage is the
one, quoted earlier, in which Eve sews fig leaves after having
eaten the apple of knowledge. The interspersion is powerfully
revealing. With the shift from the tree known for its fruit as
subject to the kind "not . . . for Fruit renown'd"—with the
lapse from natural fruit as subject to the Fall as subject—
comes a host of adhering thoughts that thrust the poet further
and further from his original purpose. All at once the poet's
concerns are with women who speak out when they should
remain silent and women who burst into affirmative actions
that may prove to have infelicitous, even morbid, conse-
quences:

> They forget, ripe figs won't keep.
> Ripe figs won't keep.

Those accursed, proper voices of the poet's human education would seem by now to be writing, through Lawrence, their own poem. He is but the instrument of their agency.

And so it is with "Grapes," too. A quick perusal of the fourth book of *Paradise Lost* helps us to see all too clearly the depth and durability of Lawrence's education. With some twenty-three lines Milton's language seems to plan out Lawrence's eventual poem about getting back to an age previous to "song," "revelation," and the "eyes" that, in their blindness, "saw too much." In the passage that introduces us to our first parents for the first time (just after describing Satan's rough violation of that "steep savage Hill"), Milton describes one side of an "irriguous Valley spread" with

> Flow'rs of all hues, and without Thorn the Rose:
> Another side, umbrageous Grots and Caves
> Of cool recess, o'er which the mantling Vine
> Lays forth her purple Grape, and gently creeps
> Luxuriant.
> (4.256–60)

Milton then proceeds Miltonically. He further defines and locates this "delicious" garden of "trembling leaves" by telling us all the places where, and things that, it was not:

> Not that fair field
> Of *Enna*, where *Proserpin* gath'ring flow'rs
> Herself a fairer Flow'r by gloomy *Dis*
> Was gather'd, . . . might with this Paradise
> Of *Eden* strive; nor that *Nyseian* Isle
> Girt with the River *Triton*, where old *Cham*
> Whom Gentiles *Ammon* call and *Lybian Jove*,
> Hid *Amalthea* and her Florid Son,
> Young *Bacchus*, from his Stepdame *Rhea's* eye.
> (4.268–79)

Milton's Paradise, then, contains in immediate juxtaposition the "Rose of all the world" that Lawrence so much deplores and the "Grots and Caves" of "cool recess, o'er which" the "vine / Lays forth her purple Grape, and gently creeps / Luxuriant." Lawrence implies that our sensibility is by necessity attuned either to the explicit world of the "dark," the "blue-black" grape. Milton has the two growing on "one" and "Another side" of an "irriguous Valley," but his sensibility is deep and wide enough to contain both the bright, colorful world "of all hue[s]" and the "umbrageous" (Lawrence's "dusky") and cavernous world of the "purple Grape." The two realms co-exist as equals; Milton does not seem to think we must choose between them.

In Paradise as in Lawrence's "flowerless, tendrilled world," the "Grape" that "gently creeps / Luxuriant" is also juxtaposed with that idea of grape named Bacchus. But whereas in Lawrence's poem the two are part of one concept (wine is the "avenue" to the "long ago" world of the vine), in Milton the two are opposed. The Paradise of "creep[ing]" grape vines from which we are exiled is "not that . . . *Nyseian* Isle" where Cham hid Bacchus from "Stepdame Rhea's eye," the proving grounds of that god of drunkenness and merrymaking. That is because Milton is more nearly what Lawrence seeks to be than Lawrence, that is, the poet of a prelapsarian world, a world where Bacchus can refer only by negation to the "Luxuriant . . . trembling" realm of the grape. In Milton's Paradise man has not yet borne Bacchus. There is no jealousy or secrecy to cause anyone to hide anything, let alone a child, from anyone. As for the concept Bacchus stands for, the small populace of Milton's Paradise has not yet fallen into merrymaking, for merrymaking implies not only artifice but also the existence of an infelicitous state. In Lawrence's poem such a state exists, for to "sip" the grape is to cross the "frontiers" which separate the "perverseness" of sobriety from the "dream" world of communion. But Milton's naked, communing pair sees everywhere Paradise; only the fallen poet glimpses its Bacchanalian "frontiers."

One of the ways that Lawrence suggests his own belatedness, by which I mean the gap between himself and the naked world to which he would return us, is by building his poem around three images—rose, grape, and Bacchus—that Milton had interwoven. Milton, Lawrence knows, comes relatively closer to envisioning the world before the Fall than Lawrence can. The closest thing the later poet achieves to original vision he attains by rescrambling Milton, by binding together what Milton had put asunder (Bacchus and grapes) and putting asunder what Milton had bound together (roses and grapes). Thus if Milton is the poet of the "rose," of "revelation," of mystifying the mere fig of reality into a "rosy . . . four-petalled flower," then Lawrence is at least equally a poet of the rose. Indeed, Milton seems, to Lawrence of the second lustre, to be the parent stem from which the later poets of revelation have sprung. Lawrence, in turn, is one of the fruits of evolution, however much he may wish to be something else, to be born of the grape's stock:

> So many fruits come from roses,
> From the rose of all roses,
> From the unfolded rose,
> Rose of all the world.
>
> Admit that apples and strawberries and peaches and
>   pears and blackberries
> Are all Rosaceae,
> Issue of the explicit rose,
> The open-countenanced, skyward-smiling rose.

The predicative command "Admit" does not dare to take the pronoun "you" as its specific subject, even though Lawrence might wish that pronoun understood. "I" is the pronoun Lawrence more honestly implies, for if "Grapes" or "Figs" or "Snake" "admit" anything it is that their poet's genealogy is longer than he would like to admit, that he is so much the "issue" of the "skyward smiling" poets he would deny that his acts of defiance are doomed to end in atonement.

Another of the ways in which Lawrence's "Grapes" admits the overwhelming odds against its own project of learning to understand the world in its otherness is the deference it shows to William Butler Yeats, an intermediate product of the Miltonic evolutionary line of development. In *The Rose*, published when Lawrence was eight, Yeats had allowed a flower native to his native land to stand as a symbol both of things mortal and immortal, of "all poor foolish things that live a day," but also of "Eternal beauty wandering on her way" ("To the Rose Upon the Road of Time," lines 11–12). Yeats's rose can suggest human suffering, as it does in "The Rose of Battle," but it can just as easily signify that peace that "pledges heaven" with such eloquence that "If Michael, leader of God's host . . . / Looked down . . . / He would his deeds forget. . .":

> And God would bid His warfare cease . . .

> And softly make a rosy peace.
> ("The Rose of Peace," lines 13, 15)

Yeats's use of Milton is so clear and unmistakable that Lawrence's awareness of Yeats can hardly help him in his effort to see around the Miltonic doors of perception. But that is not the only reason that Lawrence's strong awareness of Yeats amounts to a frustrated cry. Yeats, by making the rose stand for opposite things in facing poems, made the rose *mean* what it had not meant before, namely, the power of a physical thing arbitrarily to signify entirely disparate, abstract ideas. It is, then, partly because of Yeats and his contributions to our poetic education that grapes (or figs or other fruits of still other trees) are doomed to turn quickly into "Symbols" or figures, figures for any given *idea* about the proper (or properly vulgar) mode of human being that comes into any given poet's mind.

One of the secrets Lawrence shows to those who read his poetry in conjunction with his prose, as well as with the poems of his precursors, is that Keats joins Wordsworth and Yeats in an intermediate place in the lineage stretching back from Lawrence to Milton. An apple or strawberry, Keats inherits from the roses and passes on information to a Yeatsian peach or a Lawrentian pear. As the reader proceeds from "Snake" to "Grapes" by way of *Lamia* and *The Rose* and also by way of Lawrence's essay on "The Nightingale," Keatsian elements begin to show up in "Grapes" that otherwise would remain hidden in its landscape. In that essay, Lawrence scores Keats (who, Lawrence says in another essay, wrote several of the poems which "have meant most to me"[43]) for failing to do what he wanted, to move in the direction he intended. The nightingale, Lawrence says, is "pure music," a "song . . . much purer than words, which are all tainted," a song that communicates "some sort of feeling of triumph in . . . life-perfection." Keats, "the sad human male," Lawrence says, "tries to break away, and get over into the nightingale world." He first "wants to drink the blushful Hippocrene, and fade away with the nightingale into the forest dim. . . . Wine will not take him across. Yet he will go."

> Away! away! For I will fly to thee,
>   Not charioted by Bacchus and his pards,
> But on the viewless wings of Poesy. . . .

"He doesn't succeed, however," Lawrence concludes. "The view-less wings of Poesy carry him only into the bushes, not into the nightingale world. He is still outside."[44]

Once we have read the essay, it becomes clear that the author of "Grapes" had Keats's ode in mind as well as *Paradise Lost*. Lawrence talks, in "The Nightingale," about Keats's struggle to "get over into" the dusky "other world" of the "forest dim." In "Grapes" he attempts to envision for us the "frontiers" of an "otherworld" that is "Green, dim," and that lies down "dusky" avenues. Like the Keats of his prose analysis, he hopes that he will deliver himself via wine or poetry, and like Keats before him, "he doesn't succeed." The "grape is swart," Lawrence writes, "But we, as we start awake, clutch at our vistas democratic." As for poetry, it gets us, in the words of Lawrence's essay, "only into the bushes." For the world across the fern-scented frontiers is a world of another language, a place where beings would have to be "communicating as now our clothed vision can never communicate."

Lawrence's "Grapes," then, like "Hymn to Priapus" and "Snake," involves in a new and complex way two earlier texts at once. On one level, Lawrence is looking at Keats's ode and saying that it anticipates his own later struggle to enter the world of the forest dim. But "Grapes" does more than just bewail its Johnny-come-lately status. It also contains the highly provocative and original suggestion that the desired realm in Keats's poem is Paradise, that the nightingale is in some sense Milton, and that Keats is the singer who, unlike the soaring visionary who wrote *Paradise Lost,* tried but failed to move between two realms, one of light and the other of darkness, one of the rose and the other of the grottoed grape. And at another level, Lawrence finds originality by suggesting, as neither of the earlier poets did, that although we can *only* develop the voices of our education, we can and indeed we *must* develop them. There is no return to the world of the past because our forebears, however much their words determined us, communicated as we "never communicate." We can listen to the birds that "sing on the horizons," the "voice[s] of the past, rich, magnificent" ("Poetry of the Present," p. 181), but we cannot follow them down the dusky avenues to live in the world in which they lived. We must, rather, update their song, make it say something new.

The style of "Grapes," on first or even second reading, might seem to have little to do with the liquid siftings of the "Ode to a Nightingale." Whereas Lawrence's poem seems a casual mixture of trimeter, tetrameter, and hexameter lines in stanzas of unequal length, Keats's stanzas all contain ten lines, each one of which is in pentameter except the eighth, which is a trimeter:

> My heart aches, and a drowsy numbness pains
>   My sense, as though of hemlock I had drunk,
> Or emptied some dull opiate to the drains
>   One minute past, and Lethe-wards had sunk:
> 'Tis not through envy of thy happy lot,
>   But being too happy in thine happiness,—
>   That thou, light-wingèd Dryad of the trees,
>   In some melodious plot
> Of beechen green, and shadows numberless,
>   Singest of summer in full-throated ease.
>   (lines 1–10)

The more closely we read the "Ode to a Nightingale," however, the more apparent it becomes that Keats's pentameter often threatens to be something else, sometimes four-beat lines built out of dactyls and/or anapests ("Singest of summer in full-throated ease"), sometimes hexameter ("And with thee fade away into the forest dim").

Lawrence's "Grapes," when read for its rhythmical patterns, proves the complement of Keats's work, for the threatening under-rhythm of its casual four- and six-beat lines is that of the traditional pentameter (broken by trimeter) of Keats's ode:

> For we are on the brink of re-remembrance.
> Which, I suppose, is why America has gone dry.
> Our pale day is sinking into twilight,
> And if we sip the wine, we find dreams coming upon us
> Out of the imminent night.

In "Snake," the free-verse style that Lawrence had learned towards the unrhyming end of his first lustre by marrying Swinburne's dactyls and anapests to Hardy's shorter, terser line is modified by Wordsworthian grammar. In "Grapes," Keats is involved in the second-lustre hybrid. As for the general result of the presence of Romantic syntax in both poems, it seems to be the quiet admission, through rhythm, of the continuing presence in poetry of the Miltonic voice of education. "Of which world, the vine was the invisible rose," Lawrence begins a poetic sentence in "Grapes," and some of the lines of self-address in "Snake" sound like the lines of self-examination that Satan delivers, in regular pentameter, to the sun—minus or plus a stressed syllable:

> Was it cowardice, that I dared not kill him?
>
> .   .   .   .
>
> Was it humility, to feel so honoured?

If we look carefully at the style of "Grapes," then, or if we read the poem in the contexts provided by Keats's poem and Lawrence's essay on it, we can discover Lawrence acknowledging the past even while putting it to work for him. More blatant elements of "Grapes," however, will not admit that we are our heritage and that our challenge is to work creatively within its contexts. Through the explicit genealogical theme, for instance, the poet seeks to claim a different genealogy by aligning himself, not with the "So many fruits" that "Issue from the explicit rose," but, rather, with the "flowerless, tendrilled" family of vines. Lawrence wishes he were descended, not from a singer and seer, but, like "the ancient Bushman," from men who were "dark and evasive," "soft-footed and pristine," "Audile" and "tactile."

This is a desire evident in a number of Lawrence's mature poems. The turn away from Milton as a great white father and towards the "negroid" race, the lineage of "the ancient Bushman," is recapitulated in poems that, although published in *Birds, Beasts and Flowers*, were written after Lawrence abandoned even Italy in 1922 for India, Australia, and finally the Americas. In "The Red Wolf," the poet's conversation with an American Indian in the Taos desert amounts to an attempt to deny or repress his true heritage and to claim a different father. The Indian asks his English visitor to call him "Old Harry" or "Old Nick," and Lawrence responds by admitting,

> Well, you're a dark old demon,
> And I'm a pale-face like a homeless dog
> That has followed the sun from the dawn through the east,
> Trotting east and east and east till the sun himself
>   went home,

And left me homeless here in the dark at your door.
How do you think we'll get on,
Old demon, you and I?

Where's your God, you white one?
Where's your white God?

He fell to dust as the twilight fell
Was fume as I trod
The last step out of the east. . . .

Thin red wolf of a pale-face,
Thin red wolf, go home.

I have no home, old father,
That's why I come.

As in "Grapes," written over a year earlier, the poet seems to feel he is on a "brink" of some kind of important "re-remembrance," that he is close to coming up against a primitive world which preceded and will follow the blinding bright world of day. As in "Medlars and Sorb-Apples," written in Italy at the same time as "Grapes," Lawrence looks to the "dark," the "hellish experiences." He justifies his turn to the "old demon" with the claim that the "white God" of daylight is dead and that he, therefore, has "no home" and "no . . . father." This attempt to claim an old Indian as a new parent, like the adulation of the Negroid race in "Grapes," grows out of both reverence and condescension. Part of Lawrence does respect what he believed to be the less intellectual, more sensual life of the nonwhite races. But part of him chooses to be Indian—or Bushman—because of feelings of inferiority. As the son of white deities, Lawrence fears, I will never attain preeminence. As the son of a demon Apache I could, myself, issue in a new day.

This is racism, of course, and it is a form racism takes throughout Lawrence's poetry and in much of his fiction as well. In the "Moony" chapter of *Women in Love*, Rupert Birkin sees a statuette from West Africa and looks forward to the "fall" of European culture from "knowledge" and into "the long, long African process of purely sensual understanding." His vision of white and non-white cultures, moreover, seems to include the principle of inverse developments: "He realised now that this is a long process—

thousands of years it takes, after the death of the creative spirit. He realised that there were great mysteries to be unsealed, sensual, mindless, dreadful mysteries, far beyond the phallic cult. How far, in their inverted culture, had these West Africans gone beyond phallic knowledge?" In *The Plumed Serpent,* written in Mexico in 1923–24, Kate Leslie is similarly attracted to a nonwhite culture that she, nonetheless, feels is utterly different and apart from her own. "'You don't like brown-skinned people?"' Don Ramon asks her.

> "I think it is beautiful to look at," she said. "But"—with a faint shudder—"I am glad I am white."
> . . . "It is as you feel," he said.
> And as he said it, she knew he was more beautiful than any blond white man, and that, in a remote, far-off way, the contact with him was more precious than any contact she had known. (Chap. 12)

In Lawrence's poetry, perhaps more than in his novels, this kind of backhanded admiration is put to a meta-artistic end; that is to say, it becomes part of the highly original fiction the artist writes about his own liberation from the oppressive brilliance of an European literary tradition. The association of the realm of the wolf/ Indian/grape/Negroid race with hell (the Indian in "The Red Wolf" is called "demon" and "Nick"; the route to the tendrilled world takes us "down dark avenues . . . crossing frontiers") is partly an attempt by Lawrence to value a naked world of dark, torrid feelings over our "clothed vision" of "skyward-smiling . . . vistas democratic." But it also borders on an attitude not unlike Satan's, who in the first book of *Paradise Lost* tells Beelzebub that it is "Better to reign in Hell, then serve in Heav'n" (line 263). Lawrence craves poetic primacy, but he feels like a "second-comer, waiting." If preeminence demands that he move his poetic realm to hell (or to New Mexico), that he become the poet of the dark (and of "touch" and of the "dusky" races), then that, he thinks, is what he'll do.

In "The Revolutionary" Lawrence finds this role as the poet blind to the blinding visions of the past, the iconoclastic poet of touch and of feeling and of sensual darkness, by merging himself with Samson, the hero who in his blackness brought down the superstructure of established oppression. Dwarfed by the mighty temple, he stands between supportive white caryatids. In poetic terms the caryatids represent the great white precursors whose bright erections Lawrence feels he must destroy. Although he does not see them anymore, he cannot bear them "standing there in authority." "Pale-faces," he says, they are but

> Pale-face authority,
> Caryatids,
> Pillars of white bronze standing rigid, lest the skies fall.
>
> What a job they've got to keep it up.
> Their poor, idealist foreheads naked capitals
> To the entablature of clouded heaven.

"Oh and I wish the high and super-gothic heavens would come down now," Lawrence goes on to say, "The heavens above, that we yearn to and aspire to."

> I do not yearn, nor aspire, for I am a blind Samson.
> And what is daylight to me that I should look skyward?
> Only I grope among you, pale-faces, caryatids, as among
>   a forest of pillars that hold up the dome of high
>   ideal heaven
> Which is my prison.

"I shall be so glad when it comes down," the poet cries out, "I am so tired of the limitations of their Infinite. / I am so sick of the pretensions of the Spirit."

> See if I don't bring you down, and all your high opinion . . .
> See if I don't move under a dark and nude, vast heaven
> When your world is in ruins, under your fallen skies.
> Caryatids, pale-faces.
> See if I am not Lord of the dark and moving hosts
> Before I die.

The at once patricidal and erechthean moment is a terrifying but necessary one in which Lawrence hopes not only to "bring . . . down" those paternal, "pale-face" poets of "Infinite" spiritual "pretension" but also to become "Lord" of "the dark . . . hosts." It will be, Lawrence knows, an anxious moment of fearful confrontation, of (in the words of "Medlars and Sorb-Apples") final lone-liness." And yet, the poet asks himself,

> Am I not blind, at the round-turning mill?

Then why should I fear their pale faces?
Or love the effulgence of their holy light,
The sun of their righteousness?

The "staring caryatids" who offer only "the effulgence of their holy light" too pure (or artificial) for natural men to see surely include Milton, whose "holy Light," "Bright effluence of bright essence increate," leaves Lawrence "blind, / Sightless among all your visuality." They may also include such unlikely neighbors as the Jewish patriarchs, John of Patmos, and Shelley. The "column must always stand for the male aspiration," Lawrence wrote in the *Study of Thomas Hardy* (p. 460). And Shelley, he says, is pure "abstraction," the "pure male." In *Apocalypse* Lawrence will associate Shelley with the John who wrote the book of *Revelation*. Both of these visionaries in different ways, he says, appeal to the "negative power of the masses," cry "*anathema! anathema!* to the natural proud self of power, and try deliberately to destroy all might and all lordship." Lawrence goes on to speak of the revelation of John, and by implication of Shelley, as being essentially Jewish, by which he means interior. "Everything Jewish is *interior,*" he writes. "Even the stars of heaven and the water of the fresh firmament have to be put inside the curtains" of a "stuffy tabernacle or temple."[45] Thus Shelley and John, along with Milton and his prophetic Old Testament precursors, are likely to be among the "caryatids" of "The Revolutionary," for the temple in Lawrence's poem is a place where "the stars of heaven" and the "firmament" are but ceiling and wall frescoes. The white, anthropoidal, "pure male" columns not only "aspire . . . skyward", they actually dedicate their "naked capitals / To the entablature" of a "clouded heaven." This heaven, in turn, is opposed by the poem to the "dark and nude, vast heaven" that the speaker hopes to "move under" once he has smashed the stuffy, visionary world that is his prison.

Though one is forced to become even more speculative, it is probably fair to say the caryatids may also count Whitman in their number. Although Lawrence, during his first two poetic lustres, has words of praise for Walt Whitman the father of free verse, he has little sympathy with Walt Whitman the democrat, whom he associates with Shelley the idealist. For Lawrence all vistas democratic are fanciful, entablatured heavens which have blinded man to the importance of pure separateness, individual distinction. Shelley's hope that, through social love, man could become "one harmonious soul of many a soul, / Whose nature is its own divine control" (*Prometheus Unbound,* 4.400–401) much as lovers could become one spirit, has led to a "poor, idealist" democratic society. Lawrence does ,not specifically scorn political idealism in "The Revolutionary," but he does in its companion poem, "The Evening Land." And that poem, though it addresses an "ideal" called "America," seems as well to talk directly to Whitman:

> I confess I am afraid of you.
>
> The catastrophe of your exaggerate love,
> You who never find yourself in love
> But only lose yourself further, decomposing.
>
> .   .   .   .
>
> You who in loving break down
> And break further and further down
> Your bounds of isolation,
> But who never rise, resurrected, from this grave of
>   mingling.

The problem is that for Lawrence to bring down "democratic . . . idealists"—including John of Patmos, Milton, Shelley, and Whitman—would be to bring down the very temple in which he stands. To bring down Whitman or Shelley would be to bring down no small part of Lawrence's "own" language; to "smash" Milton is to smash that very part of Lawrence which sees himself as an individual "Sightless" amongst "visuality." Lawrence, of course, annihilates neither his precursors nor himself in the *Bird, Beasts and Flowers* volume. To portray himself as "The Revolutionary" he adopts the figure of Samson, but to adopt the figure is the ultimate act of reverence, an admission of influence, a reinforcement—not a "smashing"—of the "forest of pillars that hold up" the all-inclusive "dome." To represent oneself as Samson is to place oneself within the framework of *Samson Agonistes,* a construct within the framework of *Judges,* an artful representation within a world in which the events it sets forth may have taken place. Even as the poet makes a final prediction of absolute sovereignty, he qualifies it out of existence by a combination of conditional mood and negative syntax. "See *if* your skies *aren't* falling," he admonishes; "See *if* I *don't* bring you down," "See *if* I am *not* Lord of the dark and moving hosts / Before I die" (italics mine).

In all cases the attempt to deny a heritage is precluded by the fact that man *is* his heritage. Indeed, even the attempt to sidestep the white, European heritage through self-identification with hell or the "dusky" races has been precluded by European originators of a diabolical tradition that stretches from Blake to Baudelaire. Lawrence might like "The Revolutionary," "Grapes," "Snake," and "Figs" to be poems "not of that kind" spawned by the gardens of Genesis and *Paradise Lost*. Nonetheless, he grew up—and knows he grew up—in those seminal bowers that, like the fig trees in Paradise, "spread" their "Arms / Branching so broad and long, that in the ground" new trees

> take root, and Daughters grow
> About the Mother Tree, a Pillar'd shade
> High overarch't, and echoing walks between.
> (*Paradise Lost*, 9.1104–7)

To disclaim one's sources, to reject the bowers of generation, is to cut oneself off from the only roots sustaining life. To raze what Lawrence, in "The Revolutionary," calls the "forest of pillars" is to destroy the "Pillar'd shade" from whose roots one grows.

* * *

The very act of cutting down the "Pillar'd shade," of bringing down the "super-gothic heavens," is, then, a "revolutionary" one that takes place more in the young poet's psyche than in the world of possibility. On one hand, the hope for pure if deracinating self-liberation is the very fantasy that makes new poetry (or painting or music or fiction) possible. On the other hand, the knowledge that the poet's life is within the bowers he dreams of destroying tempers the revolutionary act, which is doomed to futility, to self-destruction.

In Wordsworth's "Nutting" we see this interplay of fantasies and facts, hope and guilt. The Wordsworthian boy wades into the bower to smash it, and it almost seems that this is what he does. But the bower has its curious revenge, for the act of sullying the bower somehow boomerangs back into the guilt that, even as it advises future generations to go gentler in hallowed ground, repairs the bower within the young poet's own poem. It is guilt that causes the poet to recall the iconoclastic day, and the mnemonic poem that results recalls the action both in the sense of remembering and rescinding or reversing. "Nutting"—unlike earlier and more antitraditional ballads such as "Simon Lee" or "The Idiot Boy"—is written in iambic pentameter, elevated in tone, rich in allusions, and respectful in attitude towards the old poets. The act of ravishing the bower is, paradoxically, the act of repairing it; at the risk of overextending Wordsworth's sexual metaphor it might be fair to say that the vicious rape renews the life of the bower by bringing into being an offspring (in this case "Nutting"), a new poetic generation whose heritage, if not its heart, is pure.

The paradox that we might define as "the revivifying rancor" has already been seen in "The Revolutionary." To bring down the temple one must be inside its perimeters; to be an insider is not to want to bring the temple down; to enter without carrying out the intended destructive purpose is, however we explain it, to become the newest parishioner. For Wordsworth the symbolic structure of this same psychological and aesthetic condition of being is the bower within bower. To destroy the past one must journey to the heart of its matter, the quick of its being, the "dearest nook" within its well-built outer wall and its tangled inner thickets. But to make the journey to destroy the inner sanctum is to find yourself become the heart of the still enwalled construct. Wordsworth describes himself entering but not leaving the virgin scene. Lawrence positions himself, psychologically, within the temple; he can only talk hypothetically about bringing it down.

In both cases the will to survive, which is the will to be traditional, would seem to turn upon the destructive will. The dialectic of violence and self-protection is however a psychological and aesthetic structure through which each poet suppresses his belief that, no matter how hard he tried, no matter how little he cared for his own poetic life, he could not raze the temple, destroy the bower. Lawrence, like Wordsworth, may pretend that he could bring down the "roofed-in erection" of tradition, that he could "let in," in the terms of Wordsworth's dubious claim, an "intruding sky." But the syntax of his final assertion suggests that the painted sky on the temple "roof" or "ceiling" is the only one he has ever really seen. Like Keats's

Lycius, Lawrence's Samson cannot be sure what kind of world—or if a world—lies beyond the columned peripheries of his sweetly suffocating bower.

To return, finally, to "Grapes" is to see, in the simplest structures of poetic language, Lawrence's second-lustre sense that his existence and art are always embowered. The poet would break out of poetic convention by seeing the world as it was before it became "the universe of the unfolded rose." When he tries to do so, however, he finds that he has no vine vision, no vine language at his command. Rather, he must show us things that are not flowers in negative (or not-flower) language. He shows us this is so by writing of a place and time "Before the glaciers were gathered up in a bunch." How does he speak of the world "Before the rose began to simper supreme," before the first "petals spread" or "colour made its disturbance"? He speaks of a "world" where "the vine was the rose of all roses," or, even better, "Of which world, the vine was the invisible rose." He takes us back to a time when men neither sought nor spoke of divine revelations by saying that back "When the vine was rose, Gods were dark skinned." The "open-countenanced" bower of "Rosaceae," of "apples and strawberries and peaches and pears and blackberries," is the developed state of the poet's language in the poet's time. He can hardly ravish it in poetry.

Chapter Four

The Buried Life

Michel Foucault, in *Les mots et les choses,* suggests that all texts are imaginatively composed mosaics, the individual pieces of which are radical events, some of them literary, in the history of consciousness.[1] The suggestion is a provocative one. On one hand it implies the degree to which all works are authored by the dead. On the other hand it implies that a writer may precipitate a radical event, that some mosaics are better than others even though they may be composed of the same elements, that a medley has the potential to be as "shock[ing]" and "effect[ive]" as any of the relatively original tunes from which it is made. The Lawrence we have heard in "Snake," "Figs," "Grapes," and "The Revolution-ary" does not seem quite so optimistic. These works often come to be about their own derivations and even about derivation in general; the original insights they offer are as often as not into the difficulty of seeing as far as the great seers of the past. If these works believe themselves to be as powerful and effective as the works that have informed them, they hold to that belief quietly and convey their optimism indirectly—by means of their own merits and considerable power.

We can meet this same D. H. Lawrence in prose, this Lawrence who talks much more about the burdens of influence than the way in which Moses and Dante and Milton and Keats managed to be radical influences in spite of the fact that their words were dic-tated by paternal voices. In an essay written and published in the *English Review* in 1917 Lawrence anticipates by three years the Samson imagery of his poem "The Revolutionary" to imply that we are imprisoned and powerless in old artistic visions, for to be original would be to commit suicide. "Once the temple becomes our prison," he writes, "we drag at the pillars till the roof falls crashing down on top of us and we are obliterated."[2]

But we can find another Lawrence in the prose, too. For instance, in a 1913 review of the 1911–12 volume of *Georgian Poetry* in which the poetry of Thomas Hardy appeared, Lawrence works with the same figures. But this time he suggests that thanks to writers like Hardy—Samsons giving their lives to the cause of tearing down the temple—later writers like himself may breathe a little more freely. "The last years have been years of demolition," he writes. "Faith and belief and the Temple must be broken. . . . And art has been demolishing for us: Nietzsche, the Christian religion as it stood; Hardy, our faith in our own endeavor; Flaubert, our belief in love. Now, for us," he continues, "it is all smashed, we can see the whole again." Man was "in prison," but "the great prisoners smashed" the prison down. "And behold, out of the ruins leaps the whole sky."[3]

In an essay published in 1929 but written earlier, a piece entitled "Chaos in Poetry," Lawrence revises the terms slightly, adding a symbolic umbrella to his practiced temple and prisoner scheme. "Man cannot live in chaos," he writes; only animals can. So man "must wrap himself in a vision." In his terror of chaos he begins by "putting up an umbrella between himself and the everlasting whirl. . . . Then he parades around, lives and dies under his umbrella. Bequeathed to his descendants, the umbrella becomes a dome, a vault." The poet, in Lawrence's terminology, is the man who comes along and, because he is the "enemy of convention, . . . makes a slit in the umbrella; and lo! the glimpse of chaos" is a "window to the sun." However, "not liking the genuine draught from chaos," man "after a while . . . daubs a simulacrum of the window that opens on to chaos, and patches the umbrella with the painted patch of the simulacrum. . . . So that [in time] the umbrella at last looks like a glowing open firmament. . . . But alas! it is all simulacrum, in innumerable patches. Homer and Keats, annotated and with glossary." The "sky of fresh air" under which we think we live, according to Lawrence, is "a fresco on a . . . roof." Civilization is "man . . . completing its own painted prison"; "Beethoven or Whitman" are but "paint" on "the plaster of our vault."[4]

These statements may raise profound questions, but at least they do not exhibit an absolute, cynical certainty about the artist's ultimate motive, capability, or fate. To be sure, Lawrence knows, with Wallace Stevens's "Man with the Blue Guitar," that "Slowly the ivy on the stones / Becomes the stones" (11.1–2). And he is every bit as convinced as Wordsworth seems to be in "Nutting" that all iconoclasm turns to worship, that every aesthetic act of tearing or ravishing is destined to become in short time but a new faerieland fresco. Nonetheless, he does ascribe to the poet the power to strip off what once was ivy, to tear the umbrella—even to know that there is a facade or a painted and patched parasol to penetrate. The poet is the one who has the originality to see that man, in Blake's words, "has closed himself up" in a prison the walls of which grow thicker day by day.[5] He may know that, ultimately, each liberating rupture contributes to the completion of the vault and the consequent suffocation of the race, but he also knows that the poet who makes the slit, opens new doors of perception, gives joy. "The joy men had when Wordsworth . . . made a slit and saw a primrose," Lawrence exclaims, sounding excited. "Since then," he continues, "we have come to see primavera" as "nothing but primrose." Thanks to Wordsworth, who showed us an element of chaos, we are farther from seeing the earth in spring than ever: "So the umbrella is absolute. . . . What about the poets, then, at this juncture? They reveal the inward desire of mankind. . . . They show the desire for chaos, and the fear of chaos. The desire for chaos is the breath of their poetry. The fear of chaos is in their parade of forms and techniques. Poetry," Lawrence concludes, "is made of words" even though the "breath" which "fills them" is the poet's "longing for chaos."[6]

In these last two essays, one written late in Lawrence's first lustre on the paternal Hardy, the other composed during the poet's third and last poetic period, Lawrence is as concerned as he is in second-lustre poems like "Snake" and "The Revolutionary" with the possibility that the reality we think we glimpse beyond the myth in which we live may be part of the myth, that our windows may only be proscenium arches, that the world beyond them is but painted scenery. But he is also aware of other things, too. What makes these essays different from most of the second-lustre poems is that, first, they seem to believe that there is a bright, chaotic world somewhere outside the vision, the temple, the umbrella. Second, they would seem to believe that some poets can occasionally tear through and momentarily capture the world that Wordsworth called "intruding sky." That which is seen may soon get painted over the window that exposed it and thus incorporated into the fresco of the protective umbrella, owing both to the conservative nature of the poet's audience and to the fact that the poet's medium invites such patchwork repairs. Words, after all, may be able to force an opening in the umbrella, but they are also made out of its fabric.

Nonetheless a great poet is more than the sum of the words he uses; he is language, but he is "breath," too. Words could not tear the umbrella if breath power—which Wordsworth defined through the figure of adolescent heat and Lawrence calls a powerful "desire for chaos"—were not behind them, "fill[ing] them," hardening them. Shakespeare and Samuel Daniel grew up with, and passed on, the same words, the same tools. But Shakespeare became a radical event, even though by now, Lawrence tells us, "the roof of our vault is . . . painted dense with Hamlets and Macbeths, the side walls too." For a time Shakespeare showed the West a new potential, "emotional, wistful man outside in the chaos, beyond the conventional idea and painted umbrella."[7] In spite of the "parade of forms and techniques" he was condemned by his humanity to adopt, Shakespeare filled them with so much breath that they did what Wordsworth's did two hundred years later. They "made a slit" and temporarily gave "joy" to that part of man that craves the dark unknown.

Lawrence makes a convincing case for his own breath power in a few of his best second-lustre poems. No less than Wordsworth or Shakespeare he seems capable, in works that are every bit as engaging but somewhat less self-conscious than "Snake" or "Figs," of exposing a reality that has long remained unknown. In these works we often are confronted with images of the world that seem startlingly original, perturbingly independent of Shakespeare, Milton, Wordsworth, Coleridge, and Keats. Take, for instance, some of the lines from "Fish," which Lawrence wrote in Austria nearly a year after completing most of his poems on Italian birds, beasts, and flowers and six months before he and Frieda were to set sail for India, Australia, and finally America.[8] In "Fish" there are moments in which the poet and all the voices of his education seem to disappear entirely and leave us with the closest thing to the unmediated reality of a fish that human language can possibly offer:

> Your life a sluice of sensation along your sides,
> A flush at the flails of your fins, down the whorl of your
>   tail,
> And water wetly on fire in the grates of your gills;
> Fixed water-eyes.
>
> .   .   .   .
>
> Himself,
> And the element.
> Food, of course!
> Water-eager eyes,
> Mouth-gate open
> And strong spine urging, driving;
> And desirous belly gulping.
>
> .   .   .   .
>
> Fishes
> With their gold, red eyes, and green-pure gleam, and
>   under-gold . . . .
>
> .   .   .   .
>
> Fishes . . .
> Lift and swim and go their way.
>
> .   .   .   .
>
> I have . . .
> Unhooked his gorping, water-horny mouth,
> And seen his horror-tilted eye,
> His red-gold, water-precious, mirror-flat bright eye;
> And felt him beat in my hand, with his mucous, leaping
>   life-throb.

In the final passage Lawrence may give us a moment's doubt that he has shown us a fish as we have never quite seen it before. We are at first suspicious of his attribution of horror to a creature suddenly bereft of its natural element. But in the last analysis the violation seems a small one, for creatures react both to alien beings and against death, and the reaction can only be evidence of some kind of inner state. In any case, in this and all the passages quoted above Lawrence has avoided the pathetic fallacy he indulged in "Snake." The "horror" we see in the eye of the fish does not seem to express any horror the poet feels, and if Lawrence momentarily stretches his credibility as a revealer by asking us to see emotion in a pike's eye, he surely doesn't stretch it as much as he did when he told us that a serpent "looked at me vaguely . . . and mused a moment."

In the last lines of "Snake," Lawrence had subtly indicated his failure to liberate himself from a tradition which has long appropriated the world as a symbolic expression of human ideas and emotional states. He had done so when he "expiated" the "pettiness" of trying to kill the serpent as if it were some kind of evil by thinking "of the albatross" and, consequently, by sympathetically calling the serpent "my snake." The fish of "Fish," however, would seem to stand further outside Lawrence than his mind and soul and heart—educated to see "reality" only and always as a convenient system of symbols—can reach. Lawrence, reacting against Milton, can come to feel the kind of "liking" for the snake that makes it stand less for Miltonic evil than for his own quarrel with Milton. But in "Fish" he tells us that even if he *were* to attempt to like or hate his subject, he could not fully annex and thus annihilate it. Every time he tries to see or measure a fish by human standards, he finds himself in a solipsistic world where he only looks at himself, talks to himself, accuses himself:

> And my heart accused itself
> Thinking: *I am not the measure of creation.*
> *This is beyond me, this fish.*

Lawrence has couched what appears to be an admission of limitation or even failure within a poem which elsewhere makes bold claims of poetic achievement. In the lines quoted above, "Fish" seems to be saying outright very nearly what "Snake" suggested, that there is a central self or "heart" of being, an inherited system through which we can attempt to understand, "measure," explain, even write poems about the world (own it, make it "mine"),

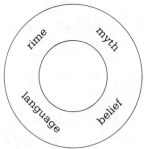

and there is a world that lies "beyond" our grasp of comprehension or communication, partially and paradoxically because of the illusions, the myths, the conceptual projections which have enthralled our eyes and ears to the point that we can see and hear nothing but them.

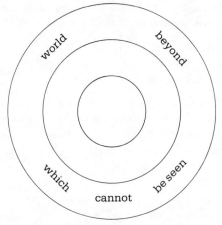

The "tremendous *non-human* quality of life," as in the words of the poet's letter to Gordon Campbell (*Collected Letters,* p. 291), would necessarily seem to be always beyond the poet's vision and grasp.

But we have already seen that "Fish" seems somewhat more successful at getting beyond unoriginal language than "Snake," that although Lawrence claims the serpent as "my snake" the snake is beyond him and although he says the fish is "beyond" him he would seem to have caught the sensual reality of a fish in the lines of his poem as surely as he has "pulled a gold-and-greenish, lucent fish from below" on the "line" of his "long rod." (Angling is as much a metapoesis in "Fish" as it is in John Donne's "The Baite.") Thus, while "Snake" never really does what it hopes it does, "Fish" in its best moments does surprisingly well what it worries it can't do: it breaks us out of our stuffy temple and brings us up against a primordial element of the original world through poetry. Lawrence positions his italicized claims that the fish is "*beyond me,*" that he is only a "heart" talking to "itself," between unitalicized and understated stanzas in which he seems to perceive not a beloved fresco but a "creature" unencumbered by old and arbitrary signs, taboos, or symbols of any kind.

Has the poet succeeded, and if so, how? "Snake" suggests that, whatever we see, we see it through the superimposed fictions that are like negatives held by history and language between our eyes and the light of the world (which may, for all we know, be just an illusion, a bright spot, in one of the older, more deeply hidden negatives). How does Lawrence, in "Fish," arrive at the notion that there actually *is* a "gorping" fish and come up with fresh, unspoiled words with which to reveal it to us?

Both his quiet optimism and his apparent success might seem to have something to do with his choice of subject. The wet slit of a juicy fig may turn a poem about fruit into a diatribe against women who are "bursten into self-assertion." But not the "water-eyes craning" of a fish. And its "gold-and-green pure lacquer-mucous" probably offers fewer invitations to indulge symbolic rhapsodies on evil, influence, and self-assertion than does a forked-tongued serpent. After all, when Lawrence says the "water-horny" fish is "beyond" the human heart—and all its anthropocentric ways of understanding or "measuring" creation—his words cut two ways. They explain the reasons not only for his fear that the fish will remain unseen and unknown but also for his hope that it won't. There are other occasions, moreover, on which the poet seems even more consciously to recognize both the importance of finding a relatively new, unusual, and elusive subject and the fact that this time he has found one. He does so in one passage that would seem to betray a thought about "Snake" and another that momentarily relies, quietly but surely, on Coleridge's transfixing *Rime.*

Whereas "Snake" deals primarily with the temptation to eat of the tree of unoriginal thoughts or language and even suggests that the temptation is a kind of fate we call life, "Fish" twice feels the same temptation, recognizes it as temptation, but decides that somehow it can escape its fate by sticking to its subject. "Fish" thus suggests, hopefully, that we may be fated to unoriginal behavior only in the presence of certain particularly word-spoiled objects or relations.

The first moment of temptation is slight and barely noticeable. It comes early in the poem when Lawrence, frustrated by his inability to relate to, understand, dislike, sympathize with, or in any way enter into the life of the fish, thinks of and then dismisses a more approachable and, paradoxically, more comfortable subject. After that amazing stanza in which Lawrence speaks of the fish's life as "a sluice of sensation"—as "the flails" of "fins," the "whorl" of a tail, "water wetly on fire" in the "grates" of gills, and "Fixed water-eyes"—he suddenly seems to look in another direction. The result is a single-line stanza:

> Even snakes lie together.

Then, quickly, he recovers his subject in a new stanza:

> But oh, fish, that rock in water,
> You lie only with the waters;
> One touch.

The intimation is that the poet is somewhat more at ease with snakes than with fish because snakes, like men, "lie" with their mates and not just with their element. Therefore it is easier for a man to project himself into a snake than upon fish, to make snakes over in man's own image than fish. Lawrence says of the fish, "I didn't know him" because man has not spent his history invading the fish with those metamorphosing mental projections which are counterparts to carnal knowledge. Snakes have been so impregnated through that intercourse we call language with a familiar system of anthropocentric thoughts and feelings that we can almost believe they love and cling to and hate and deceive ("lie" or "lie together" in its other sense; the figure humanizes the snake still more) as we do. When Lawrence says that fish, unlike snakes, feel only "one touch," that of "the naked element," it is as if he were also speaking, indirectly, of the strange feeling he feels when he sees or touches a fish (in fact or in poetry). It is the feeling, rare in "Snake," of being in contact with the naked element, of what Lawrence would call "unadulturated relationship" (*Collected Letters,* p. 467). It is the feeling of contact which has not been desensitized by a sheath of human associations, traditions, and language. The fish as subject would seem to make possible a creative ejaculation of words that, unlike the clumsy log jaculated by words, is stimulated by and directed into the naked element even as the fish "ejects his sperm to the naked flood." If the poet proves proficient, he might end up "extracting fish-fire" from the primeval fish, even as the "fish-blood" extracts oxygen "from the flood at the gills."

The second moment in which Lawrence is tempted to change subjects comes when a water-serpent enters the field of his vision. When Coleridge's Mariner first saw water-serpents, he saw "slimy things" upon a "slimy sea," but later his "tongue . . . declare[d]" their beauty. The influence of that tongue and its ongoing tale allows Lawrence an affectionate vision of a snake "swim[ming] across the Anapo." He can "*look at him*" easily and feel that "he belongs" because, in fact, he is not looking at a water-serpent at all but is, rather, merely looking through another man's poetic vision. When he says the "*rare*" creature is "*steering like a bird*" with "*his head up,*" he would seem, once again, to be "thinking of the albatross" and of the suddenly lightened head of the Mariner who had just "loved" and "blessed" water-snakes.

Keith Sagar comments on the water-serpent's appearance in "Fish" by saying that "nothing natural is to be rejected" by "human consciousness" lest "the spring of love" be "dam[med] up."[9] This interpretation misses the point; Lawrence does not care to "love" a fish, or even see a fish as he has been taught to see the water-serpent. Sagar implies that snakes and fish are—or should be—analogous, that Lawrence is struggling hard, in "Fish," to be as big-hearted and open-minded where fish are concerned as Coleridge's Ancient Mariner was towards water-snakes. In fact, the radical difference between the two subjects is important to Lawrence, important enough to receive several kinds of poetic emphasis.

First of all, "seeing" the water-serpent turns out not to be seeing at all. Certainly, seeing the snake is not "ventur[ing] . . . upon the coasts of the unknown" (*Collected Letters,* p. 318). Rather, the water-serpent is only an inducement to the poet to start speaking with his own heart, a "heart" for water-serpents that, in turn, has been created by the "spring of love" which "gushed" into words "from the heart" of Coleridge's ancient rime-maker. Lawrence uses both italics and language at once figurative and allusive to claim a shift in poetic mode when his poem stops struggling to describe what it sees in the world and begins to converse with his own conversant self, that is, begins to speak with those voices of education that inevitably lie within:

> I saw a water-serpent swim across the Anapo,
> And I said to my heart, *look, look at him!*
> *With his head up, steering like a bird!*

When Lawrence suddenly returns his eyes and his address outwards, to the fish that does not seem to "belong," he interjects a separating ellipsis and drops the italics. Also, he shifts the setting from "the Anapo" back to "Zeller lake" and abandons both the anthropocentric personal pronoun (*he*) and the artifice of simile. Perhaps most important, he effects a syntactic double reverse by repeating the conjunction "but." The result is that he fully returns himself and us to the poetic place, subject, and mode he almost left for the tempting lapse into unoriginality:

> *He's a rare one, but he belongs* . . .
>
> But sitting in a boat on the Zeller lake
> And watching the fishes in the breathing waters
> Lift and swim and go their way—
>
> I said to my heart, *who are these?*
> And my heart couldn't own them.

Lawrence, a belated mariner in a modern bark safe on inland waters, nonetheless feels primitively alone when he looks at the fish. He can look away and within, he can ask his heart for words which assure that the fishes "belong," but his heart seems to have no words of reassurance. He is challenged to talk, not of reptiles that are like birds that are like mariners that are like himself "steering" a boat, but of fish which are perfectly other to the poetic self, things which simply and inexplicably "Lift and swim and go their way." He is, in some sense, like the man who has come through one definition of love to another one in which to "love" is not to better "know [one]self" but, rather, to recognize the uncomprehended otherness of the other and consequently "explore . . . the unknown" (*Collected Letters*, p. 318).

It is when Lawrence finds himself in such a place that he often appears to find his new, clear poetic language. It is in such places that the poet, bereft of the honied peace of old poems, comes up with the "Poetry of the Present," as he would seem to do when he describes the "gorping, water-horny" mouth of a fish, or when he describes in a poem he wrote even later, in Sydney, Australia, in 1922, the "dangle" of a kangaroo's paw. There are moments in reading Lawrence's *Birds, Beasts and Flowers* volume in which we feel, in amazement, that we are seeing a familiar object for the very first time. At these moments Lawrence's assertion in prose that words not only seal us off from reality but may also be used by the poet to reveal that which lies beyond our enclosure becomes as difficult to dismiss as it is maddening.

Of course this claim of Lawrence's, made in his essay "Chaos in Poetry," is tempered by a considerable amount of skepticism. The poet who gives us a glimpse of something new, as Wordsworth did the primrose, also condemns us, if gradually, to seeing spring as "nothing but primroses," thus blinding us further to the "chaotic" realm outside ourselves. And the primrose revealed, once it becomes a word for a season, dies to us forever. A poet is breath, but he also works with "words," "forms," and "technique[s]" that reveal an inward desire *not* to see anything in chaos but, rather, to exclude it from the life of our world.

In spite of the bravado of its rather unusual subject, images, rhythms, and rough and scaly neologisms, "Fish," too, worries that it buys us our sight of its subject at a high price. For although the poem presents us with a fish, to do so it has to snag, suffocate, and kill it. What we are left with is a creature that has been caught by and that has died in the lines of Lawrence's poem. Seized out of its element and displayed with its increasingly horror-tilted eye, drying mucous, and colors rubbing off, the fish symbolizes the perhaps slow but nonetheless inevitable death of reality that is seen and pulled by a poet into the realm of human language. Someday a poet may be so hooked on Lawrence's lines that he cannot look at or think about "fish" without thinking about "Fish." At that point the reality exposed will have become only a lifeless simulacrum, a "patch" of Lawrence, "annotated and with glossary." The poet who manages originality (as Lawrence does if, in fact, he is the first to pull a fish fully into the human—read "linguistic"—element) must commit murder. The poet who truly catches a creature and makes it his for all time ("my snake" or "my fish") will inevitably end up with the liquid of life—be it mucous or blood—on his hands.

Maurice Blanchot, in *La part du feu,* has more recently expressed in prose an idea rather similar to the one that Lawrence implied in "Fish" almost sixty years ago. Poetry always ends up knowing a thing by its "absence," he tells us, and "absence" means the reality falsified each time an object is named. "Death [is] the transformation of personal identity," Blanchot further explains,

> that occurs as a part of the literary act. . . . My speech is the warning that death has been, at this very moment, let loose in the world, that it has abruptly loomed up between me speaking and the being to whom I speak: it is between us like the distance that separates us. . . . Death alone permits me to grasp what I wish to attain. . . . Before I can say: this woman, I must take from her her flesh and blood reality in one way or another, must render her absent and annihilate her. The word gives me the being, but it gives it to me deprived of being.

"Similarly," Blanchot concludes, "objects find a 'death' or 'absence' when they are named."[10] Like Lawrence, then, Blanchot sees the poet as one who ultimately annihilates reality, even as he also sees the poet as the only one who "gives [us] the being." The poet's language is a kind of "death" that alone, while it transpires, "permits [us] to grasp what [we] wish to attain." It is, he says, elsewhere, "the distance which separates us" and also the "distance [that] contains the condition of all understanding."[11]

In another work, entitled "Le regard d'Orphee" in *L'espace litteraire,* published in 1955, Blanchot reviews this notion that words deal in death or absence by seeing the writer as an Orpheus. Eurydice, according to the analogy, is the buried reality or fundamental being that, in Lawrence's words, is "beyond me" and even beyond "the pale of my being." What the writer does is to create a work in which he fails to bring her back to light. She exists in the text, but as a vague remembrance or as a name signifying the something that is missing.[12]

Lawrence does, for the time it takes the fish to die, seem to see and show us his Eurydice. Blanchot's analogy, nonetheless, seems more applicable than not to Lawrence's poem. For the poet to truly show us a piece of chaotic, primordial reality he would have to keep it alive. To leave us with a dead fish or flower, a dissectible cadaver, is to afford us no look at all. As soon as the fish dies in "Fish," it is but a word for the thing that the author failed to bring back alive. In fact, this happens sometime before the fish breathes its last, for the poet is careful to show us how the texture, color, "contour," and thus identity of the object changes as soon as it enters the zone in which we can view or (for the two are the same) talk about it. The Orphean poet cannot seem to return to us even glimpses of the unseen, unpossessed, vital world. Or if he can, it is only for the blink of an eye. In the short, perhaps immeasurable time it takes to change, the fish disappears and becomes, like Eurydice, a name signifying something that is missing.

"Fish," then, is full of individual lines that seem to capture the living reality of a fresh poetic subject. The lines, nevertheless, cluster around and point to a crucial symbolic scene that qualifies and even casts doubts on all the apparently successful moments. It does so by suggesting that, at best, the poet reveals for the short time it takes him to annihilate. (Lawrence ends up showing us his subject's "white meat"; he murders to dissect.) The worst the scene can imply is that an object, not shortly after but rather as soon as it is pulled from one medium into another, ceases to be what it was. It is therefore a remembrance, absence, or corpse that offers us, small consolation, what Blanchot calls the condition of all human understanding.

In a work such as "Fish" Lawrence implies by way of a subtle, reverse analogy the difficulty the poet faces when he attempts to live in the realm of animals and send back messages. To enter fully the world of living creatures, a man would need to leave the waters of the "womb-element" in which he "lies," the "wave-mother" of the language which has always "enwombed" him in a soft "sluice" of fanciful "sensation." He would cut himself off from the environment in which he has his very identity, the world where men "sink, and rise, and go to sleep with the waters," where they first "breathe from the flood" and then, almost as automatically, "speak . . . wavelets into the wave." Lawrence wants to avoid "visions" and render clear descriptions of the fishes' world, the merely "Loveless, and so lively" world which apparently exists through and beyond that apparently separating surface or film on which we apparently see. But to do so he would have to dive through the mirroring or distorting or "creative" surface of figures, forms, techniques. Shortly after if not instantly, his human vision, his "mirror-eye" as we know it, would be dead, would "tilt" as "flat" and useless as the fish eye does in air. If he saw, he would see as a fish, and what he saw we could not. A "fish out of water," he would cease to be human and thus become inarticulate to us, just as the "speak[ing]" fishes that remain in the water uncaught are "inaudible" to Lawrence's landward ears.

Lawrence takes no such dive. The fish suggests, via reversible analogy, not only the reality beyond our ken but also, potentially, the poet who might leave the flow of his element for the dark, fearsome, unknown other world. But this "fish" chooses to remain human, audible, and right where he is; instead of entering the living but deadly depths he pulls the other fish—the so-called real one—into the bright, killing world of words. In "Snake" there seemed to be two snakes: one that symbolized the all-too-tempting voices, the other that couldn't quite be seen because of those voices. "Fish" would like to believe that there could be two "fish" in one plane, as there would be if the poet could fully enter the realm of his subject. But he can't, so he ends up with no fish at all. Or, to put it another way, he ends up—as he did in "Snake"—with two versions of the same "reality falsified," two interchangeable significations of the same absence. There is the dead, dry creature and the poet who could not take the plunge.

It is important to keep in mind, however, that if Lawrence takes on the spoiler's role—that is, fails to cross the boundary and fully enter the world of living animals that lies, unknown, beyond the pale of human being—he does so only after amazingly imaginative, well-calculated, and momentarily revealing efforts to avoid the role fail him in frustrating, almost paradoxical ways. For example, what Lawrence sets out to do in "Fish" is struggle to see a reality men have not really seen. Consequently, he finds, he cannot quite say that living fish are beyond him, for that might imply sight and understanding of his subject. What he ends up saying is that "fish" is his name for something "outerwards" of human experience and that he looks for something beyond the known world as a fisherman might try to catch glimpses of a prospective catch. "They are beyond me, are fishes," he says, in a curious turn of phrase that seems to want to edge into general equation:

> I stand at the pale of my being
> And look beyond, and see
> Fish, in the outerwards,
> As one stands on a bank and looks in.
> I have waited with a long rod.

The "As" takes us by suprise. Is he *not* standing on a bank and looking in? He forces us to wonder whether, when he said he saw "Fish" in the "the outerwards," he saw what we thought he saw. Even the "rod" he waits with suddenly seems more metaphorical than real.

The closer we inspect the poem the more it seems that, in almost every instance Lawrence speaks of a "fish," he is seeing a sign for some quality of being beyond his ken more than he is a finny prey:

> Fish, oh Fish,
> So little matters!
>
> .   .   .   .
>
> So utterly without misgiving
> To be a fish
>
> .   .   .   .
>
> Admitted, they swarm in companies,
> Fishes.
>
> .   .   .   .
>
>   Neapolitans . . .
> Thirst for fish as for more-than-water;
> Water-alive.
>
> .   .   .   .
>
> Fishes
> With their . . . pre-world loneliness,
> And more-than-lovelessness.
>
> .   .   .   .
>
> This intense individual in shadow,
> Fish-alive.

This happens because of the nature of language itself. If "fish" is the name of something beyond your comprehension, and if you don't understand—but wish you did—states of intense individuality, social coexistence, man's thirst for more than water, or life without guilt or misgiving, then "fish" is all too ready to become the name of those elusive qualities. That is one of the ways language falsifies or "kills" that which it began by seeking to reveal.

The other way is even more maddening. A word is given to refer to that which exists beyond the pale of a man's being. It is immediately clear that, by definition, to go beyond the palest edge of being would be to die, to lose the battle to experience and describe. The rod of language, we suddenly realize, is simultaneously the tool the poet has to speak of that which is beyond the limits of ordinary experience and proof that life, for man, is the language that sets his limits. The quest for the nameless becomes impossible the moment the nameless is named. As soon as "fish" signifies the unknown then the poet will never know a fish. All Lawrence can find thereafter is something else or his own word, and that is what he gives us to see— "Fish"—a word which, like "Eurydice," speaks of a something missing. Paul de Man, writing in *Blindness and Insight*, at one point suspects that "blindness" is "inextricably tied up with the act of writing itself."[13] Lawrence would seem not only to bear out the hypothesis but even to extend it to encompass all language. It might at first seem that, by making the name of the living object that he would know and show us into a poem's one-word title, Lawrence is claiming success in his quest for understanding and description. The title might seem to claim that the poem to follow is a veritable icon, what Jonathan Culler has most clearly described as an entity in which "*significant*" actually "resembles *signifié*."[14] In fact all such a poem can do or promise to do is to be itself, something that begins as the name of an elusive thing and becomes, finally, the name of a struggle to know that thing which, by definition, is elusive.

Like "Snake" and "Grapes," then, "Fish" gropes for experience beyond the range of present human intercourse. When Lawrence tries to find words which will allow him to touch something at that pale boundary of separation, however, he often ends up with words like "fish" (which signify the unknowable or an attempt to know it) or with words that describe ideas or things that fishes are not. At these points, the poet recognizes that a purely negative strategy can never describe fishes but only affirm their utter beyondness, and these moments of recognition seem to break sentences up and stanzas off and force Lawrence to struggle for a new beginning:

> No fingers, no hands and feet, no lips;
> No tender muzzles,
> No wistful bellies,
> No loins of desire,
> None.

> You and the naked element. . . .

Fish "Never know," Lawrence goes on to say, and adds that they are that which "Never grasp," that which remains an "Almost . . . voice" that "almost screams," forever "inaudible." They are

> No more.

> Nothing more

than object in element. They are "Without love," for they are "All without love." They must also therefore be "utterly without misgiving" for the things they do. The effect of such words, of course, is that they inevitably describe a creature with loins of desire, feet and hands and fingers which grasp, and audible voices, creatures able to love and feel misgiving for their sins. What the poet's words do best is describe what they know best— man. Perhaps that is why, in a paradox symptomatic of the situation in which he finds himself, the poet once deems fishes to be "unnatural."

When he is not describing what fishes are not, Lawrence seems to find himself with essentially two poetic options. He can ask questions to which the only response is "fish," the word for that unreadable underworld of idealess experience into which he would but cannot descend. "Who is it ejects his sperm to the naked flood? / In the wave-mother?" Lawrence asks. "Who swims enwombed?"

> Who lies with the waters of his silent passion,
>   womb-element?
> —Fish in the waters under the earth.

Or he can talk, in positive syntax, about people while he pretends to describe fish. We hear of the "gay fear, that turns the tail" of a small fish "from a shadow" of a slim pike, "with smart fins" (the phrase seems almost synonymous with "fancy duds" or "cool threads") that is "slouching . . . / Like a lout on an obscure pavement." We learn of a fish "in the know" and of another with a "monotonous soul."

John Locke had known, in an earlier century, that "he that imagines to himself substances such as never have been . . . to which yet he gives settled and defined names may fill . . . another man's head with the fantastical imaginations of his own brain, but will be very far from advancing . . . knowledge" (*An Essay Concerning Human Understanding*, 3. 10. 30). The fact that Lawrence fears he is not making a slit, not advancing any knowledge of reality through his "settled name" (fish), is evident enough in the extravagance of his imaginings. It is, moreover, made more abundantly clear when the poet suddenly calls attention to his distance from knowledge of the subject by switching to another language to describe it:

> Quelle joie de vivre
> Dans l'eau!

What the lines may suggest by way of something like analogy is that, just as there is no English equivalent for the French phrase, so a phrase like "joy of life"—which is the poor way we might translate it—can in no way convey the true reality or meaning of the elusive fish. Rather, we suddenly realize, the fish-absence is being used, arbitrarily, to talk about or name an elusive quality of human thought, attitude, feeling. When it is, it seems that the umbrella is indeed absolute.

*   *   *

"Fish" is a poem in which an author's uncertainties about his world, his medium, and his ability to make the latter mirror the former (and not vice versa) result in several currents of poetic discourse. Within those currents, moreover, exist powerful countercurrents. For instance, on one level the poem claims—as not all Lawrence poems do—to be able to lift its unseen subject out of the unknown. The image of Lawrence as fisherman with a "long rod" belongs mostly to this level of the work. Perhaps because of the angling metaphor itself, however, a worry develops. If the process of elevation and revelation involves alteration, even annihilation, then what does the poet accomplish and what kind of understanding does he bring to light?

On a somewhat deeper level of the poem's flow, the poet is not even assumed to be the one who could catch up primordial reality on the lines of language. On a rereading of the poem the fisherman image becomes less convincing. The lines in which Lawrence "suddenly" finds himself with a real and functioning fishing pole seem erratic afterthoughts (or perhaps forethoughts); they are not very smoothly interwoven with the ones in which the poet struggles, without rod and without success, merely to see things that "move" in other circles. According to this current of thought, the poet couldn't annihilate a fish with words even if he wanted to; killing would entail proximity, and words are always pointing him in some other direction. If he were to find himself pulling a fish through the separating surface of rhyme and myth, the dying fish would prove to be a part of the rhyme or myth and the ripple on the broken surface a simulacrum.

At this level, "Fish" is comparable with poems discussed in Chapter 3. And yet this discourse, too, contains a countercurrent of thought, one that I cannot find in poems like "Figs" or "The Revolutionary" or any of the *Birds, Beasts and Flowers* poems written before the summer of 1921 but one that will be the driving force of Lawrence's later and last poems. This countercurrent suggests that the poet's "deepest desire" may be fulfilled, that pure relation to the primordial realities may be accomplished, and that it may be accomplished by the indirection of language. This end can only be achieved, however, once the poet discovers that the true and primordial objects of desire are not really fish or snakes or grapes at all but rather the gods and godliness that inhere in them. This powerful and important countercurrent in a poem by a man often said to be a naturalist, must be reached by way of an appreciation of "Fish" as yet another second-lustre poem that worries that it is a belated text, a commentary on commentaries.

One of the best pieces of evidence for this kind of anxiety is often, of course, a poet's attempts to seem relatively free of debts to his literary antecedents and thus relatively free of the burdens of the past. Even as Lawrence realizes that fish are beyond him, that he can talk about a word signifying what he cannot talk about (or well-dressed loiterers on a city sidewalk or something like the joy of life) but never that which lies beyond the capabilities of his language, he tries to console himself with the hope that he can talk about people, language, and ideas within a rather original and soon to be influential myth. He would seem to hope that because fewer of his predecessors have battered old subjects around after assigning to them the arbitrary symbols of fish and water than, say, snake and garden, he will at once be comprehensible (because his concerns and epistemology are filial) and seem paternal (because his choice of signs is relatively seminal).

When Lawrence says that the fish is "in front of my sunrise, / Before my day," when he says of the fish, "He outstarts me" for he was "Born before God was love" and remains "Beautifully beforehand with it all," he wants to make himself, via his central figure, seem a poet older than Coleridge and older than Milton, maybe even older than that Biblical voice of the "New Adam" which spoke of fishes and fed multitudes with two of them. That is why Lawrence develops the theme of the "flood" in "Fish." He speaks imaginatively of the waters which "rise and cover the earth," of a creature that can "breathe from the flood at the gills" and execute a "slap on the face of the flood." If he could seem to have on his line some primitive planetary inhabitant whose history or whose identity was not altered by the Flood—or by the equally effacing Flood of words—then he could perhaps seem miraculously to antedate his own history, which derives from that most ancient second comer of all time, namely Noah, the second Adam and an early type of Christ. If Lawrence could somehow seem a poetic "last comer" who completes his precursors ("Tessera" is Harold Bloom's word for this) and yet somehow seem more primitive too (through the strategy of Apophades), then he could seem to be, like the Jesus of the poem's final lines, "In the beginning . . . / And in the end." He would be the poetic Alpha and Omega, the apocalyptic voice that can be neither revised nor eclipsed.

Being a last comer is not difficult for Lawrence, naturally, but being first is a different matter, and to seem such a thing he must do far more than merely speak of the waters which "rise and cover the earth." The Flood, after all, is a most ancient event that takes place in a more recent text. One of the things the poet does is to make this thing he calls a fish into a father figure. Then he suggests that this symbolic father, unlike the snake, is not even partly a figure for the paternal past—the corrupting voices of education. Rather, the fish father symbolizes a quality unknown to man: elementary sensual contact. He is pictured as a "barrel body," a "long . . . nose" that "wash[es] in oneness / And never emerge[s]." His lover is the primeval water which has covered the earth since the first day; he "lies with the waters of his silent passion," the "wave-mother" that is both his lover (he "ejects his sperm to the naked flood") and his mother (he "swims enwombed").

The fish of Lawrence's myth, then, exists in a state of being that no man since Adam has known, for it is born of maternal elements and then becomes the proper lover of the same elements. That is to say, it washes in and drinks of the waters not as a second comer but as if it had no father, no original who had been there first. When Lawrence claims to be a son of a snake, he must grudgingly concede that Keats, Coleridge, Milton, and Moses, to name a few, are fathers and grandfathers of himself and his poem. When he portrays the fish as father, on the other hand, he would make it seem that his poem is not the offspring of other men, of their language, or even of language in general, but rather that it is spawned of direct intercourse with original reality.

In some sense, Lawrence's poem even seeks to seem older than the son of original experience with a thing; it seeks to seem the thing itself. As I have suggested earlier, by making the titles of his *Birds, Beasts and Flowers* poems out of the names of their respective subjects, Lawrence half-suggests that these poems *are* the objects they pretend to describe, so that when someone wants to spend an hour trying to get to know an elusive creature like a fish or a bat, he may well take his quest to a library instead of a pond or barn. In this sense the poet's portrayal of the fish as father can be seen to be a disguised form of patricide. He pulls a paternal fish into "Fish," kills it in the process, and makes his poem seem not like the offspring of experience, something generated by a fish, but "Fish"—experience itself. The poem is the most audacious attempt Lawrence can make to be what he cannot be, namely, a first father, "beforehand with it all."

Thus many of the events, images, and symbols that make up what I have had to describe as the poem's top level are also present in its deeper one. This, in spite of the fact that the meanings suggested by these parallel particulars by no means corroborate or necessarily even relate to one another. For instance, the feeling that the fish is a good choice of subject—a feeling permeating that level of the poem that believes itself to be catching and revealing the object world—at a deeper level of discourse holds out the promise that an effective, intellectual, and influential myth can be made. More interesting still is the involvement of the angling scene in several streams of poetic movement. The current of the poem that is concerned with a sperm-ejecting male fish not as object but as symbol of poetic origins has the fish dying to symbolize not, as Blanchot puts it, the death that objects find when named, but rather a literary strategy by which a poet alleviates what has been called the anxiety of influence by way of a myth of precedence.

Such a myth—that to which the dead fish as patriarchal absence (read absent external inspiration) belongs—has as a catalyst the longing for artistic originality that is particularly powerful when poets feel strongly overshadowed by certain predecessors. In an earlier part of this chapter I have discussed Lawrence's encounter with a water-snake, an act of avoidance that, at the anxious level of "Fish," can be taken as evidence of Coleridge's abiding power. Lawrence's longing but fundamental inability to envision the dark deeps and remain alive, moreover, surely indicates his feelings towards Milton, whose most famous invocation in *Paradise Lost* addresses Light and says:

> Thee I revisit now with bolder wing,
> Escap't the *Stygian* Pool, though long detain'd
> In that obscure sojourn.
> (3.13–15)

The poet has returned, of course, from that great flood wherein float powers "in bulk as huge" as

> Leviathan, which God of all his works
> Created hugest that swim th'Ocean stream.
> (1:200–2)

Though "the dark descent, and up to reascend" has been "hard and rare," the mermanlike Milton admits, "thee I revisit safe, / And feel thy sovran vital Lamp" (3:20–22).

Strange as it may seem, however, "Fish" may be most indebted to Matthew Arnold, whose poem "The Forsaken Merman" passes its own debts to Milton, Coleridge, and another "holy book" on to Lawrence in radically innovative and especially influential ways. Arnold's poem expresses, in part, the feeling that the modern poet must struggle to climb out of the romantic places of the imagination into the cold and even restrictive prosaic reality of the here and now. It does so by setting forth a rich symbolic setting in which the place that must be abandoned if the "white" of the "town" on a "windy hill" is to be seen is a place of "surf and . . . swell," of "Sand-strewn caverns, cool and deep," a world apart with a "pavement of pearl" and an opaque "ceiling of amber" (lines 71–74, 33–35, 118–19). To continue to live in that reigning world of the past (Arnold speaks of the "red gold throne in the heart of the sea") seems to amount to some kind of fall into rich if primitive waters:

> Down, down, down!
> Down to the depths of the sea!
> (lines 85–86)

It seems, moreover, to be a fall into poetic unoriginality. We can see this through the fact that while the lapse leads into a world of imagination, it is, at the same time, an unoriginal act with Adamic and Miltonic precedents. But Arnold is not concerned merely with these most original precedents, for he also sees the choice of a poet in his time as being between the mundane world of the mid-nineteenth-century and the richer world where "sea-beasts" "come sailing by / . . . with unshut eye," more specifically, where Coleridgian

> sea-snakes coil and twine,
> Dry their mail and bask in the brine.
> (lines 39–44)

The poem claims that a woman—perhaps the wave of the future—has broken out of the gentle undercurrents of the sea and through the mediating watery surface that makes the real world imperceptible from below. But the woman never seems more than an inimitable possibility, for the poem is spoken entirely by a merman who, because he is half fish, could never make the upwards dive the miraculous Margaret has made, even if he more than half wanted to. He can leave the water for a moment or two and stand along the shoreline dividing the two realms, just as men can momentarily enter and glimpse the watery world, but he must always return to the nurturing life below. His offspring, moreover, are mermen and mermaids too, and they will, like their father, be drawn by the life above the surface but unable to enter it except for momentary "far-off" surveys.

To the extent that Arnold's poem is a symbolic metapoesis I think that it suggests this: the poet can never break out of the world in which he was born. For Arnold that world is one of coiling, twining sea-snakes and of the life-in-death of Romantic imagination ("cool and deep," the undersea kingdom is one "where the winds are all asleep; / Where the spent lights quiver and gleam" [lines 35–37]). It is a stratified realm in which to be influenced is to be fallen "down," a realm out of which ascent is as impossible as uninfluenced being.

Arnold would seem to confirm this reading of the poem through his treatment of Margaret. Her "achievement," that of taking her "unshut" underwater eye out into the mundane, may not be the achievement it seems, for she enters that superficial world beyond the surface only to enter a church and say "Long prayers" with her "eyes . . . seal'd to the holy book" (lines 66, 81). Margaret has escaped one world of unoriginal knowledge in imaginative figurative language only to be "seal'd" to another. She has escaped one life in mythical language about life, death, salvation, and sympathetic imagination for another. Both worlds are, in a sense, worlds of the book, and the books are similar enough to speak of some common, lost source. Indeed, the two realms are in many ways alike. Both are essentially restrictive, and both allow their inhabitants intimations of the other life.

We have seen already this kind of dichotomy that is not quite a dichotomy in the poetry of D. H. Lawrence. Seeing the serpent as hero is much the same as seeing him as archenemy; Milton's book seals the unoriginality of our fate either way, and there is no escape. The landward world is one where people live but fish cannot, and the "pavement" of the undersea world is populated with "louts" in "grey-striped suits." Arnold's poem seems to provide many of the most basic structures as well as the most superficial details of Lawrence's later attempt at mermanhood. There are repeated words in "Fish," like "pavement"; there are moods, like that evoked in the claim that fish "sink, and rise, and go to sleep with the waters"; and there are larger, symbolic patterns in Lawrence's poem that extend and reinvigorate Arnold's language. The poet's positioning himself "on a bank" at "the pale [his] being" so that he can attempt to "look beyond, and see / Fish, in the outerwards," for instance, turns inside out the symbolic structure of the "Forsaken Merman," where the poet-as-fish stands "on the shore" at the pale of his being and attempts to see, talk about, and communicate with a world whose contours and a human being whose behavior seem equally loveless, ineffable.

Though Lawrence's poem first appears to reverse Arnold's, it is more nearly an elaborative parallel that widens and deepens the older poem. Both works treat the wish to escape influence, and both do so by chronicling the attempt of a person to escape the comforts of a familiar haven and enter into a zone from which that person has long been exiled. The voice of both poems, on the other hand, is that of a being who never even attempts such a voyage beyond the coasts of the unknown other. Journeying to that pale zone where a rare atmosphere begins, he returns to the comforts of the familial realm to see ("Sail and sail, with unshut eye"), but to see the familiar sights of the past with never a glimpse of the world "beyond" the ensecreting "pearly" surface. Lawrence sets out to see and show us a fish. He says he ends up with one "like a halo round my head," but that enwreathing "Fish" is surely a successful, revisionary poem, not a beast from the watery deep.

"The Forsaken Merman" finds its way into the profound currents of Lawrence's text no doubt because it reminds us just how impossible it is to break out of these words we call our perceptions; even Lawrence's turning away from the poetically propelled water snake and towards a fish that ends up looking more than half human has been precisely anticipated by Arnold. And Lawrence's debt to Arnold—in "Fish" or elsewhere—hardly stops with "The Forsaken Merman." The idea that language may throw some barrier between ourselves and some possible experience from which we have been in exile—an idea that Arnold inherited from the Romantics and revised slightly before passing on—can be found in such poems by Lawrence as "Southern Night" and "Tropic." The idea that it is important to touch things directly and not figuratively is the subject of "The Buried Life," a poem by Arnold that provides both ideas and, along with "The Forsaken Merman," a structural framework in which Lawrence can "catch fish."

Arnold, in "The Buried Life," says that "even love" is "too weak / To unlock the heart, and let it speak" of "The unregarded river" of life, the long "buried stream" over which "Light flows our war of mocking words."

> But often, in the world's most crowded streets,
> But often, in the din of strife,
> There rises an unspeakable desire
> After the knowledge of our buried life.
> (lines 1, 12–13, 39–48)

That "unspeakable desire" for "knowledge," Arnold says, is not assuaged by or through language. It is

> Only—but this is rare—
> When a beloved hand is laid in ours

that a person

> thinks he knows
> The hills where his life rose,
> And the sea where it goes.
> (lines 77–78, 96–98)

To be sure, Arnold searches for a buried spiritual essence to which a loving touch seems the only remaining access, while Lawrence, in "Fish," grasps for a deep "liveliness" of being antecedent to any Cartesian split into body and spirit. The state Lawrence yearns for is one to which love provides no access, for it is a state of being that existed before "life knew loving." It is a condition of human experience that Rupert Birkin had referred to as "a river of darkness, darkness, . . . putting forth lilies and snakes, and the ignis fatuus, and rolling all the time onwards. That's what we never take into count—" he tells Ursula in the "Water-Party" chapter of *Women in Love*, "that it rolls onwards."

"What does?"

"The other river, the black river. We always consider the silver river of life, rolling on and quickening all the world to a brightness, on and on to heaven, flowing into a bright eternal sea, a heaven of angels thronging. But the other is our real reality."

Still, there remain important parallels. Although much of Arnold's "The Buried Life" is lost on "Fish," even as it is on *Women in Love,* much abides. The deep waters into which Lawrence would "delve" with words that touch "the naked . . . element" are below visible surfaces, exactly as are the "streams" and "seas" of the buried essence, the Eurydice, Arnold fails to bring to light. Even the elder poet's specific figure—that of burial—is quietly reaffirmed. Lawrence's address to the inhabitants of the deep, after all, sounds suspiciously like the "what matters it now" address by the living to the interred:

> Fish, oh Fish,
> So little matters!
>
> Whether the waters rise and cover the earth
> Or whether the waters wilt in the hollow places,
> All one to you.

There are, furthermore, curious passages in Arnold's poem which, if read with a wry smile and willing suspension of disbelief, would suggest exactly that which Lawrence's angling poem will be seen quietly to imply: to fish the deep waters of the buried life successfully might be to catch our own elusive selves. What all of us know least about is what we were before the "flow" of "mocking words" made us lose sight of the now "indiscernible flow" of the now "unregarded river," in other words, of what life really is and what we really are. "Many a man . . . delves," Arnold cries out, but never "deep enough," and although

> we have been *on many thousand lines,*
> And we have shown, on each, spirit and power;
> . . . hardly have we, for one little hour,
> *Been on our own line,* have we been ourselves.
> ("The Buried Life," lines 39–40, 55–60; italics mine)

Whether or not these lines from "The Buried Life" pointed Lawrence towards specific images and themes is not as important as the fact that Lawrence deepens our understanding of Arnold by showing us what he has become.

Lawrence does as much in "Fish," but also in other second-lustre poems, like "Tropic," where, in a quest for his "Negroid" essence, the poet suddenly wonders,

> What is the horizontal rolling of water
> Compared to the flood of black heat that rolls upwards
>   past my eyes?

In "Southern Night," a poem written in the same place (Taormina), at the same time and published in juxtaposition with "Tropic," Lawrence again employs Arnold to speak of his own search for the subconscious floods of his "blood-dark" being. This time, however, he calls upon Arnold's "A Southern Night" instead of "The Buried Life." In that poem, the elder poet stands by "The sandy spits" where the "soft Mediterranean breaks / At my feet," where "Gibraltar's cannon'd steep / O'er frowns the wave" (lines 1–4, 23–24). The night is "so soft, so lone, / So moonlit," that the "memory" of a brother who died at this very site, Arnold says, "Possesses me quite" (lines 13–14, 18–20). The poem contains, however, a somewhat uncomplimentary note, the poet remarking that

> In cities should we English lie,
>   Where cries are rising ever new,
> And men's incessant stream goes by.
>   (lines 61–63)

Arnold argues that those who pursue only idle "talk" and "business" in a cold country do not deserve burial in the beauties of a vibrant, lovely nature they never had time to see:

> Not by those hoary Indian hills,
>   Not by this gracious Midland sea
> Whose floor to-night sweet moonshine fills,
>   Should our graves be.
>   (lines 73–76)

Lawrence seizes the poem and rewrites it into his own. He, too, stands by the Mediterranean (the Arnoldian "place" for southern nights). He speaks of a moonrise, of memories, and of the cold English climate, all of which once "bore" (and now "bore") the mature poet struggling for a more "tropical" identity:

Come up, thou red thing.
Come up, and be called a moon.

The mosquitoes are biting to-night
Like memories.

Memories, northern memories,
Bitter stinging white world that bore us.

Using Arnold's basic symbolic landscape and the Arnoldian themes of Nature and English self-consciousness, Lawrence adds several dimensions to the scene which Arnold either was not aware of or did not quite articulate. Lawrence's poem, more than Arnold's, speaks of the awful grip a heritage can have over our consciousness, our perceptions. In front of a landscape more explicitly erotic than Arnold's "hoary Indian hills" or moon-bathed "Midland Sea," watching a throbbing southern moon rise from the Mediterranean waters, Lawrence's mind is still made bitter by the lingering "northern memories" of the cold "white world that bore" him. Of course, for Lawrence, Arnold and his unquiet Mediterranean meditation are amongst those memories. Indeed, the thought of a bitter "white world" seems to break into Lawrence's meditation in darkness as it broke into Arnold's previous meditation; Lawrence, because he remembers the poem, seems compelled enough by it to follow more or less in its course. Put another way, Lawrence chooses to write about a "Southern Night," moons, memories, and the north because he has the poetic memories that almost guarantee the impossibility of the new blood consciousness unconvincingly heralded by the moon. Arnold, if not quite the poetic parent who bore Lawrence, is at least a dead elder brother he half-resents and half pays tribute to. Arnold, standing by the Mediterranean and remembering his elder brother, wishes he were interred in a distant northern clime. Lawrence, remembering Arnold as he stands by the same sea, wishes his elder brother were more dead than he is, less a part of the seas into which Lawrence vainly looks for a fresh experience, idea, sign.

Indeed, Lawrence gives us some evidence that he never really even sees a "real" moon on a "Southern Night," only a sign most recently invested with meaning by Matthew Arnold, who thought about the "gracious" natural world that seemed to mock man's frantic pursuit of money and talk and "called" it a "moon."

Returning to the poem's opening lines, we notice that just as Lawrence never quite says he looks for fish but, rather, that fish is a name for the unseen, so, in "Southern Night," he speaks of something that has not yet arisen and tells it to

Come up, and be called a moon.

"Moon," after all, would be the likeliest name to give to that which represents all that modern man leaves foolishly unregarded, for as Lawrence almost blatantly reveals through his title, his poem "Southern Night" is not written within the "real" contexts of a southern night but, rather, within the established linguistic contexts of "A Southern Night." (Once again, Lawrence's title appears to refer to a thing but in fact refers to words.) Even if Lawrence is looking at his own phallus, which is what he may be doing in this poetic scene, the phallus represents the unappreciated natural source and therefore, after Arnold, may properly be called a "moon." "In the beginning," we might say revising "Fish," the vital existence from which man is cut off "was called the moon / And in the end." And the nature of language, that system of appellations and figures we pass down from father to son, elder to younger brother, is what guarantees our continued separation.

*   *   *

Critics of our own day, of course, have written exhaustively about the problems of perception and language that Lawrence struggles with in "Snake," "Figs," and to some extent in "Fish." Where Lawrence feels frustrated by the inability to see or say anything originally, they would tell him that although a clean break with the past and the cold knowledge it imparts is impossible, poetic frustration with that fact is the source of all those poems that offer relatively original perceptions by way of powerful reflections and elaborations. David Caroll, writing on "*Mimesis* Reconsidered" in *Diacritics,* would assure Lawrence that "the eye-witness always *constructs* his stage, determines its boundaries and the field of his perception, and reduces its complexity—he never really sees what *is* in a random, natural way as he pretends. 'Pure perception' is thus a mystified concept, an ideolog[y]."[15] In George Steiner's 1977 review of Gombrich's *Heritage of Apelles,* Lawrence could confirm that which, in "Snake," he shows us he so often suspects, namely, that the eyewitness constructs his stage in accordance with the old and well-worn blueprints. "The eye is never naked," Steiner writes. "Normal vision derives from education and choice." The "controlling factors are essentially cultural. The information, the external data gathered by the eye, has to be interpreted to make sense, and this interpretation will vary according to historical inheritance" and the "aesthetic conditions" under which the viewer views. What we see is what the "controlling" voice of our "education . . . allows us to see."[16] Lawrence's declaration, in *Etruscan Places,* that "men can only see according to a convention," and that "we haven't exactly plucked our eyes out, but we've plucked out three-fourths of their vision,"[17] is somewhat less sophisticated and considerably more evaluative than is Steiner's analysis. But it is also remarkably prescient.

Paul de Man would tell Lawrence that "even if pure perception *were* possible," the attempt to render it in language would contaminate it, convey something different from that which was perceived. De Man speaks in *Blindness and Insight* of the inevitability of "mystification," of "the impossibility of making the actual expression coincide with what it signifies." He goes on to say that the very "conception of literature . . . as a demystification [is] the most dangerous myth of all."[18] If de Man is right, then whether we "see" an object or read a poem about one, we get very little sense of the thing at all.

Immanuel Kant, who argues that the hypotyposis or sensible illustration is always symbolical, also tells us that "judgment"— an act we inevitably perform when we experience either a fig or a poem about one— "teaches us nothing about the nature of objects, only about the conditions under which we view them."[19] Jonathan Culler, speaking of Gerard Genette, would seem to agree with Kant on this issue; many anti-ideological writers of the past century, he says, have searched for "*vraisemblance,*" that "middle distance" in which they are neither closer to nor farther from an object than men "ordinarily are" in their "daily business." What they have not realized, Culler points out, is that *vraisemblance* is already an "ideology." It begins, that is to say, with the undemonstrable assumption that "ordinary people in ordinary situations view things truthfully, objectively, as they really and truly are."[20] D. H. Lawrence, like the anti-ideological writers of which Culler speaks, wishes he could know the world uninfluenced but then significantly influence the world. This is not possible; like all men he has been conditioned to view things in a certain way even as he conditions us to even more conditions under which to view and judge his poems and, later, the world itself.

If what seem to be original representations in language were not conditioned judgments, displaced quotations, could they possibly mean anything to us in the first place? Probably not. Culler, speaking of Sigmund Freud in his study of Ferdinand de Saussure, makes the statement that "linguistic communication is possible because we have assimilated a system of collective norms which organize the world and give meaning to verbal acts."[21] Its complement would be equally true: a man seeking to present a world unorganized by collective norms does not achieve linguistic communication, that is to say, does not give meaning to his verbal act. Maurice Blanchot, in the *Journal des Débats*, would go so far as to say that language can convey no "pure" meaning as opposed to "cliché" or "rhetorical convention." All literature must "accept" and "work with" and "make" its meanings out of all possible accumulated meanings. If "literature were to be absolutely unique, a pure personal expression, it would be a perfect silence, unflawed by public language." Blanchot knows what Lawrence knows: "At the heart of each writer there is a demon urging him to strike dead all literary forms, . . . to interrogate in an inexpressible manner what he is and what he does." But if "he gives in to this as a Terrorist in search of perfect expression, he must give up his craft in despair."[22] Blanchot hardly thought these thoughts with Lawrence in mind. And yet Lawrence spoke, in the note he prefixed to *Collected Poems* in 1928, of a proper young man, himself, who always seemed to be "interfering" with his wilder "demon within," always felt the need to put "his hand over the demon's mouth . . . and speak . . . for him."[23] Lawrence must have realized that poetic speech demanded the gagging. For rather than giving up his craft in despair and turning to silence, like a proper young man he continued to frame mediated conceptions in monologues that are, in fact, collages of displaced quotations.

In *Speech and Phenomena*, Jacques Derrida makes the claim that "any meaningful monologue is redundant speech."[24] Heidegger, before Derrida, had told us that "language speaks. Not man. Man speaks only in so far as he artfully complies with language."[25] There is evidence that Lawrence, too, knew in happier moments that the best (and only) "originality" is creatively redundant speech. There is even reason to believe that far from despairing at a creation like "Snake," "Tropic," "Lamia," "Nutting" or "Fish," far from hating its inability to simply see some physical subject, he thought the best art to be that which can see a thing as an almost infinite layering of dream, speculation, association, myth, fancy. In an essay entitled "Art and Morality" Lawrence speaks out against "photographic art," which he believes is a contradiction in terms. He says, "You've got to see in the apple the bellyache, Sir Isaac's knock on the cranium, the . . . insect [laying] her eggs . . . , the . . . unknown quality which Eve saw hanging," and the "glimpse the mackerel [must get of it] as he comes to the surface." (We can only assume he would think "you've got to see" every bit as much in a mackerel or fig.) Calling Van Gogh a "true artist," he says: "His painting does not represent the sunflower itself. We shall never know what the sunflower itself is. And the camera will *visualize* the sunflower far more perfectly than Van Gogh can."[26]

Nothing can tell us what a sunflower really is. A camera can visualize one. An artist can tell us something interesting and important by incorporating one in his art. These statements point towards those made in the last few decades by critics such as Marcel Raymond and Michel Foucault. In sympathy with Lawrence's feeling that when an artist really "sees" an apple he thinks about Eve, feels Isaac Newton's bump on the head, and imagines the way one looks to a surfacing mackerel, Raymond writes that the Baroque, Romantic, and now Modernist impulses lead "towards a view of art in which existential perception is both the means and end of creation, where 'frontiers disappear between objective and subjective.'"[27] Even more like the Lawrence of "Art and Morality" is Foucault, who says that "to know an animal or a plant, or any living terrestrial thing whatever, is to gather together the whole dense layer of signs with which it or they have been covered." In *Les mots et les choses* he focuses his attention on the work of the naturalist Aldrovandi, whose writings, he says, are "an inextricable mixture" of "descriptions,"

fables without commentary, remarks dealing with an animal's anatomy, its use in heraldry, its habitat, its mythological values, or the uses to which it could be put in medicine or magic. And indeed, when one goes back and looks at the *Historia serpentum et draconum,* one finds that the chapter 'On the serpent in general' is arranged under the following headings: equivocation (which means the various meanings of the word *serpent*), synonyms and etymologies, . . . anatomy, nature and habitats, temperament, coitus and generation, voice, movements, diet, . . . death and wounds caused by the serpent, . . . remedies, epithets, denominations, . . . monsters, mythology, gods to which it is dedicated, fables, allegories and mysteries, . . . proverbs, coinage, miracles, riddles, . . . heraldic signs, historical facts, dreams, . . . miscellaneous uses.

The reason, Foucault says, that for Aldrovandi and his contemporaries the world was "all *legenda* . . . was not because they preferred the authority of man to the precision of the naked eye." Rather, it was because they believed that "nature, in itself, is an unbroken tissue of words and signs, of accounts and characters, of discourse and forms."[28]

This is not to say, of course, that Foucault believes this "tissue of words and signs" we call "nature" to be man's original and essential element. "In its original form," he writes, "language was an absolutely certain and transparent sign for things, because it resembled them, just as strength is written in the body of the lion, regality in the eye of the eagle." (What "God introduced into the world," Foucault believes, "was written words; Adam, when he imposed their first names upon the animals, did no more than read those visible and silent marks." This linguistic "transparency" was "destroyed at Babel," whereupon "languages became separate and lost" their "original resemblance to . . . things." Foucault goes on to say that even though language no longer bears an immediate likeness to the things it names, "this does not mean that it is separate from the world; it still continues, in another form, to be the locus of revelations and to be included in the area where truth is both manifested and expressed. It is rather the figuration of a world redeeming itself."[29]

Language—*legenda*—is thus for Foucault both the evidence of an exile from reality and, paradoxically, the way back. "There is nothing now . . . that still recalls even the memory of primitive being. Nothing, except perhaps literature—and even then in a fashion more diagonal than direct."[30] The diagonal fashion of literature is, of course, attributable to the fact that literature comments always on other literatures, whether it wishes to or not. Foucault would not disagree in letter with Montaigne, who sounded like a frustrated academic when he said that "there is more work in interpreting interpretations than in interpreting things; and more books about books than on any other subject; we do nothing but write glosses on one another" (*Essays*, bk. 3, chap. 13). But he would disagree in spirit, for he holds to the paradoxical belief that the way out is somehow going to turn into the way back. "The task of commentary," writes Foucault, "can never be completed."

> And yet commentary . . . calls into being, below the existing discourse [of the language being commented on] another discourse that is more fundamental and, as it were, "more primal," which it sets itself the task of restoring. There can be no commentary unless, below the language one is reading and deciphering, there runs the sovereignty of an Original Text.[31]

In Foucault's view, then, it is possible for a writer, by commenting on an earlier writer, to expose a lost and more fundamental discourse that, because it is "more primal," brings more meaning into the present and future than the predecessor brought into the past. This amounts to something slightly different from what Harold Bloom describes by way of the word *Apophades,* that rhetorical method by which a belated poet reduces his anxiety by making himself seem older than his great precursor, father to his father. To Foucault it actually seems possible for a writer to be both "younger" and "older" than a predecessor. The great poet moves present and future man closer to the goal of "truth . . . manifested and expressed" by finding the almost invisible contours of that truth latent in the precursor's text, which he then develops (in the photographic sense) into his own at once new and older vision of the world. Any work, no matter how recent it may be, may thus radically change the nature of our individual and collective being.

The Jean-Jacques Rousseau reconstructed by Jacques Derrida, a contemporary of Foucault's, would agree with the notion that the written word is both a "diagonal" supplement to primitive being and, paradoxically, the "way back" to it. The Rousseau of the *Grammatology,* who was "straining toward the reconstruction of presence" or original being, "raised above writing . . . speech as it should be or . . . *should have been.*" Consequently, Derrida argues, he "valorizes and disqualifies writing at the same time."

On one hand Rousseau sees writing as "a destruction of presence and . . . disease of speech." On the other, he thinks it alone "promises the reappropriation of that which speech allowed itself to be dispossessed of"; a "dangerous means, a menacing aid," writing is thus "the critical response to a situation of distress." Just how it is that Rousseau can see the menace as a means, Derrida explains by supplementing his precursor's statement that "writing is nothing but a supplement of speech." The slow "movement of supplementary representation," Derrida points out, "approaches the origin as it distances itself from it. Total alienation is the total reappropriation of self-presence. Alphabetic writing, representing a representer [i.e., a more literal picture-writing], supplement of a supplement, increases the *power* of representation. In losing a little more presence, it restores it a little bit better."[32]

Whether we believe that "commentary" can help us "approach . . . origin" because total alienation equals primitive self-presence, or whether we think, with Foucault, that commentary can illuminate that which remains of the Original Text in belated ones, certain facts remain. The idea that a primordial future can be developed out of a belated past can be found in those early poems by D. H. Lawrence that are at once devoted to Shelley and trying not to be, and it can be found again as a countercurrent within that stream of discourse by which "Fish" declares the redundancy of its own speech, indeed, of all language. Present even in those lines the texts of which were prescribed by Milton and Matthew Arnold, the notion can be found perhaps most easily in the work's maddening reminder that "In the beginning / Jesus was called The Fish. . . . / And in the end."

It is easy to see this conclusion as but the final evidence of Lawrence's authorial frustrations. Indeed, it is hard to see that the three lines could offer anything more than a simple reiteration of the fact that human beings always attempt to know the unknown by giving it a name, but that the name is as arbitrary as it is necessary to discussion. After all, "Jesus was called The Fish" largely for the reason that the trope "Iēsous Christos, Theou yious, sōtēr" could be abbreviated by the word *ICThys*, "fish." Since Jesus happened to be signified by the very "thing" Lawrence claims he is talking about in his poem, the poet must be reminding us conclusively that what a man might wish to know as things in the world are, in fact, only short names for other words he calls his abstract ideas. The conclusion, in other words, seems like the poem's final admission that man has never—or at least has not since the beginning—been talking about things, because things are the terms in which he talks.

But "Fish," though it may suggest the arbitrariness of all signs, does more than that, too, through its ambiguous axiom about the beginning, the fish, and the end. It makes a suggestion that becomes more convincing with every return we make to the previous stanzas of the text. It intimates that the primordial reality which the poet seeks is, in the last analysis, not a creature but, rather, something for which the fish, in Foucault's terms, may have originally been a transparent sign that original man clearly read. The poet speaks, for instance, of a time "before God was love" and of a God "outside my God." "God" is a word by which English-speaking people have traditionally signified a desired presence or essence "beyond" the "pale" of present "being." A significant group of English-speaking people have, following a certain Western tradition, chosen to call God "love." Man does not have to say "God" is "love"; indeed, in the beginning even "Jesus was called The Fish," by which Lawrence means (below the most literal level of discourse) that before Western man approximated the beyond by projecting on it an arbitrary but known human quality such as love, before he called it humanity that is perfect, and even before he called humanity that is perfect by the name Jesus, he signified the object of his most profound desire by a creature. Since Lawrence says that the signifying fish is "loveless, and so lively" but that he, himself, was born after "life knew loving," the lost and elusive reality from which the poet is separated and for which he searches, the God beyond his gods, is simultaneously a primitive deity and a lost mode of existence.

However inconceiveable to us such a unity may be, it is in using the old fish sign that Lawrence comes closest to rediscovering it:

> To have the element under one, like a lover;
> And to spring away with a curvetting click in the air,
> Provocative.
> Dropping back with a slap on the face of the flood.
> And merging oneself!

The fish, here, is a figure which allows the poet to speak

provocatively of an elemental being, state, and relation that antedates Christian "love" and its God. It seems to me that, in these lines, Lawrence does not even pretend that his deepest desire is for the object world. That world itself is a figure for what he desires. And do a fish and its element really "provoke" the poet to thoughts of a lover, which is what he implies? (He has already told us that the idea or practice of love is foreign to fish, which do not even have "loins of desire.") It seems more likely, rather, that it is thought which has been "provocative"—provocative of description. The fish proves to be a powerful way of intimating a condition of freedom that interests the Lawrence who has come through the first lustre and into the second. It is a condition of freedom that antedates the flood, one in which lovers merged with their earthy counterparts but then could spring away—intense, individual, alive "clicks" in the air. The fish speaks of a way of being in which one is "alone with the waters" though "one . . . with the rest."

This primal loneliness—as Lawrence describes it in "Medlars and Sorb-Apples," one of the several *Birds, Beasts and Flowers* poems in which he shows interest in the state—is equally paradoxical in that it is one in which God or the divine—that beyond the pale of being—can be felt as presence. To be truly lonely is to see everyone, everything, and indeed the entire "element" as being beyond the boundaries of empathy, sympathy, and personal comprehension. It is, therefore, to see the element and all its inhabitants as a vast mystery. The Greeks, according to Lawrence, came far closer than the sons of Milton, Coleridge, and Arnold can to such an appreciation. "Today," Lawrence writes in *Apocalypse,* it is almost impossible for us to realize what the old Greeks meant by god, "or Theos."

> Everything was theos; but even so, not at the same moment. At the moment, whatever *struck* you was god. If it was a pool of water, the very watery pool might strike you: then that was god; or a faint vapour at evening rising might catch the imagination: then that was *theos;* or thirst might overcome you at the sight of the water: then the thirst itself was god; or you drank, and the delicious indescribable slaking of thirst was the god; or you felt the sudden chill of the water as you touched it: and then another god came into being, "the cold": and this was not a *quality,* it was an existing entity, almost a creature, certainly a

theos .... Even to the early scientists or philosophers, "the cold," "the moist," "the hot," "the dry" were things in themselves, realities, gods, *theoi.* [33]

In this ancient epistemology the quest for things and for abstractions could coincide. God, the word meaning God, a thing, and the self experiencing the sublime mystery of the thing all momentarily coalesced as a single powerful identity. The epistemology, moreover, is perfectly pointed towards by the sign of a fish, for the fish makes us think of a being in which that which is perfectly sensual, perfectly other, and perfectly mysterious adheres perfectly to the boundaries of self.

When such a way of being is seen as the proper end of a poetic quest, Lawrence can feel quite optimistic. In an essay entitled "The Proper Study," an essay that he wrote at the same time as "Fish" and published in *Adelphi* in 1923, Lawrence says that the "business of knowing myself has led me slap up against the forbidden enclosure" in which the "God mystery is kept in corral." The enclosure protects him, he says, from "a precipice on which stands up a signboard: Danger! Don't go over the edge!" But "I've *got* to go over the edge," Lawrence says; "Flop! Over we go, and into the endless sea. There drown."

No! Out of the drowning something else gurgles awake. And that's the best of human consciousness. When you fall into the final sea of *I Don't Know*, then, if you can but gasp *Teach Me,* you turn into a fish, and twiddle your fins and twist your tail and grope in amazement, in a new element.

That's why they called Jesus: The Fish. . . . Because he fell, like the weariest river, into the great Ocean that is outside the shore, and there took on a new way of knowledge.[34]

As long as the linguistic quest is not for mere scales and gills and tails, paradoxically, the poet *can* gurgle awake in the longed-for element beyond what was once a separating surface, *can* become a "fish out of water" and yet be alive and able to impart a "new way of knowledge."

The "new way" is signified here by the Fish Jesus, a fact which implies that the way forward must always be found by the way back. The historical "river" of "consciousness," Lawrence writes, starts with "the God of the Beginning, call him Jehovah or Ra or

Ammon or Jupiter or what you like." It begins "to meander and to doubt. Then fall slow. Then . . . pass into the great Ocean, which is the God of the End. In the great ocean of the End, most men are lost. But Jesus," he says respectfully, "turned into a fish. . . . And then like a salmon he beat his way up stream again." That is why, Lawrence concludes, "the river of human consciousness . . . goes in a circle." Great men bring history into a new era by swimming upstream, that is, by "speak[ing] from the source." Jesus had what Lawrence calls the "sixth sense," the "sense of the God that is the End and the Beginning." Lawrence, two thousand years later, stands "in the deep, muddy estuary of our era, and terrified of the emptiness of the sea beyond." His role as poet is to create in this empty beyond a possible future, to make "the End . . . the Beginning" ("Proper Study," p. 721). To do so he will have to speak from the source.

That does not mean, however, that he has to recover Christ's message. "Jesus, the Saviour," Lawrence says, "is no longer our Way of Salvation. He *was* the Saviour" (ibid., p. 729). Christ, rather, is a figure for a rich and diverse poetic past, even as the "river of consciousness" is a figure. "We are at the end of the great road," Lawrence writes elsewhere in the same essay, "that Jesus and Francis and Whitman walked. We are on the brink of a precipice" (ibid., pp. 721–22). To find a beginning in the end by speaking from, say, a Whitmanian source is not to restate the general view of things that Whitman's poems have been thought to have presented. The author of the end must, rather, find a new way of beginning from the old text. Jesus, who knew well the voices of his paternal education, returned man from "doubt" to "God" as the "source," but he did not return man to Jupiter or Ra or even Jehovah. In this sense Lawrence is closer to Derrida than Foucault; the "supplement" reapproached God in the very act of distancing Himself *from* the Old Text. As for the poet of our own day, supplement to countless supplements to the Christian supplement, he must be equally deft if he is to bring us closer to a new beginning:

Get a glimpse of this new relation of men and women to the great God . . . and you get a glimpse of the new literature. Think of the true novel of St. Paul, for example. Not the sentimental . . . Christian novel, but the novel looking out to sea, to the Source,

and End, of all beginnings. Not the St. Paul with his feelings
repudiated, . . . [n]ot the St. Paul violent in reaction against
worldliness and sensuality, and therefore a dogmatist with his
sheaf of Shalt-Nots ready. But a St. Paul two thousand years
older, having his own epoch behind him, and having again the
great knowledge of the deity, the deity which Jesus knew, the
vast Ocean God which is at the end of all our consciousness.
(Ibid., p. 723)

The mind boggles. Is not a novel like *Women in Love* or *The
Rainbow* or even *Lady Chatterley's Lover* being presented impli-
citly and simultaneously on "the new literature," the "novel of St.
Paul," and the work of a "St. Paul two thousand years older," some
theos-bathed Greek, perhaps, who knew "the deity which Jesus
knew, the vast Ocean God . . . at the end of all . . . consciousness"?
"Turn into the Fish," Lawrence concludes the essay, "take a new
way of knowledge," and "you'll start to swim again in the great life
which is so frighteningly godly that you realize your previous
presumption. And then you realize the new relation of man. Men
like fishes lifted on a great wave, . . . swimming together, and
apart" (ibid.).

This, of course, is the "relation of man" that Lawrence speaks of
by way of the sign of the fish. "Admitted, they swarm in
companies, . . . / But soundless, and out of contact," he writes in
"Fish." They are, he continues, "Many suspended together,
forever apart." The idea that "the great life is so frighteningly
godly that you realize your previous presumption" is also instinct
to "Fish," with its "God of love," its "Other Gods / Beyond my
range," its "gods beyond my God." The fish, to return for a
moment to the terminology of *Apocalypse,* is the thing that
"struck" Lawrence as theos, as a relation between self and other
in which theos is most manifest, and as a way of referring to,
describing, "calling," the divinity and relation. Through the fish
Lawrence finds that he can "Turn into the Fish" and begin to
"return" us to the new "way of knowledge."

Why through the fish? It seems doubtful that Lawrence would
honestly answer the question by posing as one of those Greeks
accustomed to seizing on whatever caught his imagination at the
given instant. Lawrence, after all, seeks to point us towards a
world of being that is also, in Foucault's words, an "Original Text,"

and therefore he can hardly recall this "memory of primitive being" by arriving at his sign so arbitrarily, by using whatever sensation is the order of the moment. He would probably admit, rather, that he has been led to the fish because, for some reason, that sign has persistently spoken of a living godliness throughout history and its various cultures and languages.

In his writings on the pictorial literature of the Etruscans, Lawrence speaks of his belief that, even more than to a Greek, "to the Etruscan . . . the whole universe . . . was alive, like a vast creature. [It] had a great soul, or *anima:* and in spite of its one great soul, there were myriad, roving, lesser souls." These "ancients" therefore subscribed to the belief that "no part of us nor of our bodies shall be, which doth not feel religion." This "idea of the vitality of the universe was evolved long before history begins," he continues, "and elaborated into a vast religion before we get a glimpse of it. When history does begin, . . . the Egyptians and Babylonians and Etruscans" communicate their "active religious idea" through their "idols or symbols."[35]

One of the favorite symbols of these earliest groups, Lawrence says, was that of the fish. Because "the sea is that . . . womb of all things, out of which all things emerged," it was representative of that mysterious and divine "oneness of which the people knew nothing." The fish, which "leaps in and out of it suddenly," like the "phallus carrying the spark of procreation," came to symbolize "the *anima,* . . . the very clue to the vast sea. For this reason," Lawrence concludes, "Jesus was represented in the first Christian centuries as a fish, in Italy especially, where people still thought in the Etruscan symbols."[36] Thus although the "Etruscan tongue is dead" ("Cypresses"), the people who spoke Latin (and those who now speak any language derived therefrom) to some extent think in Etruscan signs.

What is interesting to any student of Lawrence's poetry is his belief that the other persistent, ancient symbol of "great soul-*anima*" was the snake. "If we remember that in the old world the centre of all power was at the depths of the earth and in the depths of the sea," he says, "and that the serpent represented the vivid powers of the inner earth . . . while the fish was the symbol of the depths of the waters, whence even light is born, we shall see the power these symbols had over the imagination." So much power had the snake symbol that, Lawrence argues, the "ancient idea" of the "king-god" derives from it. Pharaohs, kings of Ninevah, and Etruscan lucumones were clothed in scarlet and gold so they would appear to be, like serpents, "bodily a piece of the deepest fire." They thus became the "vermillion clue to the mystery . . . for their people." The "warriors and slaves," he says, were "kept *in touch* . . . with the mysteries. . . . But 'knowing' belonged" to the king.[37]

To reflect again on "Snake," then, is to widen and deepen our understanding of that earlier and more famous second-lustre poem by realizing that it forms a kind of diptych with "Fish," one of the last poems Lawrence wrote before making the passage to India in 1922 that was to lead him towards America and, eventually, a new poetic lustre. Both works would reawaken in Western man an *anima* alive to the vast, creaturely life and power of the universe. "Snake" does so by indirection; it takes as its object one that has lost or had compromised its original symbolic power. The snake recalls somewhat the "king" to whom "cosmic . . . knowing belonged," but it stands far more squarely for that knowledge that keeps us in continual exile from the mysteries of creation. "Fish," on the other hand, seeks to work on us more directly. It does so by tapping the power of a sign that, Lawrence feels, throughout the history of languages and their literatures has pointed towards an original, "great wave" of "life which is . . . surprisingly godly."

Literature, through what Foucault has termed its "diagonal . . . fashion," can help us to "restore another discourse that is more fundamental." Past literatures give the new poet a "locus" of possible and still deeper "revelations"; they provide a stream by which the source may be returned to and thus a method with which the world may "redeem itself," strange as it may seem, via "commentary." Matthew Arnold pointed back to a world of being infused with beauty and magic and mystery. He did it using images of fish, sea, and a being capable of "gurgl[ing] awake" in a different realm where there is "a new way of knowledge." Not the Matthew Arnold half in love with the piously industrious little town, and the Arnold comparable to the Saint Paul "who was against sensuality" and "therefore a dogmatist." That is the Arnold of what Foucault would call the "existing discourse." Lawrence eats away, burns off, gets rid of, this intervening text, the Victorian Arnold, by revealing in his commentary on "The

Forsaken Merman" that he calls "Fish" the Arnold "two thousand years older." This "more fundamental" voice speaks as Lawrence's own, moreover, not at those points where the verbal echoes are most obvious but, rather, where "Fish" suggests that the lost state of being is not one of love but of fishlike autonomy, that the unfathomable beauty of the undersea world is a function of its loneliness, and that the religion of love cuts us off from a rich and primordial mode of being.

Lawrence develops "The Buried Life" by separating out the vision of a divine life flow rolling under that conscious stream of our "mocking words" from the poem's perhaps more obvious idea, namely, that through romantic love we can come closest to catching some of the sublinguistic, subterranean, and submarine essence "on our line." He develops that earlier revision of Arnold to be found in the "Water-Party" chapter of *Women in Love* by deciding that "the dark river" of the buried life is not the opposite of the heavenly flow but, rather, is the stream of being in which divinity is to be found. He finds the primitivism of Milton by suggesting that the longing for the incomprehensible draws us towards the dark depths of the unreasonable Leviathan's element, and thus he wonders, via Christian tradition, if Jesus weren't "called The Fish" for reasons that even the first abbreviators didn't understand.

The fish in its deep and all-enclosing element, then, is not just something that for no reason struck the poet's signifying fancy. If it were that, he could have interchanged it for the suddenly appearing water snake; instead, he clung to it and dealt with the coiling piece of Coleridgiana by way of a careful literary act. The fish in water comes to Lawrence by way of innumerable layers of reflexive discourse in which brief stirrings of a lost world of pure, unadulterated, and unmediated relation inhere mysteriously but persistently in the fish sign. Lawrence, through the realization of that fact and the careful critical commentary on his predecessors' language, hopes he can direct us towards the sought-for "end," the original world he foresees as our best future.

The finding in words of the lost, primitive fish and its world, then, may not be precluded, in the last analysis, either by the search for "Jesus" or by the careful scrutiny and elaboration of a precursor's fishy metaphors. In the first place, as John Freccero has pointed out in a paragraph on Saint Augustine, "Short of the Word made flesh, there can be no bridge between words and things."[38] In the second, we might pay heed to Derrida's argument with Husserl, in which Derrida declares that all "seeing" is "seeing as."[39] We do not see the apple less because of Genesis and the writings of Newton; rather, we are more likely to see it—as Lawrence several times does—in all its original, plump, sensual, pendant heaviness because of them. However we explain it, the poet's fear that what Geoffrey Hartman calls the "negative progress" or the "centrifugal character" of poetry[40] leads him further and further from primordial being gets superseded by a paradoxical equation of endings and origins. For the late-coming poet powerfully to recall the intermediary Jesus is also to recall him in the other sense by finding, keeping, developing only the wellsprings or sources from which he spoke. The fear that, in the words of "Fish," the last "admission" life has to "wring from" us will be wrung is swallowed up by the victorious poet who finds a beginning in the end. "He wanted to see and not be touched by blue," says Wallace Stevens of his own angler for unmediated reality in "Landscape with Boat."

> Nabob
> Of bones, he rejected, he denied, to arrive
> At the neutral centre, the ominous element,
> The single-colored, colorless, primitive.
>
> .   .   .   .
>
> He never supposed
> That he might be the truth, or part of it,
> That the things he rejected might be a part. . . .
>
> .   .   .   .
>
> He never supposed divine
> Things might not look divine, nor that if nothing
> Was divine then all things were, the world itself.
> (lines 4–5, 9–12, 31–33, 38–41)

If the test of Lawrence's success, of his poetic voice or "breath," is the world that germinated in the lyrics of his poetic followers, then it is clear that modern poetry has much good to say for Lawrence and his ability to make the slit, show the new way. Elizabeth Bishop, in "The Fish," for instance, seems to have caught none other than Lawrence's "Fish" on her line. She pulls a "tremendous fish ... / Half out of water," watches its "gills breathing in / the terrible oxygen," thinks of its "coarse white flesh / packed in like feathers," and makes the sidewards turn of fish eyes suggest her own difficulty in seeing the fish as it really is. ("They shifted a little but not to return my stare," she writes of the "yellowed" irises "packed with ... tinfoil." Bishop finally "let[s] the fish go" because of what might be deemed the unoriginality of her catch, for from the fish's lower lip are suddenly seen hanging "old pieces of fish-line" attached to "hooks ... / Like medals with their ribbons / frayed and wavering." The poet may wish to imply by her poem's ending that the fish as a subject can never be poetically "caught," but all her preceding lines would seem to admit that it has been once and for all pulled into poetry; anglers subsequent to Lawrence have caught and will continue to catch Lawrence's fish only to see it in Lawrence's way.

Ted Hughes' poem "Pike," published in *Lupercal* in 1960, is certainly one of those Lawrentian catches. Hughes speaks of the "green tigering the gold" of his subject, of the "submarine delicacy and horror" of fish moving "Over a bed of emerald ... a hundred feet long in their world," and of pike "Logged on last year's black weeds, watching upwards":

> The jaws' hooked clamp and fangs
> Not to be changed at this date;
> A life subdued to its instrument;
> The gills kneading quietly, and the pectorals.

Hughes even tells of how "The outside eye" of his catch "stared," as "its film shrank in death."

Hughes' "Pike," however, offers far more than these images as examples of Lawrence's poetic "breath"-power; it apotheosizes the very environment Lawrence created, one in which the deep mystery of the planet envelops us in our loneliness like a God. "A pond I fished," Hughes says, "Whose lilies" had "outlasted every visible stone / Of the monastery that planted them":

> Stilled legendary depth:
> It was deep as England. It held
> Pike too immense to stir, so immense and old
> That past nightfall I dared not cast

But silently cast and fished
With the hair frozen on my head
For what might move, for what eye might move.
The still splashes on the dark pond,

Owls hushing the floating woods
Frail on my ear against the dream
Darkness beneath night's darkness had freed,
That rose slowly towards me, watching.
(lines 29–44)

"Cast thy bread upon the waters," the Preacher of Ecclesiastes admonishes his audience in what seems almost a pre-Lawrentian pun, "for thou shalt find it after many days." Lawrence says of the fish, with his "Absurd fish voice," that he is always only "himself . . ."

In the element,
No more.

Nothing more.

He only "ejects . . . sperm" into the "naked flood"; he has neither lover nor child to claim his seed:

What price *his* bread upon the waters?
Himself all silvery himself.

There are drawbacks to being human, but there is no value in being less.

Third Lustre: 1923–1930   Poetic Gods

Chapter Five

Passage to More Than India

If originality is the greatest challenge that any creative artist constantly faces, then the characteristic way out of all those binds that tradition imposes is the distinctive feature of any creative period. D. H. Lawrence, during his first lustre, makes his way by recalling and recombining the works of several influential predecessors, hoping to forge in the process a new style and a new paradoxical belief in the ideality of the body and the wonder of unsponsored chaos. During Lawrence's second lustre his problem is somewhat different, for it is language itself and not idealism that seems the obstacle to original relation and expression. The way out must therefore also be different; the poet's best hope for "coming through" his creative frustration lies, first, in generalizing his own problem through the myth of the Fall and, second and implicitly, by claiming himself to be part of the banishing process. (Anyone who has read William Carlos Williams' elegy for Lawrence or Denise Levertov's poem "To the Snake" or Robert B. Shaw's still more recent work entitled "Snake Crossing" knows that Lawrence did, to no small extent, make the snake "his.")[1]

The way out of unoriginality that Lawrence discovers during his second lustre is somewhat more cynical than the one that he had believed in earlier, however superb the poems expressing that cynicism may be. Keith Sagar, in *The Art of D. H. Lawrence*, characterizes the years between 1917 and 1924 as Lawrence's one truly troubled period. "I hope to demonstrate that [Lawrence's] works fell into a well-defined pattern," he writes:

(1) 1906–11: a period of gradual discovery and growth;
(2) 1912–16: the first phase of mature achievement;

(3) 1917–24: a period of moral and artistic uncertainty or even perversity;

(4) 1925–30: regeneration to a new art and vision.[2]

My quarrels with Sagar's outline of the chronological watersheds are few, and quibbling at best. He breaks into two parts the period beginning in 1906 and ending in 1916—but then his focus is on the novels, and the differences between *The White Peacock* and *The Rainbow* are indeed far greater than those between "The Wild Common" and "Song of a Man Who Has Come Through." Because Lawrence, as far as we know, completed no poems between 1923 and 1928, 1925 could certainly be defended reasonably as the beginning of the last lustre. But since "Fish" contains many of the elements of the later and last poems, positing the new way out of the fix of unoriginality that the poet will explore until his death in 1930, I am using the 1923 publication date of *Birds, Beasts and Flowers* to mark the beginning of the last phase.

The exact number and length of Lawrence's periods, or lustres, is arguable; that his life and art fell into phases is not. Frieda, writing in *Not I, But the Wind,* speaks of 1917 in the contexts of the political troubles the Lawrences were having during the war, recalling specifically their expulsion from their cottage on the fifteenth of October. "When we were turned out of Cornwall," she writes, "something changed in Lawrence forever."[3]

Evidence exists that the poet was beginning to change again by 1921. In a letter he wrote from Baden-Baden on the lonesome trip without Frieda that would take him to Zam-al-See (where one poem, "Fish," would be composed), he not only anticipates the concerns of that crucial, transitional poem but also reveals attitudes far different from the ones he revealed in his 1916 letters on love, marriage, and a pure relation with the universe of objects. The letter was written to E. H. and Achsah Brewster, who were about to leave for Kandy, Ceylon, where they would live and study in a Buddhist monastery that Lawrence would leave Italy for in 1922:

I here and now, finally and for ever give up knowing anything about love, or wanting to know. I believe it doesn't exist, save as a word: a sort of wailing phoenix that is really the wind in the trees.—In fact I here and now, finally and for ever leave off loving anything or everything or anybody. . . . As for *Die Liebe, Minne, l'amour, love, l'amore, Amor* and the two blessed Greek words which we pretend stand for love: look at 'em . . . . Give me *differences.*

"Leave me my tigers, leave me spangled leopards, leave me bright cobra snakes," Lawrence says elsewhere in the same missive. "I wish I had poison fangs and talons as good. . . . I *believe* in fear and in pain and in oh, such a lot of sorrow":

> Oh, may each she-tigress have seventy-seven whelps, and may they all grow in strength and shine in stripes like day and night, and may each one eat at least seventy miserable featherless human birds, and lick red chops of gusto after it. (*Collected Letters,* pp. 651–52)

There is much here, obviously, of the sensibility that wrote the whole *Birds, Beasts and Flowers* volume. But there is something else too, something mystical, visionary, and prophetic in the manner of Blake.

How much of Lawrence's changing attitude and style can be attributed to a changing relationship with his wife can only be guessed at. It may bear mentioning, however, that beginning in April of 1912, when Frieda went home to be with her sick mother and Lawrence took the long journey during which he was to write "Fish," the two separated more often and for longer periods of time than they had in previous years. On August 18, 1923, Frieda was to leave Lawrence behind in Mexico and to remain apart from him for almost four months. It was during that stay in England that she was to fall briefly in love with Middleton Murry, traveling with him from London to Germany only to become the object of what he was to call his "great renunciation." ("No, my darling, I couldn't let Lorenzo down," he is reputed to have said to her.)[4] Lawrence, in a letter he sent to Frieda's mother during this period of separation, says that "if Frieda finds it such hard work to love me, then, dear God, let her love rest, give it holidays. Oh, mother-in-law, you understand, as my mother finally understood, that a man doesn't . . . ask for love from his wife, but for strength, strength, strength" *Collected Letters,* p. 763). On the very same day, November 10, 1923, he wrote to Frieda as well, and it is clear from what he says that he considered their life together a thing of the past—at least for awhile. The letter, which is cool in tone throughout ("We've had several thundershowers"; "the *barranca* . . . is very impressive—you never saw that"), ends almost frigidly. "The egg is addled," Lawrence says, ostensibly of England and Europe. "But I'll come back to say how do you do! . . ."

> I am glad if you have a good time with your flat and your children. Don't bother about money—why should you. When I come home we'll make a regular arrangement for you to have an income if you wish. I told you the bank was to transfer £100 to you. —I wonder if Seltzer is in England. I haven't heard a word from him or Adele for three weeks, so know no news.—The Australian novel is very nearly done. —*Tanti saluti*. (Ibid., p. 762)

We can hardly say that Lawrence had entirely given up on marriage by the early years of his last lustre; he and Frieda were reunited, after all, within a month after he wrote to speak of a "regular" transference of funds, and they lived together, more or less, more or less happily until his death in 1930. What we can say is that, beginning in 1921, Lawrence was struggling—in art and in life—less and less to attain pure and unmediated relation with objects and in marriage, and more and more for knowledge of what might be called godliness. The Lawrence who had once left metaphysic behind for a new kind of matrimony was gradually becoming something of the lonely metaphysician, and that tendency began with a desire to withdraw, even from the natural world. "I am weary of Taormina," he writes in January of 1922. "I have decided to go to Taos in New Mexico. There are Indians there, and an old sun magic," he tells his friend Brewster (*Collected Letters*, p. 681). "But I have changed my mind," he then says two weeks later to Catherine Carswell, in a letter from Sicily.

> I want to go east before I go west: go west via the east. . . . We had almost booked our passage to America, when suddenly it came over me I must go to Ceylon. I think one must for the moment withdraw from the world, away towards the inner realities that *are* real: and return, maybe, to the world later,

when one is quiet and sure. I am tired of the world, and want the peace like a river. (Ibid., p. 687)

Lawrence didn't find his spiritual nirvana in Ceylon; he found mainly "the thick, choky feel of tropical forest, and the metallic sense of palms and the horrid noises of the birds and creatures, who hammer and . . . clack and explode all the livelong day" (ibid., p. 699). He did catch one "glimpse into the world before the Flood," the world he had glimpsed by looking at fish, when he heard "the clanging of great mud-born elephants." Other than pachyderms, though, the only thing lonely and fishlike he saw in Ceylon was "The Prince of Wales, . . . a lonely little glum white fish . . . sitting up there at the Temple of the Tooth with his chin on his hands gazing blankly down on all the swirl of the East" (p. 701). As for Buddhism, the passage to India had only brought him to see "a very conceited, selfish show, a vulgar temple of serenity built over an empty hole in space" (p. 700). He decided to continue his move eastwards, to turn his travels into a passage to more than India, "to America," where the search for the "inner reality"—what Whitman called "primal thought"—might be more successful, not amongst "the awful 'cultured' Americans with their limited, self-righteous ideals," but amongst the Indians of the New World (ibid.).

As often happened, Lawrence didn't end up going where he had planned on going, and in the letters he wrote from Australia he seems to be attributing his presence down under to the fact that he has lost his recently acquired hunger for things spiritual. "There seems to be no inside life" in Australia, he writes to Catherine Carswell from Wyerwurk, only a "fascinating indifference . . . to what we call soul or spirit" (*Collected Letters*, p. 711). To S. S. Koteliansky he says, "One can be . . . absolutely indifferent to the world one has been previously condemned to . . . here." He likens his Australian sojourn to "falling out of a picture and finding oneself on the floor, with all the gods and men left behind in the picture" (ibid., p. 712).

When Lawrence arrived in America in September of 1922, he spoke of its West, not as the place he had come to as the result of a spiritual quest recommenced but, rather, as some kind of Australian double. "It's free enough out here," he writes back to Brewster in Ceylon, "if freedom means that there isn't anything in life except moving *ad lib.* . . . It is just the life outside, and the outside of life" (ibid., p. 717). Such claims though are as misleading about what Lawrence sought—and found—in America as earlier ones are with respect to his two-month Australian sojourn. In fact, Lawrence, as he came from Australia to Taos in the fall of 1922, was verging on both a new spiritual breakthrough and a new aesthetic tack. It was to be a second breakthrough, as it were, to the style of the casual, a style that—far from being only a "life outside, and the outside of life"—allowed the development of the "sacred spontaneous life" that the poet spoke of in a letter from Taos (ibid., p. 722) and that he had never known before, not even during his first lustre. Lawrence's letter about "going east" to "go west" is roughly apt as a metaphor for his own development. Its only inaccuracy lies in the fact that the casually spiritual world view he was to come back to was not the same one he had set off from; the phoenix, when it renewed its youth, did not sail into old skies.

Evidence for the fact that, in spite of Lawrence's protestations to the contrary, America nurtured rather than starved the poet's growing spiritual sensibility lies once again in letters. And, once again, the letters carry on an important theme of "Fish," namely, that an original godliness that has been called by different names at different times lies around us as perfectly as does water around a lonely fish breathing in at the gills. With Frieda away in England for four months, Lawrence writes to Mabel Luhan:

> You have striven so hard, and so long, to *compel* life. Can't you now slowly change, and let life slowly drift into you? Surely it is even a greater mystery and preoccupation even than willing, to let the invisible life steal into you and slowly possess you. Not people, or things, or action, or even consciousness: but the slow invasion of you by the vast invisible god that lives in the ether. . . . Instead of projecting your will into the ether of the invisible God, let the invisible God interpenetrate into you. . . . And one can make a great, great change in all one's flow of life and living, from the power of output to the mystery of intake, without changing one's house or one's husband. "Then shall thy peace be as a river." (*Collected Letters*, p. 757)

There is a change that *is* required before the peace of the God or gods of the waters of the world can be known, however; one must, like an Australian, be indifferent "to what we call soul or spirit" or, like an American, "mov[e] *ad lib*." "One can do it only by *not* caring, by . . . having a bit of stark trust inside oneself. Stark trust in a Lord we have no name for. . . . My gods, like the Great God Pan, have a bit of a natural grin on their face" (ibid., p. 771). The principle of "not caring" brings with it a belief in many gods (for the "monotheistic" view belongs to the grinless "monomaniac") and requires the willingness to live as an isolate, unmarried individual. There can be "no more unison among man" than among "wild animals," Lawrence writes from Questa, New Mexico, on the Fourth of July, 1924:

> And I have known many things, that may never be unified: Ceylon, the Buddha temples, Australian bush, Mexico and Teotihuacán, Sicily, London, New York, Paris, Munich—don't talk to me of union. . . .
>
> To me, chaos doesn't matter so much as abstract, which is mechanical, order. To me it is life to feel the white ideas and the 'oneness' crumbling into a thousand pieces, and all sorts of wonder coming through.
>
> . . . there has to be a return to the older vision of life. But not for the sake of unison. And not done from the *will*. It needs some welling up of religious sources that have been shut down in us: a great *yielding*. (Ibid., p. 796–97)

The letter suggests that Lawrence believes he now knows why, in his earlier "Song of a Man Who Has Come Through," he could never quite "come at" the world's wonder but only found the mythical Hesperides. It was because he said "*we* shall come at the wonder, *we* shall find the Hesperides" (italics mine), because he had yet to learn the life of the fish, the way of being that is "out of contact," "forever apart," "alone."

*   *   *

Just as Lawrence's early love affairs cannot be separated from those early readings in old poems that Jessie Chambers describes in her article "The Literary Formation of D. H. Lawrence,"[5] so Lawrence's turn to loneliness and religious sources is partly to be explained by—and partly the reason for—his turn to Blake and Whitman as last mentors, final contexts. Of course, Lawrence had been reading and responding to these two poets since as early as 1908.[6] He had written the first version of his chapter on Whitman in *Studies in Classic American Literature* in 1918, and he had already acknowledged Blake's thought, in poems such as "Snake," by suggesting that there are secret doors to reality that lie beyond the blinkers of man's limited vision. Sandra Gilbert has argued persuasively that even some of Lawrence's very early poems, such as "Love on the Farm," are written out of deep familiarity with Blake, and Tom Marshall has made a similar case for Whitman's influence on "Dreams Old and Nascent."[7] But Gilbert implies about Blake what Marshall explicitly states with regard to Whitman, namely, that he "is a stronger presence in . . . the later poems."[8]

That fact has, I think, something to do with the casual styles of Blake and Whitman, those two Romantic predecessors who must earlier have seemed but poets of self. Once Lawrence, embracing both his new loneliness and a pantheistic vision of godliness, is no longer intent upon the pure objectivity that no longer seems possible anyway, he is able to appreciate for their style these two predecessors who, like Lawrence's Americans, seem always to "mov[e] *ad lib.*" The reverse, moreover, is equally true: the informality of style common to Blake and Whitman, because it is part of a spiritual principle, a morality of what could be called "not caring" or even of "yielding," came to guide Lawrence through his final spiritual quest.

It is grossly misleading, of course, to speak of Blake and Whitman as if their poetries were nearly the same; they are alike only in their looseness of structure, their moral liberalism, and what might reductively be called their pantheism. Of the poems Lawrence wrote after his travels east had brought him back west to Europe in 1925, some are more nearly Blakean, others are more in debt to Whitman, and a few are written in a composite style that fuses the elements of Blake and Whitman in the way that "Hymn to Priapus" fused Swinburne and Hardy or "Grapes" grafted to Lawrence's earlier style the pentameter of Milton, as modified by Keats.

In "Desire Goes Down into the Sea," one of Lawrence's *Pansies*,[9] the poet speaks as if he were one of the fish in his own poem, "Fish," one of the pike that "rock in water," that "lie only with the waters; / One touch." He speaks of a fishlike existence in which he says he has "no desire any more / towards woman" or "creature or thing," and he does so with a slow prosody reminiscent of Whitman's endlessly rocking elegies:

> All day long I feel the tide rocking, rocking
> though it strikes no shore
> in me.

In other *Pansies* Lawrence sounds more like the Whitman of "Song
of Myself" than like the Whitman of the *Sea Drift* volume. He
speaks of the desire to know the gods in their primitive essence,
those gods of the lonely pike who are, in the words of "Fish,"
"beyond my range," "outside my God," "in front of my sunrise." In
a poem that begins "Give us gods, Oh give them us!", Lawrence
goes on to qualify his request by adding that he has no desire for
"gods grey-bearded and dictatorial, / nor yet that pale young man
afraid of fatherhood":

> Give us gods before these —
> Thou shalt have other gods before these.
>
> Where the waters end in marshes
> swims the wild swan
> sweeps the high goose above the mists
> honking in the gloom the honk of procreation. . . .
>
> Mists
> where the electron behaves and misbehaves as it will,
> where the forces tie themselves up into knots of atoms
> and come untied. . . .

Lawrence "refuse[s] to name" these gods in a poem entitled
"Name the Gods!" Like Whitman before him, though, Lawrence
constantly pictures godliness in a whirl of images:

> But all the time I see the gods:
> the man who is mowing the tall white corn,
> suddenly, as it curves, as it yields, the white wheat
> and sinks down with a swift rustle, and a strange,
>   falling flatness,
> ah! the gods, the swaying body of god!
> ("Name the Gods!")

What are the gods, then, what are the gods?

>The gods are nameless and imageless
>yet looking in a great full lime-tree of summer
>I suddenly saw deep into the eyes of god:
>it is enough.
>("What Are the Gods?")

>People were bathing and posturing themselves on the
>   beach
>and all was dreary, great robot limbs, robot breasts
>robot voices, robot even the gay umbrellas.

>But a woman, shy and alone, was washing herself under a
>   tap
>and the glimmer of the presence of the gods was like lilies,
>and like water-lilies.
>("The Gods! The Gods!")

The gods always reveal themselves to the self alone, it seems, or in images of another person or creature in unselfconscious, casual relation to the world. Very often that relation is described, as it first was in "Fish," in terms of a self alone in water; a woman washes herself and glimmers under a tap, a wild swan swims where "the waters end in marshes," a goose honks from the "Mists / where the electron behaves and misbehaves as it will."

In Whitman's poetry, loneliness is not so important a condition for the discovery of godliness except to the extent that Whitman, because he annexes all other men to himself, speaks of a kind of collectively lonely experience of the world. Otherwise, however, the American poet's view that Nature, at first a silent incomprehensibility, eventually yields up divine vistas perfectly anticipates Lawrence's *Pansies* (or *pensées*) on the manifold godliness of the universe. "Allons!" Whitman begins the ninth meditation of "Song of the Open Road" (1856):

>. . . The earth never tires,
>The earth is rude, silent, incomprehensible at first,
>   Nature is rude and incomprehensible at first,
>Be not discouraged, keep on, there are divine things well
>   envelop'd,
>I swear to you there are divine things more beautiful
>   than words can tell.

In his later and better-known poem, "Passage to India" (1868), Whitman speaks, in the seventh meditation, of beginning "a circumnavigation" that will take him "to primal thought" and back again. ("I want to go . . . west via the east," was what Lawrence was to write to a close friend; one must withdraw "towards the inner realities that *are* real: and return.") Then, in the eighth meditation, Whitman describes to his soul what he expects to find on his trip that is "Not" to "lands and seas alone":

> Ah more than any priest O soul we too believe in God,
> But with the mystery of God we dare not dally.
>
> O soul thou pleasest me, I thee,
> Sailing these seas or on the hills, or waking in the night,
> Thought, silent thoughts, of Time and Space and Death,
>   like waters flowing,
> Bear me indeed as through the regions infinite,
> Whose air I breathe, whose ripples hear, lave me all over,
>   Bathe me O God in thee, mounting to thee,
> I and my soul to range in range of thee.

Whitman speaks here as if there were but one God, and in that respect a poem such as the one entitled "With Antecedents" might seem to be more properly "Lawrentian." In that poem, Whitman says he respects the gods of "Assyria, China, Teutonia, and the Hebrews" and every "god, and demi-god" that has ever been named because the whole universe is divine and therefore all "bibles" that were written in "past days" that "were what they must have been" are "true." In most ways, however, "Passage to India" is the richest antecedent to Lawrence's *Pansies*; its refusal to "dally" with the "mystery of God" provides contexts for Lawrence's later refusal to "name" or "describe" the gods, and its almost un-Whitmanian insistence on loneliness as a prerequisite for knowing godliness looks forwards to Lawrence poems from "Fish" to a remarkably Whitmanian later poem entitled "There Are No Gods." Left "alone" in his room, the speaker suddenly wonders whose "presence" makes the air "still and lovely" and

> . . . touches me over the heart
>   so that my heart beats soothed, soothed, soothed and at
>   peace?

> Who is it smooths the bed-sheets like the cool
> smooth ocean where the fishes rest on edge
> in their own dream?
>
> .   .   .   .
>
> I tell you, it is no woman, it is no man, for I am alone.
> And I fall asleep with the gods, the gods
> that are not, or that are
> according to the soul's desire,
> like a pool into which we plunge, or do not plunge.

The casualness of Lawrence's last lustre is apparent above in phrases ("that are not, or that are"), in images ("bed-sheets like the cool / smooth ocean where the fishes rest") and in rhythm ("rest on edge / in their own dream"). The casualness of *Pansies* can take Blakean as well as Whitmanian forms, however, and when Blake provides the literary contexts of a Lawrentian pensée, the poem's casualness tends either towards the moral indirection of Blake's *Songs of Innocence and of Experience* or towards the proverbial style of *The Marriage of Heaven and Hell.*

Many of Blake's *Songs* are little dramas of limited points of view. It is through the apparent limitations of a speaker's consciousness that the poet reveals by indirection his own larger moral vision, be it satirical or prophetic. "The Little Black Boy" dramatizes more than a black child's limited perspective; the speaker reveals indirectly Blake's condemnation of colonialism. When "The Chimney Sweeper" ends his song by claiming "if all do their duty, they need not fear harm," more than a child's pathetic innocence is being exposed by the poet.

What often makes Blake's work so perplexing, paradoxically, is the very clarity of the difference between the poet's view and that of his speaker. So obvious is it sometimes that poet and speaker do not agree that a treacherous relation is set up: the speaker may sound like a terribly unsuspecting innocent, like a pointedly satirical commentator calling attention to his or her own false inflections, or like a voice sliding up and down a whole range of possibilities between the extremes of naivete and full knowledge. The speaker who holds forth "On Another's Sorrow" can sound alternately and even simultaneously like a sentimental Nonconformist Christian or like someone making fun of one:

He doth give his joy to all;
He becomes an infant small;
He becomes a man of woe;
He doth feel the sorrow too.

.   .   .   .

O! he gives to us his joy
That our grief he may destroy;
Till our grief is fled & gone
He doth sit by us and moan.
(lines 25–28, 33–36)

Lawrence, in more than a few of the *Pansies* that he began writing in 1928 after his return to Europe, similarly dramatizes limited points of view and, by so doing, tries to widen the doors of perception. One such poem, "When I Went to the Film," might seem to have affinities with Whitman's "When I Heard the Learn'd Astronomer," but the complicated relation of narrator and poet and the difficult-to-measure gap between the speaker's point of view and the author's make the poem more nearly like one of Blake's *Songs*. The speaker says that when he went to a film and heard the audience "sighing and sobbing" over "all the black and white kisses" that "nobody felt,"

It was like being in heaven, which I am sure has
     a white atmosphere
upon which shadows of people, pure personalities
are cast in black and white, and move
in flat ecstasy, supremely unfelt,
and heavenly.

The speaker sees that "nobody felt" the emotions they saw, but is he an advocate of feeling? The tone of the last word, "heavenly," is surely as treacherous as the tone of "moan," the last word in Blake's song "On Another's Sorrow." Is the speaker implying that heaven *is* a place without passion, or is he merely having fun with the way upper-class Englishmen put to meaningless use words like "heavenly" and "ghastly"? If he does think of heaven as a place of supreme unfeeling, does he offer his thought as a criticism of heaven?

The position of the speaker and his or her relation to the poet is easier to pin down when the speaker has just transcended former innocence, has just narrowed the gap between what he or she previously thought and what the poet thinks. "The Saddest Day," whose second through tenth stanzas are hybrids of various stanzas from Blake's *Songs*, begins with a parody of the last stanza of a hymn, "The Son of God Goes Forth to War." Lawrence's parody recalls Blake's half-parodies of the Church of England hymnal, some of which were later adopted as hymns in their own right.[10] The speaker describes a steep ascent towards heaven

> "Through peril, toil and pain.
> O God to us may strength be given
>   To scramble back again."
>
> O I was born low and inferior
> but shining up beyond
> I saw the whole superior
> world shine like the promised land.
>
> So up I started climbing
> to join the folks on high,
> but when at last I got there
> I had to sit down and cry.
>
> For it wasn't a bit superior,
> it was only affected and mean;
> though the house had a fine interior
> the people were never in.
>
> I mean, they were never entirely
> there when you talked to them;
> away in some private cupboard
> some small voice went: *Ahem*!

Sometimes Lawrence's songs of education, of innocence-become-experience, retrace a development more surprising in its direction and final turn. "Chastity" is a poem whose speaker, the reader gradually realizes, has come through even Blakean experience:

O leave me clean from mental fingering
from the cold copulation of the will,
from all the white, self-conscious lechery
the modern mind calls love!

From all the mental poetry
of deliberate love-making,
from all the false felicity
of deliberately taking

the body of another unto mine,
O God deliver me!
leave me alone, let me be!

More often though, Lawrence, like Blake, does not speak through people whose consciousness has been widened. In "True Democracy" the poet records a conversation between an English working-class man and an American who claims that, "in my country, just over the way / we are *all* kings and queens!" What makes the poem pointed is the fact that its speakers are, on one hand, limited in their notions of what gentility entails and, on the other, hopelessly misguided in their very desire to be genteel. Thus, like Blake, Lawrence does a delicate balancing act; he satirizes simultaneously the limited view of his speakers and the system of life that so limits their views and values.

Sometimes such conversations, recorded in prose-poetry, approach the black humor of Blake's diabolical interchanges. "Canvassing for the Election" is an example of this kind of "pansy." The man doing the canvassing explains to a man on the street that he is making a survey of all the "*really* patriotic people":

So *would* you mind giving me your word?—and signing here, please—that you *are* a superior person—that's all we need to know—
—Really, I don't know what you take me for!
—Yes I know! It's too bad! Of course it's perfectly superfluous to ask, but the League insists. Thank you so much! . . . I've never been denied a signature!

Once again Lawrence indirectly offers a view of things large enough to contain satires that are dangerously close to contradicting each other, one of a nation in which every ordinary person feels

superior, one of the very idea of superiority. He accomplishes his
end by staging an interchange in which ostensible adversaries,
like Blake's devils and angels in *The Marriage of Heaven and Hell*,
prove themselves to be in league.

Not all of *The Marriage of Heaven and Hell*, and certainly not all
of Blake's poetry, is so indirect in communicating meaning, and
neither are all of Lawrence's pensées. Some of the *Pansies* are, in
Sandra Gilbert's words, "squibs crackling with the intensity of
Blakean proverbs."[11] She mentions the two-line "Retort to Whit-
man" and the equally brief "Retort to Jesus" as examples of
Lawrence's proverbial style. Read with "Fish" and Lawrence's
more Whitmanian poems in mind, the two "retorts" suggest that
Lawrence, even in his last lustre, sometimes struggles against
strong influences even as he struggles to bring them into his
poetry. He uses the style and world view of one (in this case Blake)
to recall some destructive element from the poetry of the other (in
this case Walt Whitman, who in Lawrence's view seems to be the
name Jesus the God of Love was called by in the nineteenth
century in the West):

> Retort to Whitman
> And whoever walks a mile full of false sympathy
> walks to the funeral of the whole human race.

> Retort to Jesus
> And whoever forces himself to love anybody
> begets a murderer in his own body.

Some of the *Pansies* in which Lawrence directly states his points
of view, to be sure, lack what might be called the biblical
eloquence of Blake's proverbial style and even of the two "retorts"
quoted above. A few of the poems so fervently believe, in the
words of one entitled "Dark Satanic Mills," that "The dark satanic
mills of Blake" are "much darker and more satanic . . . now" that
they sacrifice all subtlety on an altar of urgent necessity. "How
beastly the bourgeois is / especially the male of the species,"
begins one of Lawrence's impatient proclamations that flames
more than it crackles:

> Presentable, eminently presentable—
> shall I make you a present of him?
> ("How Beastly the Bourgeois Is")

Another, entitled "All That we Have is Life," might be said to be proverbial in the manner of Blake, but it exceeds in both petulance and anger the *Proverbs of Hell*. Blake's "mighty Devil folded in black clouds" had written no proverb more scathing than the one that says that

> As the caterpillar chooses the fairest leaves to lay
> her eggs on, so the priest lays his curse on the
> fairest joys.[12]

The figure with which Lawrence characterizes the bourgeois work ethic is so much more unseemly that it takes over the poem it was meant to serve and turns it into something of an obscene parody of a parable. "Work is life," Lawrence writes in "All That we Have is Life," to all those men and women who are not "wage-slave[s]":

> While a wage-slave works, he leaves life aside
> and stands there a piece of dung.

Not all of Lawrence's Blakean *Pansies* fall into the ways of excess. (Those that do, like "All That we Have is Life," typically end up sounding as much like Thomas Carlyle's most Swiftian excretions as anything in Blake.) "Let the dead go bury their dead," Lawrence begins a poem that has the same theme as "All That we Have is Life"—but considerably more tact. "Leave them to one another, / don't serve them":

> Trust the mills of God, though they grind
> exceeding small.
> But as for the mills of men
> don't be harnessed to them.
> ("Let the Dead Bury their Dead")

"Things made by iron and handled by steel / are born dead," Lawrence begins yet another of his *Pansies*; "they are shrouds, they soak the life out of us" ("Things Made by Iron"). The poet defines life as opposed to "A Living" even more successfully:

> A bird picks up its seeds or little snails
> between heedless earth and heaven
> in heedlessness.

When Lawrence thus tempers irritation with image, his *Pansies* are as teasing, provocative, and subtle as the best of Blake's *Proverbs of Hell*:

> New brooms sweep clean
> but they often raise such a dust in the sweeping
> that they choke the sweeper.
> ("New Brooms")

> Desire has failed, desire has failed
> and the critical grasshopper
> has come down on the heart in a burden of locusts
> and stripped it bare.
> ("Grasshopper is a Burden")

Lawrence meant, of course, for his Blakean *Pansies* and *Nettles* to be abrasive. The fact remains, however, that the less abrasive works, like "A Living" or "Grasshopper is a Burden," better succeed in challenging the reader. Lawrence may succeed best at divining the godliness of the cosmos when he speaks as a man alone, but he is most successful as a social critic when he remembers that Blake's proverbs were not written in a combative, one-on-one, author versus reader style. Indeed, he succeeds best when he utilizes Whitman's most common mode of address and speaks to a collective reader with a narrating "I" that sounds more like a large-souled "we."[13] It is in these poems that Lawrence sounds like Blake's Los—a voice at once in time and above it— and it is in these poems that he most nearly attains the ambitious goal he set for himself in the "Introduction" to *Pansies*. His stated purpose, after all, was not to confront the reader with the world's utter hypocrisy but rather to achieve Whitman's stated goal, in *Song of Myself*, of expressing "thoughts of all men . . . , not original to me" (*Song of Myself*, 17.1). "This little bunch of fragments is offered as a bunch of . . . thoughts," Lawrence writes in his introduction, "thoughts which run through the modern mind and body," thoughts that make up "the modern temper," belong to the "same nest," each "having its own separate existence, yet each of them combining with all the others to make a complete state of mind."[14]

"You" is one of those poems that combine the epigrammatic indirection of Blake with the large-souled narrative voice of Whitman in order to sing a subtle love song of mankind to mankind. I quote the poem in its entirety:

You, you don't know me.
When have your knees ever nipped me
like fire-tongs a live coal
for a minute?

Some of the hybrid *Pansies* are more critical of the collective reader
than is "You"; "Beware, O my dear young men, of going rotten,"
one of the more stridently admonishing of Lawrence's large-
souled pensées begins. But even those poems that lament the
gap between the world view of the "You" and that of the speaking
"I" soften their satire with Whitmanian sympathy and a casual,
"American" optimism. "Do you lack vitality?" Lawrence asks
young men in the first two lines of one poem:

Well well, if it is so it is so;
but remember, the undaunted gods
give vitality still to the dauntless.

And sometimes they give it as love,
ah love, sweet love, not so easy!
But sometimes they give it as lightning.
("Vitality")

The gods of both lamb and tiger are not necessarily or always gods
of love; the vitality they give does not always come in comfortable
forms. Lawrence offers this sobering warning, this Blakean
challenge, with the kind of nonchalance he spoke of, as early as
1922, in letters that urged correspondents to allow "the invasion of
you by the vast invisible god that lives in the ether," in letters that
counseled "yielding" and a fishlike life of "not caring" in the
elements. The paradox the poem suggests by leading up to the
image of lightning with an enervated prosody is that in the
moment we realize we lack vitality and respond to our knowledge
with an Australian or American offhandedness ("Well well, if it is
so it is so"), in that moment lightning strikes.

The spiritual passivity that Lawrence advocates must begin,
according to several *Pansies*, with the abandonment of rationality
as the end of being. In "Climb Down, O Lordly Mind," the poet's
opening, imperative address is to something like what Blake
named Urizen. Then Lawrence shifts his interest to the whole
human being, his audience:

Thou art like the moon,
and the white mind shines on one side of thee
but the other side is dark forever,
and the dark moon draws the tides also.

Thou art like the day
but thou art also like the night,
and thy darkness is forever invisible,
for the strongest light throws also the darkest shadow.

The poem is one of Lawrence's better—and certainly one of his quintessential—*Pansies*. It combines the indirection, the mythopoeic style, and the general world view of Blake with the generous outlook, affectionate voice, and sensual imagery of Whitman. It suggests, finally, that there is a dark, buried life that goes on in each one of us and that we know little more about it than we know about the fish that swims submerged in its subaqueous element.

*   *   *

Of the poems Lawrence wrote between the time of his return to Europe in 1925 and his death in 1930, all but those in *Pansies* and *Nettles* were posthumously published by Richard Aldington and Giuseppe Orioli. Together these two men brought out a volume that they entitled *Last Poems* (1932) and that printed dozens of new and previously unpublished *Pansies*, together with the handwritten contents of a "thickish, bound book" that had been discovered after Lawrence's death.[15]

In collected and complete editions of the poetry that have appeared subsequently, the posthumous *Pansies* have been separated from the other posthumously published poems, with the former printed as *More Pansies* and the latter as *Last Poems*. This has been done not only because Aldington and Orioli found the unpublished *Pansies* in a separate manuscript from the one in which they found those strange and almost mystical works such as "Silence" and "Demiurge" but also, presumably, because the two groups of poems seem so utterly different.

Yet the more we read the poems that Lawrence wrote after publishing *Birds, Beasts and Flowers*, the more of a piece—and of the same mind—they seem. A. A. Alvarez has argued for continuity in Lawrence's later poetry by pointing out that the same philosophy of composition governs all of the poems.[16] It is true, certainly, that whether they are short, staccato outbursts of temper such as "How Beastly the Bourgeois Is" or sustained lyrics of great profundity like "Ship of Death," all of Lawrence's later and last poems ebb and flow with the thought and feeling that produced them, imparting intellectual content as much through their casually shifting tempos and rhythms as through what might be called traditional, formal structure. The similarities between Lawrence's *Pansies* and those lyrics we think of as *Last Poems* do not end there, however: the themes of the vast majority of third-lustre works can be traced back to "Fish," and the poetic geniuses presiding over "Lucifer" as well as "You," "Bavarian Gentians" as well as "Vitality," are William Blake and Walt Whitman, especially Whitman.

Lawrence's *Last Poems*—and from this point on I will use the title to refer, not to the posthumously published *Pansies*, but rather, exclusively to what Aldington and Orlioli referred to as the "more serious poems"—stress the importance of informality, of moving *ad lib*, of "going [one's] way" like a lively, lovely fish. Lawrence declares, at the opening of "For the Heroes are Dipped in Scarlet," that before Plato lied to men with all of his ideals, "men slimly went like fishes, and didn't care, . . ."

> They knew it was no use knowing
> their own nothingness:
> for they were not nothing.

As in "Fish," the state of carelessness is a privileged state, one in which the mystery of existence inheres: "And enormous mother whales lie dreaming suckling their whale-tender young," Lawrence begins an extraordinarily loose sentence in "Whales Weep Not!"

> and dreaming with strange whale eyes wide open in the
>   waters of the beginning and the end.
> And bull whales gathering their women and whale-calves
>   in a ring
> when danger threatens, on the surface of the ceaseless
>   flood. . . .
> and all this happens in the sea, in the salt
> where god is also love, but without words.

"Whales Weep Not!" is unusual in suggesting that there is only one God, even as it is unusual in suggesting that "love" is an accurate way of signifying God in the landward world that is not "without words." The poem is far from unusual, however, in advancing the belief that we drift through a divine life-element and in hinting that all we need do is go "dreaming" with our "eyes open" to see that this is so. Indeed, Lawrence's *Last Poems* take the reader into a world even more divine than the one glimpsed in such early *Pansies* as "What Are the Gods" and "Name the Gods!" They explore a realm in which godliness is sensed physically, seen in embodied form, felt as a fish feels its watery element. In "The Body of God," Lawrence defines divinity as—and only as —"poppies and the flying fish, / men singing songs, and women brushing their hair in the sun." "Religion," Lawrence says in a related poem he calls "Demiurge," "knows better than philosophy."

> Religion knows that Jesus was never Jesus
> till he was born from a womb, and ate soup and bread
> and grew up, and became, in the wonder of creation,
>   Jesus,
> with a body and with needs, and a lovely spirit.

The physical component of mystery, the body of divinity that has little to do with love or spirit, is always stressed in Lawrence's *Last Poems*; since divinity can be born in many bodies and forms, moreover, these final lyrics can no more accurately be called Christian than can "Fish" or the most pantheistic of the *Pansies*. Jesus, in the view of *Last Poems*, was a body that signified God to a bygone era much as the fish itself is a physical entity that has suggested divinity over many ages. In the words of the essay entitled "The Proper Study," written at the same time as "Fish," "Jesus the Saviour is no longer our Way of Salvation. He *was* the Saviour."[17] Indeed, in "Lucifer" Lawrence suggests, through a Whitmanian mode of address and with Blake's dialectical world view in mind, that "devil" may, indeed, be the name divinity will be called by in the coming age. The poem, which might also be said to be conscious of "The Second Coming," in fact shares with Yeats's work only the common knowledge of Blake. In dark blue depths, Lawrence says, under "layers of darkness,"

> I see him more like the ruby, a gleam from within
> of his own magnificence,
> coming like the ruby in the invisible dark, glowing
> with his own annunciation, towards us.

The longing for god that in *Pansies* overlaps with the longing for unselfconscious, casual physical experience is, in *Last Poems*, part of a longing for death as the final casual, sensual experience. Thus, death itself becomes at once a sensation and a divinity, a Pluto attending the return of the absent Persephone from the daylight world of logic and idealism. In "Bavarian Gentians," the exquisite and best-known poem on this subject, Lawrence rewrites myth in the manner of Blake and borrows the prevalent blues and blacks of Whitman's "Out of the Cradle Endlessly Rocking" and "When Lilacs Last in the Dooryard Bloom'd" to assert, in his own age, the divine, even sensual, passion of death. Rather than Dante's "pearl on a white brow" (*Paradiso*, 3.15) or Shelley's "shadow of white Death" ("Adonais," line 66), darkness superimposed on darkness strikingly figures metaphysical and thus invisible presence. "Reach me a gentian, give me a torch!" Lawrence exclaims,

> let me guide myself with the blue, forked torch of this
>   flower
> down the darker and darker stairs, where blue is
>   darkened on blueness
> even where Persephone goes, just now, from the frosted
>   September
> to the sightless realm where darkness is awake upon the
>   dark
> and Persephone herself is but a voice
> or a darkness invisible enfolded in the deeper dark
> of the arms Plutonic.

One of the obvious features of the poem, which was almost certainly written during Lawrence's last year of life, is that it seems to believe in eternal life, or at least in some repeating cycle of life and death. "The Ship of Death," equally famous among Lawrence's *Last Poems*, relies on Whitman plus several other poetic mentors to make more explicit the theme of the eventual return to life in the world after death, a theme only implied by "Bavarian Gentians" through the Persephone myth. In "The Ship of Death," after speaking of the soul's disappearance in "deepening black darkening still / blacker upon the soundless, ungurgling flood" that lies across the bar, Lawrence exclaims:

> And yet out of eternity, a thread
> separates itself on the blackness,
> a horizontal thread
> that fumes a little with pallor upon the dark.
> Is it illusion? or does the pallor fume
> A little higher?
>
> .   .   .   .
>
> The flood subsides, and the body, like a worn sea-shell
> emerges strange and lovely . . . into her house again.

The poem is clearly informed by "Crossing the Bar": Tennyson's "flood," too, is "soundless" and therefore "ungurgling." Lawrence's depiction of death as a "deepening black darkening still / blacker" and rebirth as "a thread / separat[ing] itself on the blackness" may contain hints of Whitman's "When Lilacs Last in the Dooryard Bloom'd," in which signs of the "ever-returning spring" are juxtaposed with the image of President Lincoln's coffin passing "Through day and night with the great cloud darkening the land" (6.2):

> Falling upon them all and among them all, enveloping
>   me with the rest,
> Appear'd the cloud, appear'd the long black trail,
> And I knew death, its thought, and the sacred
>   knowledge of death.
>   (14.10–12)

In the early stanzas of "Ship of Death," echoes of Swinburne's youthful poetry of sighs mix and merge with the sad, autumnal tones of Tennyson's 1830 *Poems, Chiefly Lyrical:*

> Now it is autumn and the falling fruit
> and the long journey towards oblivion.

> The apples falling like great drops of dew
> to bruise themselves an exit from themselves.

> And it is time to go, to bid farewell
> to one's own self, and find an exit
> from the fallen self.

As "The Ship of Death" proceeds, the poet casts off the poem's vestiges of Pre-Raphaelitism in favor of a style that is more purely Whitmanian. The second section of the poem draws heavily on those poems by Whitman that speak of the soul's passage from life to death in terms of an ocean voyage, poems like "Aboard at a Ship's Helm," "In Cabin'd Ships at Sea," and "Sail Out for Good, Eidólon Yacht." In the latter work, the poet addresses his own soul:

> Depart, depart from solid earth—no more returning to
>   these shores,
> Now and for aye our infinite free venture wending,
> Spurning all yet tried ports, seas, hawsers, densities,
>   gravitation,
> Sail out for good, eidólon yacht of me!
> (lines 6–9)

The very moving second section of "The Ship of Death" is equally conversant with those poems by Whitman in which the poet addresses his whole readership as well as his own individual soul, poems such as "Passage to India" and "Good-Bye My Fancy." "Have you built your ship of death, O have you?" Lawrence asks urgently as much of himself as of the reader:

> O build your ship of death, for you will need it.

> The grim frost is at hand, when the apples will fall
> thick, almost thundrous, on the hardened earth.

> And death is on the air like a smell of ashes!
> Ah! can't you smell it?

Because dying for Lawrence has become what it was in the fourteenth section of Whitman's "When Lilacs Last in the

Dooryard Bloom'd," a heightened state in itself—the poet places
at least as much importance on the passage towards darkness as
he does on what awaits him in that realm where, in the words of
"Bavarian Gentians," "blue is darkened on blueness" and "dark-
ness invisible [is] enfolded in the deeper dark." Writing last poems
is, of course, a very important part of a poet's final state of
passage; it is the process of preparation that is itself something of
a sacred rite. Lawrence's image of a little boat being fitted out for
the final journey may refer, in part, to the religious, ritualistic burial
habits of his beloved Etruscans, but it is equally a self-reflexive
figure for the poet's partaking of the mysterious rite of last writing.
"Build then the ship of death, for you must take / the longest
journey, to oblivion," Lawrence suggests in the fifth and seventh
sections of his poem:

> Oh build your ship of death, your little ark
> and furnish it with food, with little cakes, and wine
> for the dark flight down oblivion.
>
> .   .   .   .
>
> A little ship, with oars and food
> and little dishes, and all accoutrements
> fitting and ready for the departing soul.

To the extent that Lawrence is speaking to himself and not to his
larger audience, his poem takes its own advice in the process of
offering it. The *Last Poems* are a dying man's attempts to come to
terms with death in poetry; the little ship of death that Lawrence
speaks of building and fitting out during the time of preparation is,
therefore, "The Ship of Death" itself. As happens so often in the
earlier *Bird, Beasts and Flowers* volume, the poem can be said to
turn into its own object. Because the object of the poems
Lawrence wrote in his third lustre is not the object world itself but
rather the divinity that inheres in everything from a nursing whale
to the most casual expressions of thought, the self-reflexiveness of
"The Ship of Death" amounts to success and not partial failure.

   To say that "The Ship of Death" *is* the ship of death the poem
speaks of—or, at least, a synechdoche for the whole volume of
poems that together amount to a poetic act of preparation—is to
raise an important question. If the bark spoken of is to be read as a

metapoesis, what then are the oars and provisions? One way of answering would be to say that the "accoutrements" of "The Ship of Death," or for that matter of any poem, include far more than just the images and techniques and ideas with which it is fitted out. The accoutrements necessarily include, in fact, the whole store of experiences that an author brings to its writing, experiences that in turn include but are by no means summed up by all the works of literature from Virgil's *Georgics* to Spenser's *Faerie Queene* to Shelley's "Adonais" to Tennyson's "The Lady of Shalott" to Whitman's many poems in which the bark has figured poetry.[18]

It does not take a very large leap of the imagination, after all, to see a possible connection between the poem's theme of rebirth and its mode, which is to recognize its own contexts in literary history and thus to allow old poems that had fallen into silence, become still-existent blacknesses on the blackness of time, to reenter the light of history and speak again in new ways. Whitman, whose poems are among the most certain forerunners of "The Ship of Death," not only went ahead of Lawrence in exploring the passage between life and death but also followed the tradition Lawrence carries on when he uses the boat as a figure for the poetry that is his best hope for life in the future.

Whitman's belief that future poets will determine his own ability to return to the world after death rests on his more fundamental belief that the living reembody the dead. In the forty-fourth meditation of "Song of Myself" he says, "I launch all men and women forward with me into the Unknown." Then he goes on to explain that "Before I was born out of my mother generations guided me, / My embryo has never been torpid, nothing could overlay it. . . ."

> All forces have been steadily employ'd to complete and
>   and delight me,
> Now on this spot I stand with my robust soul.

The very poem with which the poet "launch[es]" his readers into uncharted territory, therefore, must also have been in the making for generations.

In other lyrics Whitman is more explicit in his suggestion that generations of people are "steadily employ'd" in the making of future poems as well as future people. Whitman addresses "Poets to Come" in one of his *Inscriptions* and says, "Not to-day is to justify me and answer what I am for":

> I myself but write one or two indicative words for the
>   future,
> I but advance a moment only to wheel and hurry back in
>   darkness.
>
> I am a man who, sauntering along without fully
>   stopping, turns a casual look upon you
> and then averts his face.
> Leaving it to you to prove and define it,
> Expecting the main things from you.

The importance Whitman places on the "casual look" towards the future, together with the image of the poet "advanc[ing] a moment only to wheel . . . back in darkness," makes us think of Lawrence and his "Ship of Death," one of the "main things" that Whitman was confidently "expecting." "Poets to Come" is, moreover, not the only poem in which Whitman builds, in a poem about poetic reincarnation, towards Lawrence's image of "the deepening black darkening still" on "darkness" until "a thread / separates itself on the blackness" and "the whole thing starts again." In "Crossing Brooklyn Ferry" Whitman turns boats crossing the East River in the darkness of a December evening into a figure not only of life crossing over into death but also, implicitly, of the poetry that may guarantee the "reincarnation" of his own body of thought. "It is not upon you alone the dark patches fall," the poet assures the readers of the far-off future in the poem's sixth section: "The dark threw its patches upon me also ."

> Closer yet I approach you.
> What thoughts you have of me now, I had as much of you
>   —I laid in my stores in advance,
> I consider'd long and seriously of you before you were
>   born.
>   (7.1–3)

"I am with you, you men and women of a generation, or ever so many generations hence," Whitman had written in the poem's third section:

> Just as you feel when you look on the river and sky,
>   so I felt,

.   .   .   .

> Just as you are refreshed by the gladness of the river
>> and the bright flow, I was refresh'd,

.   .   .   .

> Just as you look on the numberless mass of ships
>> and the thick-stemm'd pipes of steamboats, I look'd.
>> (3.2–7)

The fact that Whitman recorded his feelings in a bark of poetry that carries them on across the gulf between the living and the dead is, of course, the *reason* why the future thinks about its present in much the same way that Whitman thought about his. What any generation "look[s] on" or thinks about or feels, almost instinctively, as it takes its passage through its present has been to a great extent determined by the visions of past harbor-crossers. That is surely part of what Whitman has in mind when he says "Live, old life! . . . Play the old role" and

> Consider, you who peruse me, whether I may not in
>> unknown ways be looking at you.
>> (9.10–12)

In yet another poem that considers the question of afterlife, "In Cabin'd Ships at Sea," Whitman makes even more explicit his faith that he will find his way back into life, that the "stores" he lays "in advance," in the words of "Crossing Brooklyn Ferry," will be, in Lawrence's words, the "accoutrements" of future voyagers. "In cabin'd ships at sea," Whitman declares assuredly, with "The boundless blue on every side expanding,"

> By sailors young and old haply will I,
>> a reminiscence of the land, be read,
> In full rapport at last.
> ("In Cabin'd Ships at Sea," lines 1–2, 7–8)

What follows, printed in italics, is the poetry written by one of those future readers; the juxtaposition suggests Whitman's faith that he will speak, in poetry, again in the future:

> *Here are our thoughts, voyagers' thoughts.*
> *Here not the land, firm land, alone appears,* may then by
>> them be said,

> *The sky o'erarches here, we feel the undulating deck*
>   *beneath our feet,*
> *We feel the long pulsation, ebb and flow of endless*
>   *motion,*
> *The tones of unseen mystery, the vague and vast*
>   *suggestions of the briny world, the liquid flowing*
>   *syllables.*
> (lines 9–13)

Whitman's one unitalicized phrase admits that the poet cannot exactly say what he will speak when he speaks again. Poetry resurrected—whether it be "In Cabin'd Ships at Sea" resurrected in "Ship of Death" or the casual "Hymn to Priapus" resurrected in "Name the Gods!"—is always poetry changed into something new. *"We feel the long pulsation, ebb and flow of / . . . the briny world"* is what "may . . . be said" by the future voyagers. What in fact was said by that one named D. H. Lawrence was that

> The flood subsides, and the body, like a worn sea-shell
> emerges strange and lovely.
> And the little ship wings home, faltering and lapsing
> on the pink flood. . . .
>
> Swings the heart renewed with peace
> even of oblivion.
>
> Oh build your ship of death, oh build it!
> for you will need it.
> For the long voyage of oblivion awaits you.

*   *   *

One major distinction must be made between Lawrence's "Ship of Death" and all of those poems by Whitman that might easily have been given the same title. Whitman, in "Crossing Brooklyn Ferry," foresees the immortality of his ideas through poetry; "In Cabin'd Ships at Sea" looks forward to poetry resurrected. Lawrence, in "Ship of Death," hardly disagrees with his predecessor about the way in which a poetic line, or "thread," may disappear only to reappear again, to "separate . . . itself on the blackness again," at some later time. But Lawrence looks forward to more than poetry resurrected; he looks to his own resurrection and reincarnation as well.

It is an important feature of Lawrence's thought during the final lustre that he does not believe he will return to life as D. H. Lawrence with another name. The voyage of death, the poet says no less than seven times in "Ship of Death," is "the voyage of oblivion," "the dark flight down oblivion." The poet's preference for the preposition "of" in the former phrase and the conspicuous absence of the preposition "to" in the latter serve to strengthen the power of "oblivion"; it is not a place that can be visited and left behind. Lawrence speaks of "the long and painful death / that lies between the old self and the new" and speaks of "emerg[ing] strange" at some future point. The "little ship" of the soul that "wings home" is also a ship that, however we explain it, has been entirely obliterated. "And everything is gone," Lawrence declares in his earlier description of the moment of death, "everything is . . . / completely under, gone, entirely gone."

> The upper darkness is heavy on the lower,
> between them the little ship
> is gone
> she is gone.
>
> It is the end, it is oblivion.

Lawrence's faith demands a higher tolerance for paradox than does Christianity, for in Lawrence the belief that death is, in Milton's words, "the Gate of Life" (*Paradise Lost*, 12.561) must coexist with the belief that, at the moment of death, the self is "completely" and "entirely gone" because death is "the end, . . . oblivion."

"Ship of Death" is not the only one of Lawrence's *Last Poems* to look forward to a "strange" new being. "Shadows" speaks of a rebirth of self in "new, strange flowers / such as my life has not brought forth before, new blossoms of me." It speaks of "the unknown God . . . breaking me down to his own oblivion / to send me forth on a new morning, a new man." In "Phoenix," Lawrence asks, "Are you willing to be sponged out, erased, cancelled, made nothing? / Are you willing to be made nothing?" Then he goes on to speak of the Phoenix that renews her youth in the moment of self-annihilation.

The strong cadence of the poem's repetitive opening question is so reminiscent of Whitman that this poem about becoming nothing in order to be resurrected in a new form might make us wonder if Lawrence believes himself to be Whitman resurrected, Whitman modified, Whitman "really change[d]" by Blake and Tennyson and Swinburne and others and now nearly ready to be transformed again (into a Ted Hughes or Denise Levertov). The idea is bound to remain speculative at best, but the notion that Lawrence believes himself to be a poet metamorphosed and reincarnated would go a long way in explaining the serenity of *Last Poems*, in which Lawrence shows a new and marvelous ability to rewrite the past without feeling threatened by it, without being perturbed as he had been in his two previous lustres by the persistent return of thoughts of "old love" or of "the albatross." The idea of reincarnation turns the poet whose texts always have clear contexts from an artist threatened by unoriginality into the past reoriginated.

Whitman's notion, prevalent in his poetry, that his thought will be thought again by future minds and spoken again by "Poets to Come" may or may not be responsible for Lawrence's interest, in "Ship of Death," in reincarnation. Whether or not Lawrence came to see himself as Whitman metamorphosed and reincarnated, Lawrence did find in Whitman a new kind of mentor. Whitman, rather than being a precursor whose overpowering influence Lawrence needed to work his way out of during the third lustre, was himself the way out of the problem of feeling unoriginal.

In 1918, while in Middleton, England, Lawrence had completed a draft of the essay on Whitman that was to become the last chapter of *Studies in Classic American Literature*, a volume not published until 1923, when Lawrence had reached America. In that essay, written five years before the commencement of what I am calling the last lustre, Whitman is criticized for his impure relation with the universe of objects. As he does in "The Evening Land" and in "Bibbles," Lawrence takes Whitman to task for his Romantic belief that

> The universe, in short, adds up to ONE.
> One.
> 1.
> Which is Walt.

Then he changes his tack suddenly and says:

Whitman, the great poet, has meant so much to me. Whitman, the one man breaking a way ahead. Whitman, the one pioneer. And only Whitman. No English pioneers, no French. No European pioneer-poets. In Europe the would-be pioneers are mere innovators. The same in America. Ahead of Whitman, nothing. Ahead of all poets, pioneering into the wilderness of unopened life, Whitman. Beyond him, none. His wide, strange camp at the end of the great high-road. . . . He is the first white aboriginal.[19]

This kind of adoration, however, is as instinct to Lawrence's second-lustre sensibility as is the criticism of Whitman's largeness of soul. It amounts to an attempt to say what Lawrence was to say in so many poems that he was to write between 1920 and 1922, namely, that only one man has had any real influence on him, and he is a Bushman. Or an Apache. Lawrence proves the half-heartedness of his claim that Whitman had and will stand alone by using the words "ahead" and "beyond" so loosely that both may be suspected of meaning "before." Before Whitman, there was none. But after Whitman? Doesn't the claim that Whitman was "the first white aboriginal" imply that there could be—or is—a second?

For the most part, in this second-lustre study of American literature, Lawrence values Whitman in the same way in which he values anything and everything that might or might not seem to free him from the prison house of white "English," "French"—"European"—poetic tradition. He values Whitman for different reasons in the last-lustre poems, some of which seem to delight in reincarnating that very tradition. He does so for several reasons besides the hypothetical one that Whitman led him towards the belief that poets may be their own, reincarnated precursors. One of those reasons is predicted by a prescient passage in *Studies in Classic American Literature* in which Lawrence says: "Whitman is a very great poet, of the end of life. A very great post-mortem poet, of the transitions of the soul as it loses its integrity. The poet of the soul's last shout and shriek, on the confines of death."[20] Originality, after all, is an issue grounded in "integrity." Lawrence, himself facing death, finds consolation and poetic energy through the works of a predecessor who sang from the perspective of a soul happily letting go; to wish for credit for what was first Whitman's talent—even subconsciously—would be a holding back and thus a contradiction in terms.

It is not enough to say, though, that Lawrence felt comfortable with Whitman's influence because Whitman was "a very great post-mortem poet." The American predecessor proved a way out of the bind of feeling unoriginal because of that moral and aesthetic casualness of Whitman's towards everything—including literary history—that may have been related to a kind of death-obsession but that surely cannot be equated with it. It may have been partly because Whitman could say, in "Poets to Come," that "I myself but write one or two indicative words for the future" that Lawrence could learn, in his last lustre, to admit what he admitted in *Apocalypse,* namely, that "every profound new movement makes a great swing also backwards."[21] It was in part because Whitman admitted that "Before I was born out of my mother generations guided me" that Lawrence, in "Ship of Death," can come so comfortably and eloquently to echo that elegy which many have called the greatest of all death poems:

> The breath whose might I have invoked in song
> Descends on me; my spirit's bark is driven,
> Far from the shore, far from the trembling throng
> Whose sails were never to the tempest given.
> ("Adonais," lines 487–90)

Through Whitman, Lawrence finally came to terms with Shelley. It is in "Phoenix," the last poem in *Last Poems,* that Lawrence can finally foresee the "hot . . . ash" of Shelley's former power "renewing" its "youth like the eagle." Through dying, Lawrence comes to terms with his youth. "The end," as he said in "Pomegranate," "cracks open with the beginning."

Introduction

1. D. H. Lawrence, "Foreword" to *Look! We Have Come Through!* (London: Chatto and Windus, 1917).

2. From the rejected preface to *The Collected Poems of D. H. Lawrence* (London: Martin Secker, 1928), printed in *Phoenix: The Posthumous Papers of D. H. Lawrence*, ed. Edward D. McDonald (New York: The Viking Press, 1936), p. 253.

3. *The Collected Letters of D. H. Lawrence*, ed. Harry T. Moore (New York: The Viking Press, 1962), p. 69.

4. *Ibid.*

5. D. H. Lawrence, "Poetry of the Present," the introduction to the American edition of *New Poems* (New York: B.W. Huebsch, 1920), reprinted in *The Complete Poems of D. H. Lawrence*, ed. Vivian de Sola Pinto and Warren Roberts (New York: The Viking Press, 1964), p. 182.

6. Ibid., p. 183.

7. D. H. Lawrence, *Study of Thomas Hardy*, in *Phoenix*. p. 480.

Chapter One

1. In "The Literary Formation of D. H. Lawrence" (*European Quarterly* 1 [1934]: 36–45) and in *D. H. Lawrence: A Personal Record* (London: J. Cape, 1935), E.T. [Jessie Chambers] discusses the books that she and Lawrence read together; reading and loving were inseparable components of their relationship.

2. D. H. Lawrence, *Study of Thomas Hardy*, in *Phoenix: The*

Posthumous Papers of D. H. Lawrence, ed. Edward D. McDonald (New York: The Viking Press, 1936), p. 480.

3. *The Collected Letters of D. H. Lawrence,* ed. Harry T. Moore (New York: The Viking Press, 1962), p. 474. Hereafter cited in the text as *Collected Letters.*

4. Helen Corke, *D. H. Lawrence: The Croydon Years* (Austin: The University of Texas Press, 1965), p. 9.

5. Rexroth is cited in Tom Marshall, *The Psychic Mariner* (New York: The Viking Press, 1970), p. 46.

6. Harry T. Moore, *The Priest of Love* (New York: Farrar, Straus and Giroux, 1974), p. 203.

7. From the rejected preface to *The Collected Poems of D. H. Lawrence,* printed in *Phoenix,* p. 253.

8. My ellipsis stands in place of the word "beneath." I have not quoted the word in my text because, although its presence would in no way damage my argument, it seems a wholly diversionary word the logic (or creative illogic) of which I am not sure I can explain. Why would Lawrence say that he is "beneath" his "underground" love? He cannot be accused of having sacrificed sense for a rhyming word, since "beneath" and "death" form only an eye rhyme anyway. Perhaps "beneath" is intended as a figurative, valuative word. (The mother, although dead, still reigns over her son.) Or the poet may intend to recall the downward-looking, male Orion in such a way as to make clear the status of both images as symbols of the parental past and yet confuse corpse and constellation just enough to keep either or both of them from being read too autobiographically.

9. D. H. Lawrence, "Preface" to *The Collected Poems of D. H. Lawrence* (London: Martin Secker, 1928), p. 6.

10. Graham Hough, *The Dark Sun* (New York: Macmillan, 1957), p. 191.

11. F. B. Pinion, *A D. H. Lawrence Companion* (London: Macmillan, 1978), p. 96.

12. D. H. Lawrence, *Sons and Lovers* (London: Duckworth, 1913), p. 196.

13. Ibid., p. 193.

14. Marshall, *The Psychic Mariner,* pp. 52, 204.

15. D. H. Lawrence, *The Symbolic Meaning* (London: Centaur Press, 1962), pp. 72–73. Quoted by Tom Marshall in *The Psychic Mariner.*

16. Thomas Hardy, *Tess of the d'Urbervilles.* I quote the version of the novel published in the Wessex Edition of *The Works of Thomas Hardy* (London: Macmillan, 1912), 1:77.

17. Lawrence, *Study of Thomas Hardy,* p. 459.

18. Thomas Hardy, in his elegy entitled "A Singer Asleep," refers to Swinburne's *Poems and Ballads* as "New words, in classic guise." Hardy's various testimonies on Swinburne's influence can be found in my study *Swinburne, Hardy, Lawrence and the Burden of Belief* (Chicago: the University of Chicago Press, 1978).

19. Algernon Charles Swinburne, *William Blake,* in *The Complete Works of Swinburne,* Bonchurch Edition (London: William Heinemann, 1926), 16:179.

20. Lawrence, *Study of Thomas Hardy,* p. 478.

21. D. H. Lawrence, *Sea and Sardinia,* in *D. H. Lawrence and Italy* (New York: The Viking Press, 1972), p. 123.

22. D. H. Lawrence, *Apocalypse* (New York: The Viking Press, 1960), p. 56.

23. "Poetry of the Present" was the introduction to the American edition of *New Poems* (New York: B. W. Huebsch, 1920).

24. The one critic who has spoken of the literary background to "Hymn to Priapus" is Tom Marshall, in *The Psychic Mariner,* pp. 104–5). It was he who led me to see that "Hymn to Priapus" might have been influenced by Swinburne's "Hymn to Proserpine."

25. Sandra Gilbert, *Acts of Attention* (Ithaca, N.Y.: Cornell University Press, 1972), p. 85.

26. D. H. Lawrence, "Art and Morality," in *Phoenix,* p. 525.

27. Gilbert, *Acts of Attention,* pp. 85–86.

28. W. H. Auden, *The Dyer's Hand and Other Essays* (New York: Random House, 1948), p. 279; Karl Shapiro, "The Unemployed Magician," in *A D. H. Lawrence Miscellany,* ed. Harry T. Moore (Carbondale, Ill.: Southern Illinois University Press, 1959), p. 382; R.G.N. Salgãdo, review of *The Complete Poems of D. H. Lawrence,* in *The Critical Quarterly* 7 (1965): 389–92.

29. Keith Sagar, *The Art of D. H. Lawrence* (Cambridge: Cambridge University Press, 1966), p. 242; Hough, *The Dark Sun*, p. 193.

30. Harold Bloom, "Lawrence, Blackmur, Eliot, and the Tortoise," in *A D. H. Lawrence Miscellany*, pp. 362, 363, 368.

31. A. A. Alvarez, "D. H. Lawrence: The Single State of Man," in *A D. H. Lawrence Miscellany*, p. 349.

32. Ibid., p. 356.

33. Hough, *The Dark Sun*, p. 205.

34. R. P. Blackmur, *The Double Agent* (New York: Arrow Editions, 1935), pp. 107–15 *passim*.

35. Lawrence, *Study of Thomas Hardy*, p. 410.

Chapter Two

1. D. H. Lawrence, "Making Love to Music," in *Phoenix: The Posthumous Papers of D. H. Lawrence*, ed. Edward D. McDonald (New York: The Viking Press, 1936), pp. 160–63.

2. D. H. Lawrence, *The Rainbow* (London: Methuen, 1915), p. 170.

3. Matthew Arnold, "Byron," in *The Complete Prose Works of Matthew Arnold*, ed. R. H. Super (Ann Arbor: The University of Michigan Press, 1960), 9:218; Algernon Charles Swinburne, "Notes on the Text of Shelley," in *The Complete Works of Swinburne*, Bonchurch Edition (London: William Heinemann, 1926), 15:380.

4. Gerard Genette, *Figures* (Paris: Editions du Seuil, 1966), p. 169. Translation mine.

5. See Shelley's own footnote to this ode.

6. D. H. Lawrence, "Poetry of the Present," introduction to the American edition of *New Poems of D. H. Lawrence*, ed. Vivian de Sola Pinto and Warren Roberts (New York: The Viking Press, 1964), pp. 181–82.

7. Ibid., p. 186. Hereafter cited in the text as "Poetry of the Present."

8. William Wordsworth, "Essay, Supplementary to the 'Preface' (1815)," reprinted in *The Prose Works of William Wordsworth*, ed. W. J. B. Owen and Jane Worthington Smyser (Oxford: The Clarendon Press, 1974), 3:83.

9. Percy Bysshe Shelley, "A Defence of Poetry," in *The Complete Works of Percy Bysshe Shelley*, ed. Roger Ingpen and Walter E. Peck (London and New York: The Julian Editions of Ernest Benn and Charles Scribner's Sons), 7:116–17. Italics mine.

10. Shelley, "A Defence of Poetry," p. 117.

11. D. H. Lawrence, "Preface" to *The Collected Poems of D. H. Lawrence* (London: Martin Secker, 1928), p. 6.

12. Shelley, "A Defence of Poetry," p. 116.

13. Ibid., pp. 135, 132–33.

14. Lawrence, "Introduction" to *Pansies* (London: Martin Secker, 1929), also reprinted in *The Complete Poems of D. H. Lawrence*, pp. 417–18.

15. Shelley, "A Defence of Poetry," p. 113.

16. Lawrence, *The Complete Poems of D. H. Lawrence*, p. 27.

17. D. H. Lawrence, *Apocalypse* (New York: The Viking Press, 1960), pp. 84–85.

18. D. H. Lawrence, *Study of Thomas Hardy*, in *Phoenix*, p. 405. Hereafter cited in the text as *Hardy*.

19. Thomas Hardy, *The Woodlanders* (London: Macmillan, 1887), 1:11.

20. Shelley, "A Defence of Poetry," p. 131.

21. Ibid., pp. 112, 140.

22. Lawrence, *Apocalypse*, p. 31.

23. Ibid., pp. 48–50.

24. Ross C Murfin, *Swinburne, Hardy, Lawrence and the Burden of Belief* (Chicago: The University of Chicago Press, 1978).

Chapter Three

1. Karl Shapiro, "The Unemployed Magician," in *A D. H. Lawrence Miscellany*, ed. Harry T. Moore (Carbondale, Ill.: Southern Illinois University Press, 1959), pp. 395, 393.

2. Robert Browning, "Rabbi Ben Ezra," line 62.

3. Ibid., lines 184–85.

4. W. H. Auden, "Musée des Beaux Arts," lines 10–12.

5. Rainer Maria Rilke, *Duino Elegies*, trans. J. B. Leishman and Stephen Spender (New York: W. W. Norton, 1939), p. 67.

6. W. B. Yeats, "Those Images," lines 10–12.

7. Algernon Charles Swinburne, *The Poems of Algernon Charles Swinburne* (London: Chatto and Windus, 1904), 2:3–4.

8. *Bay*, published in 1919, contains only thirteen new poems. Some of the poems date from 1910–12.

9. Harry T. Moore, *The Priest of Love* (New York: Farrar, Straus and Giroux, 1974), p. 327.

10. Keith Sagar, *The Art of D. H. Lawrence* (Cambridge: Cambridge University Press, 1966), p. 120.

11. Moore, *The Priest of Love*, p. 203.

12. Quoted without attribution by Harry T. Moore, in *The Priest of Love*, p. 318.

13. Earl and Achsah Brewster, *D. H. Lawrence: Reminiscences and Correspondences* (London: Martin Secker, 1934), p. 27.

14. D. H. Lawrence, *Sea and Sardinia*, in *D. H. Lawrence and Italy* (New York: The Viking Press, 1972), p. 3.

15. Ibid., p. 9.

16. Ibid., p. 14.

17. Sagar, *The Art of D. H. Lawrence*, p. 120.

18. Graham Hough, *The Dark Sun* (New York: Macmillan, 1957), pp. 201–2.

19. Keith Sagar advances this view of "Snake" when he reminds us that in "'Pomegranate' and 'Figs' . . . the word 'fissure' is specifically defined as the 'female part,'" and then goes on to say that in "Snake" the "'fissure' above the water-trough . . . combines with the phallic snake in a sexual metaphor." See *The Art of D. H. Lawrence*, pp. 124–25.

20. D. H. Lawrence, *The Plumed Serpent* (London: Martin Secker, 1926), p. 210.

21. Leslie Brisman, "Coleridge and the Ancestral Voices," *Georgia Review* 29 (1975).

22. Harold Bloom, "Poetry, Revisionism, Repression," *Critical Inquiry* 2 (1975): 237.

23. Matthew Arnold, "Byron," in *The Complete Prose Works of Matthew Arnold*, ed. R. H. Super (Ann Arbor: The University of Michigan Press, 1960), 9:227.

24. See Dante's *Inferno* (14.1–60) and Milton's *Paradise Lost* (1.225–38).

25. Lawrence, *Sea and Sardinia*, pp. 1–3.

26. D. H. Lawrence, "The Crown," in *Phoenix II: Uncollected, Unpublished, and Other Prose Works by D. H. Lawrence,* ed. Warren Roberts and Harry T. Moore (London: Heinemann, 1968), p. 407.

27. Lawrence, *The Plumed Serpent,* pp. 454–55.

28. Sandra Gilbert, *Acts of Attention* (Ithaca, N.Y.: Cornell University Press, 1972), p. 174.

29. Sagar, *The Art of D. H. Lawrence,* pp. 125–26.

30. D. H. Lawrence, "Hymns in a Man's Life," in *Phoenix II,* p. 597.

31. William Blake, *The Marriage of Heaven and Hell,* in *The Poetry and Prose of William Blake,* ed. David B. Erdman with commentary by Harold Bloom (New York: Doubleday, 1970), p. 37.

32. Ibid., p. 2.

33. Ibid., p. 39.

34. Sagar, *The Art of D. H. Lawrence,* p. 123.

35. *The Poetry and Prose of William Blake,* p. 38.

36. Ibid., p. 2.

37. Hough, *The Dark Sun,* p. 207.

38. The theme of "Nutting," David Perkins argues in *Wordsworth and the Poetry of Sincerity* (Cambridge: Harvard University Press, 1964), is the "dawning" of the "recognition . . . of nature as animate and haunted by a spiritual presence" (p. 184). Only Geoffrey Hartman, in *Wordsworth's Poetry* (New Haven: Yale University Press, 1964), p. 75, suggests that there might be some connection between the grove of hazel nuts and "the bower of Romance," but he merely suggests, and he goes on to speak of "Nature's activity or pedagogy."

39. William Wordsworth, "Preface" to the 1800 edition of *Lyrical Ballads,* in *The Prose Works of William Wordsworth,* ed. W.J.B. Owen and J. W. Smyser (Oxford: Oxford University Press, 1974), 1:124, 130, 132.

40. Swinburne, *The Poems of Algernon Charles Swinburne,* 2:117.

41. John Freccero, "The Fig Tree and the Laurel: Petrarch's Poetics," *Diacritics* 5 (1975): 37.

42. Gilbert, *Acts of Attention,* p. 144.

43. D. H. Lawrence, "Hymns in a Man's Life," in *Phoenix II,* p. 597.

44. D. H. Lawrence, "The Nightingale," in *Phoenix,* pp. 42–43.

45. D. H. Lawrence, *Apocalypse* (New York: The Viking Press, 1960), p. 88.

Chapter Four

1. Michel Foucault, *The Order of Things: An Archaeology of the Human Sciences* (New York: Pantheon Books, 1970), p. 217.

2. D. H. Lawrence, "The Reality of Peace," in *Phoenix: The Posthumous Papers of D. H. Lawrence,* ed. Edward D. McDonald (New York: The Viking Press, 1936), p. 669.

3. D. H. Lawrence, *"Georgian Poetry* 1911–12," in *Phoenix,* p. 304.

4. D. H. Lawrence, "Chaos in Poetry," published as *"Chariot of the Sun,* by Harry Crosby" in *Phoenix,* p. 255.

5. William Blake, *The Marriage of Heaven and Hell.* See *The Poetry and Prose of William Blake,* ed. David B. Erdman with commentary by Harold Bloom (New York: Doubleday and Co., 1970), p. 39.

6. Lawrence, "Chaos in Poetry," pp. 256–57.

7. Ibid.

8. Most of the poems that were written in Italy and that appeared in *Birds, Beasts and Flowers* seem to have been written, at least in draft form, in 1920. Twenty of thirty-three are known to have been composed by the fall of 1920; there is no evidence of which I am aware that any more than four of the remaining thirteen were written after that time.

9. Keith Sagar, *The Art of D. H. Lawrence* (Cambridge: Cambridge University Press, 1966), p. 126.

10. Maurice Blanchot, *La part du feu* (Paris: Gallimard, 1949), pp. 325–26. I was pointed to these passages by Sarah N. Lawall, who translates and discusses them in her book *Critics of Consciousness: The Existential Structures of Literature* (Cambridge: Harvard University Press, 1968), pp. 229–30.

11. Blanchot, *La part du feu,* p. 326.

12. Maurice Blanchot, "Le regard d'Orphée" in *L'espace litteraire* (Paris: Gallimard, 1955).

13. Paul de Man, *Blindness and Insight* (New York: Oxford University Press, 1973), p. 106.

14. Jonathan Culler, *Structuralist Poetics* (Ithaca, N.Y.: Cornell University Press, 1975), p. 16.

15. David Carroll, *"Mimesis* Reconsidered," *Diacritics* 5 (1975): 10.

16. George Steiner, "The Kingdom of Appearances" (a review of *The Heritage of Apelles* by E. H. Gombrich), *New Yorker,* April 4, 1977.

17. D. H. Lawrence, *Etruscan Places,* in *D. H. Lawrence and Italy* (New York: The Viking Press, 1972), p. 76.

18. De Man, *Blindness and Insight,* pp. 11, 14.

19. Immanuel Kant, *Critique of Judgment,* trans. J. H. Bernard (New York: Hafner, 1951), p. xvii.

20. Jonathan Culler, *Structuralist Poetics,* pp. 143–44.

21. Jonathan Culler, *Ferdinand de Saussure* (New York: Penguin Books, 1977), p. 76.

22. See Maurice Blanchot's essays "La terreur dans les lettres" in the *Journal des Débats* (October 24, November 25, and December 2, 1941). Sarah Lawall translates the phrases I have quoted in *Critics of Consciousness,* p. 226.

23. D. H. Lawrence, "Preface" to *The Collected Poems of D. H. Lawrence* (London: Martin Secker, 1928), p. 6.

24. Jacques Derrida, *Speech and Phenomena and Other Essays on Husserl's Theory of Signs,* trans. H. Allison (Evanston, Ill.: Northwestern University Press, 1973), p. 51.

25. Martin Heidegger, *Der Satz vom Grund* (Pfullingen: G. Neske, 1957), p. 161.

26. D. H. Lawrence, "Art and Morality," "Morality and the Novel," in *Phoenix,* pp. 524–25, 527.

27. Marcel Raymond, preface to *Baudelaire au surrealisme* (Paris: Corti, 1952), p. 13. Translation mine.

28. Foucault, *The Order of Things,* p. 39.

29. Ibid., pp. 36, 38.

30. Ibid., p. 43.

31. Ibid., p. 41.

32. Jacques Derrida, *Of Grammatology,* trans. G. C. Spivak (Baltimore: Johns Hopkins University Press, 1976), pp. 131–42, 144, 295. Derrida himself, of course, dismisses as metaphysical mythology the whole notion of a "first presence" (p. 296).

33. D. H. Lawrence, *Apocalypse* (New York: The Viking Press, 1960), pp. 84–85.

34. D. H. Lawrence, "The Proper Study," in *Phoenix*, p. 721. Hereafter cited in the text as "Proper Study."

35. Lawrence, *Etruscan Places*, pp. 47, 49–59.

36. Ibid., p. 53.

37. Ibid., pp. 107, 51–52.

38. John Freccero, "The Fig Tree and the Laurel: Petrarch's Poetics," *Diacritics* 5 (1975): 35.

39. See Newton Garver's preface to Jacques Derrida's *Speech and Phenomena*, p. xxii.

40. Geoffrey Hartman, "Monsieur Texte II," *Georgia Review* 30 (1976): 184, 192.

Chapter Five

1. See Williams's "An Elegy for D. H. Lawrence" in *Selected Poems* (New York: New Directions, 1964). "To the Snake" is in *With eyes at the backs of our heads* (New York: New Directions, 1959). "Snake Crossing" is in *Comforting the Wilderness* (Middletown, Conn.: Wesleyan University Press, 1977).

2. Keith Sagar, *The Art of D. H. Lawrence* (Cambridge: Cambridge University Press, 1966), p. 4.

3. Frieda Lawrence, *Not I, But the Wind* (New York: The Viking Press, 1934), p. 4.

4. Quoted without attribution by Harry T. Moore in *The Priest of Love* (New York: Farrar, Straus and Giroux, 1976), p. 378.

5. E. T. [Jessie Chambers], "The Literary Formation of D. H. Lawrence," *European Quarterly* 1 (1934): 36–45.

6. See E. T. [Jessie Chambers], *D. H. Lawrence: A Personal Record* (London: J. Cape, 1935), p. 122, as well as the works cited in n.7, below.

7. Sandra Gilbert, *Acts of Attention* (Ithaca, N.Y.: Cornell University Press, 1972), pp. 54–55; Tom Marshall, *The Psychic Mariner* (New York: The Viking Press, 1970), p. 106.

8. Marshall, *The Psychic Mariner*, p. 110.

9. I shall use the word *Pansies* to refer both to the poems published in *Pansies* (London: Martin Secker, 1929) and to those posthumous pieces published as *More Pansies* in *The Complete Poetry of D. H.*

Lawrence, ed. Vivian de Sola Pinto and Warren Roberts (New York: The Viking Press, 1964).

10. "The Divine Image," one of the *Songs of Innocence* written in the metrical patterns of a church hymn and meant, at best, to express a naïve view of such qualities as "Mercy" and "Pity," is reprinted as hymn 506 in *The English Hymnal* (London: Oxford Univeristy Press, 1906), p. 402.

11. Gilbert, *Acts of Attention,* p. 253.

12. See *The Poetry and Prose of William Blake,* ed. David Erdman with commentary by Harold Bloom (New York: Doubleday, 1970), p. 35.

13. Sandra Gilbert contrasts the personal stance Lawrence takes in his early poetry with Whitman's public one (*Acts of Attention,* p. 83). Tom Marshall says of Lawrence's later *Pansies* that the poet comes to believe he "experience[s] in his own being the fatal self-division of Western man" (*The Psychic Mariner,* p. 166).

14. "Introduction" to *Pansies,* reprinted in *The Complete Poems of D. H. Lawrence,* p. 417.

15. Richard Aldington, "Introduction" to *Last Poems* and *More Pansies,* reprinted in *The Complete Poems of D. H. Lawrence,* p. 591.

16. A. A. Alvarez, "D. H. Lawrence: The Single State of Man," in *A D. H. Lawrence Miscellany,* ed. Harry T. Moore (Carbondale, Ill.: Southern Illinois University Press, 1959), p. 353.

17. D. H. Lawrence, "The Proper Study," in *Phoenix: The Posthumous Papers of D. H. Lawrence,* ed. Edward D. McDonald (New York: The Viking Press, 1936), p. 729.

18. See *Georgics,* 4.116–17; *The Faerie Queene,* 1.12.42; and Tennyson's "Lady of Shalott," in which the lady, on leaving her tower, writes "round about the prow" of her "boat . . . *The Lady of Shalott*" (lines 123–25).

19. D. H. Lawrence, *Studies in Classic American Literature* (New York, 1928), pp. 247, 251, 253, 257.

20. Ibid., p. 252.

21. D. H. Lawrence, *Apocalypse* (London, 1932), p. 56.

Index